"What seems to us unique is Riccardo Lombardi's use of his own body, of embodied experiences in the analysand and in the entanglement of both analyst and analysand bodies in fantasies shared and unshared. His approach is designed to teach us confidence in our creative listening, caution in what we imagine we know, and compassionate identification with patient's suffering and our own. Lombardi strikes us as an analyst determined on the deepest possible encounter with the analysand's subjectivity at unconscious, somatic, barely figurable levels. At the same time, he is always mindful of the interdependence of consciousnesses across persons inside the consulting room and in the wider world of families and groups."
– **Adrienne Harris and Lewis Aron**, Editors of the *Relational Perspectives Book Series*

"*Body–Mind Dissociation in Psychoanalysis* is an immensely useful handbook for the practicing clinician, a guide to recognition of the crucial role of mind-body dissociation in various forms of psychopathology, as well as a compendium of helpful suggestions concerning the techniques by which mind-body dissociation can be addressed and repaired."
– **Owen Renik,** Former Editor of the *Psychoanalytic Quarterly* and author of *Practical Psychoanalysis for Therapists and Patients*

"*Body–Mind Dissociation in Psychoanalysis* is a most original contribution to the psychoanalytic literature: the reader is asked to adopt a new orientation, as if someone had suddenly changed all the subway lines and their stops. This book is extremely rich in clinical presentations, in which the analyst's interventions always surprise his patients, not to mention his readers. Like those very few authors who are able to turn our psychoanalytic knowledge upside down – as is the case with James Grotstein and Thomas Ogden – Riccardo Lombardi compels the reader to make a quantum leap. He opens the door to what has up to now been unthinkable, exploring the proto-sensorial levels of the analytic relationship in a unique way."
– **Antonino Ferro**, President of the Italian Psychoanalytic Society and Consultant Associate Editor of the *International Journal of Psychoanalysis*

Body–Mind Dissociation in Psychoanalysis

The conflict and dissociation between the body and the mind have determinant implications in the context of our current clinical practice, and are an important source of internal and relational disturbances. *Body–Mind Dissociation in Psychoanalysis* proposes the concept as a new hypothesis, different from traumatic dissociation or states of splitting.

This approach opens the door to a clinical confrontation with extreme forms of mental disturbance, such as psychosis or borderline disorders, and strengthens the relational power of the analytic encounter, through a focus on the internal sensory – emotional axis in both analyst and analysand. The book details this importance of the analyst's intrasubjective relationship with the analysand in constructing new developmental horizons, starting from the body – mind exchange of the two participants.

Body–Mind Dissociation in Psychoanalysis will be of use to students, beginners in psychotherapy, mental health practitioners, and seasoned psychoanalysts.

Riccardo Lombardi is a psychoanalyst, psychiatrist, and MD. He has a full-time private practice in Rome and teaches at the Roman Psychoanalytic Institute of the International Psychoanalytic Association. He is a Training and Supervising Analyst of the Italian Psychoanalytic Society. Among his published works is the book *Formless Infinity: Clinical Exploration of Matte Blanco and Bion*, published by Routledge in 2015.

The *Relational Perspectives Book Series (RPBS)* publishes books that grow out of or contribute to the relational tradition in contemporary psychoanalysis. The term *relational psychoanalysis* was first used by Greenberg and Mitchell[1] to bridge the traditions of interpersonal relations, as developed within interpersonal psychoanalysis and object relations, as developed within contemporary British theory. But, under the seminal work of the late Stephen A. Mitchell, the term *relational psychoanalysis* grew and began to accrue to itself many other influences and developments. Various tributaries—interpersonal psychoanalysis, object relations theory, self psychology, empirical infancy research, and elements of contemporary Freudian and Kleinian thought—flow into this tradition, which understands relational configurations between self and others, both real and fantasied, as the primary subject of psychoanalytic investigation.

We refer to the relational tradition, rather than to a relational school, to highlight that we are identifying a trend, a tendency within contemporary psychoanalysis, not a more formally organized or coherent school or system of beliefs. Our use of the term relational signifies a dimension of theory and practice that has become salient across the wide spectrum of contemporary psychoanalysis. Now under the editorial supervision of Lewis Aron and Adrienne Harris, with the assistance of Associate Editors Steven Kuchuck and Eyal Rozmarin, the Relational Perspectives Book Series originated in 1990 under the editorial eye of the late Stephen A. Mitchell. Mitchell was the most prolific and influential of the originators of the relational tradition. Committed to dialogue among psychoanalysts, he abhorred the authoritarianism that dictated adherence to a rigid set of beliefs or technical restrictions. He championed open discussion, comparative and integrative approaches, and promoted new voices across the generations.

Included in the Relational Perspectives Book Series are authors and works that come from within the relational tradition, extend and develop that tradition, as well as works that critique relational approaches or compare and contrast it with alternative points of view. The series includes our most distinguished senior psychoanalysts, along with younger contributors who bring fresh vision. A full list of titles in this series is available at www.routledge.com/series/LEARPBS.

1 J. Greenberg and S. Mitchell, *Object Relations in Psychoanalytic Theory* (Cambridge, MA: Harvard University Press, 1983).

Body–Mind Dissociation in Psychoanalysis

Development after Bion

Riccardo Lombardi

LONDON AND NEW YORK

First published 2017
by Routledge
2 Park Square, Milton Park, Abingdon, Oxon OX14 4RN

and by Routledge
711 Third Avenue, New York, NY 10017

Routledge is an imprint of the Taylor & Francis Group, an informa business

© 2017 Riccardo Lombardi

The right of Riccardo Lombardi to be identified as author of this work has been asserted by him in accordance with sections 77 and 78 of the Copyright, Designs and Patents Act 1988.

All rights reserved. No part of this book may be reprinted or reproduced or utilized in any form or by any electronic, mechanical, or other means, now known or hereafter invented, including photocopying and recording, or in any information storage or retrieval system, without permission in writing from the publishers.

Trademark notice: Product or corporate names may be trademarks or registered trademarks, and are used only for identification and explanation without intent to infringe.

British Library Cataloguing in Publication Data
A catalogue record for this book is available from the British Library

Library of Congress Cataloguing in Publication Data
Names: Lombardi, Riccardo, author.
Title: Body–mind dissociation in psychoanalysis :
development after Bion / Riccardo Lombardi.
Description: 1 Edition. | New York : Routledge, 2017. |
Series: The relational perspectives book series
Identifiers: LCCN 2016011108 | ISBN 9781138100046 (hardback) |
ISBN 9781138100053 (pbk.) | ISBN 9781315657844 (ebook)
Subjects: LCSH: Mind and body. | Intersubjectivity. | Psychoanalysis. |
Bion, Wilfred R. (Wilfred Ruprecht), 1897–1979.
Classification: LCC BF161 .L586 2016 | DDC 616.89/17–dc23
LC record available at https://lccn.loc.gov/2016011108

ISBN: 978-1-138-10004-6 (hbk)
ISBN: 978-1-138-10005-3 (pbk)
ISBN: 978-1-315-65784-4 (ebk)

Typeset in Times New Roman
by Out of House Publishing

To Carola

The contrast between man's ideological capacity to move at random through material and metaphysical spaces and his physical limitations, is the origin of all human tragedy. It is this contrast between power and prostration that implies the duality of human existence. Half-winged – half-imprisoned, this is man!

(Paul Klee, *Pedagogical Sketchbook* [1925], trans. Sibyl Moholy-Nagy)

Contents

	Foreword ADRIENNE HARRIS AND LEWIS ARON	xiii
	Permission acknowledgments	xvi
	Introduction	1
1	Body–mind dissociation and transference onto the body	21
2	Visual power, emotions, and mental growth: A clinical essay on some of Bion's earliest psychosomatic intuitions	40
3	Intersubjectivity and the body	59
4	Primitive mental states and the body: A personal view of A. B. Ferrari's concrete original object	68
5	The body in the analytic session: Focusing on the body–mind link	92
6	Body and mind in adolescence	110
7	Working with the body–mind dissociation in three psychoanalytic sessions	128
8	The body, feelings, and the unheard music of the senses	144

9 The hat on top of the volcano: Bion's O and Ferrari's
   body–mind relationship   166

10 Bodily claustrophobia and the music: A psychoanalytic
   note on Beethoven's *Fidelio*   187

   Conclusion: Art, bodily experiences, and internal harmony   203

   References   209
   Index   222

Foreword

Adrienne Harris and Lewis Aron

It is with great pleasure that we introduce to our readers the work of Riccardo Lombardi. Lombardi has a deservedly distinguished international reputation and he publishes widely, interested in a unique way in the theoretical innovations of Wilfred Bion. In this regard, he is part of the evolving group of analysts working to integrate Bionian ideas and projects into clinical practices, sometimes within a field theory perspective – in Lombardi's case more in an interweaving of his own ideas and Bion's evocative demanding challenges, along with the work of Matte Blanco and Ferrari, work on the body in psychic reality, and the unique character of the unrepressed unconscious. As contemporary analysts begin to assimilate this fascinating group, we will need to be sensitive to nuance, and to distinct and individual perspectives and ways of using Bion.

There are immediately recognizable Bionian and neo-Bionian elements in Lombardi's ways of working and thinking and feeling. We see the presence of "negative capability," the phrase from Keats and aesthetic theory indicating the capacity to work in states of uncertainty. Lombardi models for his reader a way of working in which confusion, upset, moments of creative imagination, and uncertainty are all in play in the analyst's *rêveries* and communications.

What seems to us unique is Lombardi's use of his own body, of embodied experiences in the analysand and in the entanglement of both analyst's and analysand's bodies in fantasies shared and unshared. Certainly, the work on embodied states and on what Lombardi terms dissociation rather than splitting arises with analysands experiencing significant disturbance and crises of living, working, and being. But over this volume, we see a wide range of analysands and their difficulties and see the value of Lombardi's method very generally.

Lombardi is also quite particular in drawing his ideas from early work in Bion on the body and somatic states and on working with the patient's experience or alienation with his own body. There is a transference of patient to his own body, and this, in Lombardi's view, must predate the more traditional transference interpretations. Working always along two axes, body – mind and analyst – analysand, Lombardi initially concentrates on the disjunctions and chaos in the patient's relationship and/or alienation to her own body. Thought and higher levels of representation and articulable experience await the development of the patient's capacity to be in their own body and draw on somatic experience to contact and construct affective and symbolizable experience.

Lombardi also draws important influences from two Italian analysts not well known in the contemporary analytic scene: A. B. Ferrari and Ignacio Matte Blanco, each of whom inspired elements in Lombardi's theoretical and clinical evolution. Readers can listen for the particular notes and influences of these important figures from our psychoanalytic history. Lombardi feels free to draw on thinkers whose approach is what we might think of as "one-person" but to weave these approaches uniquely into intersubjective psychic spaces. Drawing on Ferrari, Lombard's focus is on the analysand's internal experience (silent, dissociated, or articulable) of bodily sensations and experience, and the analytic work is designed to elaborate and develop the analysand's capacity to move from soma to representation, and to mentalization.

From this volume of collected essays by such a gifted thinker and clinician, we think our readers can glean many ideas of how to work and how to think clinically. Lombardi's approach has affinities with that of other neo-Bionians; it is a clinical method equally poised between daring and deep caring, designed to teach us confidence in our creative listening, caution in what we imagine we know, and compassionate identification with patients' suffering and our own. Important lessons.

Finally, with this publication the Relational Perspectives Book Series affirms its commitment to holding the tension between the relational and the intrapsychic. Lombardi strikes us as an analyst determined on the deepest possible encounter with the analysand's subjectivity at unconscious, somatic, barely figurable levels.

At the same time, he is always mindful of the interdependence of consciousnesses across persons, inside the consulting room and in the wider world of families and groups.

Permission acknowledgements

Chapter 3 was previously published as Lombardi, R. (2013). "Object relations and the ineffable bodily dimension". *Contemp. Psychoanal.*, 49: 82–102. Reprinted by permission of Taylor and Francis.

Chapter 4 was previously published as Lombardi, R. (2002). "Primitive mental states and the body. A personal view of Armando B. Ferrari's Concrete Original Object". *Int. J. Psycho-Anal.*, 83: 363–381. Reprinted by permission of Wiley-Blackwell.

Chapter 5 was previously published as Lombardi, R. (2008). "The body in the analytic session: Focusing on the Body–Mind link". *Int. J. Psycho-Anal.*, 89: 89–109. Reprinted by permission of Wiley-Blackwell.

Chapter 7 was previously published as Lombardi, R. (2004). "Three psychoanalytic sessions". *Psychoanal. Q.*, 73: 773–786. Reprinted by permission of Wiley-Blackwell.

Chapter 8 was previously published as Lombardi, R. (2011). "The body, feelings, and the unheard music of the senses". *Contemp. Psychoanal.*, 47: 3–24. Reprinted by permission of Taylor and Francis.

Chapter 9 was previously published as Lombardi, R. (2016). "The hat on top of the volcano: Bion's 'O' and the body–mind relationship". In Civitarese, G. and Levine, H.B., *The W.R. Bion Tradition. Lines of Development – Evolution of Theory and Practice over the Decades*. London, Karnac, pp. 223–238. Reprinted by permission of Karnac Books Ltd.

Chapter 10 was previously published as Lombardi, R (2013). "Music and bodily claustrophobia: A psychoanalytic note on Beethoven's 'Fidelio'". *International Journal of Applied Psychoanalytic Studies:*, 10: 108–120. Reprinted by permission of John Wiley & Sons, Ltd.

Introduction

This book focuses attention in psychoanalysis on the body and the body–mind relationship, together with the conflict and dissociation that we sometimes find there. This does not imply returning to a sort of Cartesian dualism, since in harmonious relations between body and mind the two are integrated and in dialogue with each other: instead it involves taking note of a whole series of clinical phenomena characterized by a discordant arrangement, including the situation in which body and mind tend not to interact, but instead to exclude each other. Body and mind differ in their natures, hence we are all exposed, by the very nature of things, to a conflict between something concrete and something immaterial.

According to the artist Paul Klee, in the quotation I have chosen as the epigraph to this volume, the coexistence of bodily limitation with the boundless mobility of the mind is at the root of our deepest conflicts, indeed of the intrinsically tragic dimension of human nature. My observations are the fruit of clinical psychoanalysis, but they could have implications for psychology, psychiatry, philosophy, anthropology, and culture in general. However, I shall not break down any interdisciplinary barriers, leaving it to the reader to work out the correlations. At the end of the book I shall include some references to music, prose, and poetry, but only as a reminder that I could not be a psychoanalyst without being at the same time immersed, qua *Homo sapiens*, in a world in which the various artistic forms importantly "hold ... the mirror up to nature" (*Hamlet* III.ii.24–25), continually spurring man to reflect on himself. In my clinical experience, the encounter with

This introduction is translated by Karen Christenfeld.

my analysands has increased my sensibility towards various cultural manifestations, just as, vice versa, my interest in the arts contributes to my emotional and intellectual receptiveness towards what takes place in the analytic setting.

Man's intellectual "capacity to move at random through material and metaphysical spaces" in contrast to "his physical limitations," as Klee put it, reminds us of what we might call a two-sided aspect of the psychoanalytic experience. Whereas psychoanalysis cannot, empirically speaking, exclude the need to catalyze some therapeutic benefit, at the same time it calls into play profound existential components of the personality. In my practice I regularly observe how confronting one's deepest anxieties can be significantly offset by the activation of individual creative resources, which inevitably differ from person to person.

The book is the result of research that I began thirty-five years ago as a hospital psychiatrist whose business it was to give advice about the psychological implications of organic disorders. I have continued my investigations in the subsequent thirty years of my analytic practice. The implications of this research as regards the way psychoanalysis is conceived will be explored with the help of numerous clinical histories, which illustrate my hypotheses and also show the practical consequences of the latter for analytic communication: vivid material that is accessible even to those without specialist knowledge. What has been decisive in the course of my research is the contribution of my analysands, the protagonists of a courageous exploration of themselves, but also the contribution of the colleagues with whom I have collaborated, so that what I have written here is shored up by a whole series of implicit coauthors, to whom I here express my gratitude, as I heartily do to my teachers, who formed me as a psychoanalyst and provided support in my first years in this profession.

Some personal considerations

But perhaps a few words might serve to sketch an encounter of my own with the body, prior to the psychoanalytic evolution of which I write in this volume. Not unlike what many of our colleagues who have also come from medical studies experienced, the concreteness of the body formed part of the impact I sustained in studying medicine and the empirical natural sciences in general. This impact was hardly trifling, given my quite dissimilar youthful bent for literature and philosophy. One element of my orientation towards medicine that I should not neglect to mention was my initial intention to follow in my father's footsteps by becoming a surgeon, like him. Consequently my medical training included, for some years, an internship in surgery, with brief courses in Denmark and Germany, and I participated actively for quite some time in my father's private surgical practice. It is well known that a certain affinity is necessary if one is to approach a career as a surgeon, and I was not lacking in this: I felt essentially at ease at the operating table, so that I soon progressed through the traditional stages of operating-room aide, surgical technologist, and then assistant to the primary surgeon. Having been fascinated, during my first years of studying medicine, by my acquired knowledge of the three-dimensionality of the human anatomy, I now found myself up against the corrective lesson that the operating table imparted to my expectation of scientific predictability. I learned that no anatomy is predictable and no actual body corresponds precisely to any other body, not to mention any anatomical chart. This now strikes me as not unlike the uniqueness of the experience the analysand has of his own body in analysis, and also as reminiscent of the uniqueness of the individual analytic relationship – certain institutional attempts to impose standards and standardization notwithstanding (Renik, 2003). The surgeon is obliged to work on an observational basis: every step, every movement in the operating room is based on the careful observation of the scene of action and of the segment on which she is working. I also came to realize that even meticulous visual observation can be insufficient, and that a more general sensory alertness may be called upon. I remember, for instance, an occasion when I was assisting my father, who was operating on a young woman's acute abdomen. The opening of the abdominal wall revealed that the peritoneum was flooded with blood, so that visibility was, despite diligent cleansing of the area, minimal. My father was silent: I saw that he identified completely with the pulp of his fingers as they explored the patient's internal organs by touch, in the absence of sight. After my initial surprise, I began to understand that we were facing an extrauterine pregnancy that had caused a fallopian tube to explode, with the resultant hemorrhage invading the abdomen. Unquestionably, experiences such as this remained with me even after I reached the conclusion that spending my days standing before an operating table was not altogether in keeping with my scientific curiosity and interests, so that I decided to turn to neurology, psychiatry, and psychoanalysis. I shifted gradually, working for years as psychiatric liaison in a general hospital, while also studying experimentally the changes in somatic cathexis after surgery, and the boundaries of the self.

The importance of these first medico-surgical experiences came to mind when, for example, I first read the psychoanalyst Wilfred Bion's excoriation of the use of the countertransference in psychoanalysis – referring, of course, to true, i.e., unconscious and largely inaccessible, countertransference, as opposed to the analyst's feelings. He clearly states that every analysis based on the analyst's countertransference – which has much more to do with the analyst than with the analysand – is bound to end in failure, just as, he says, would clearly be the case if a surgeon set out to operate based on the countertransference, instead of on what he saw or had discovered through anatomical and physiological examination.

A tendency to be guided by the emotional basis of their own impressions has frequently appeared when I have discussed with young colleagues their material: they would say that they acted on the basis of what they felt in their "countertransference," while they were actually quite deaf to their analysands' verbal communications and reasoning. This proclivity, with its attendant incapacity to listen to one's analysands, follow the way they think, and construct a dialogue that is consistent with their communications, leads, I observed, to relational disintegration.

I would not exclude the possibility that my surgical training has influenced my psychoanalytic approach to extreme situations like acute psychosis, which I have treated with highly frequent sessions in my office, working in dialogue with the analysand (Lombardi, 2003c) – always bearing in mind that failing to discuss a psychotic theory or to guide the confused manifestations of primitive mentalization towards more recognizable forms is more or less the equivalent of just letting an artery bleed instead of suturing it. And perhaps the idea that no psychoanalysis should be unconnected to some form of therapeutic benefit for the analysand who turns to us for help is also in part conditioned or strengthened by the imprinting of my surgical training. It was there that

I learned to consider the role of the body as inalienable, very simply because if there's no body there's no person. This idea implies a radical respect for the *person* of the analysand as one who is internally rooted in her own body, which is, clearly, distinct from our own. This elementary and basic notion has been essential to me since my first days of medico-surgery and throughout my present career as a psychoanalyst. Thus as an analyst I am careful to place my interlocutor within the three-dimensionality of her bodily space, as the only place where the analysand can experience her emotional and heedful presence. Of course, my original surgical vocation is just one aspect of the bodily world that permeates me: indeed, that world corresponds to the wide range of experiences – and sometimes conflicts – on the borderline between body and mind, which I shall be presenting in this book. The body–mind conflict belongs, in fact, no less to me than to my analysands: without recognizing it as a part of myself I would have run the risk of not understanding them. I leave it to the reader, however, to judge to what extent my clinical observations and reflections correspond to their experience of clinical reality and to the deepest needs of our analysands, and what these might contribute to an amplification of our psychoanalytic approach.

"And there is no new thing under the sun": the body in psychoanalysis

Interest in the body–mind relationship informed psychoanalysis at its inception and has continued to do so throughout its subsequent development.[1] The body–mind relationship is now taking on a renewed relevance because of the ever more common disturbances our patients show in this area. It is, indeed, a conflictual area involving many problems that have been approached in psychoanalysis in the light of different vertices, such as the essential conflict between feeling and thinking (Matte Blanco, 1988), the radical independent functions of *primordial mental activity* and mature cognition (Robbins, 2008, 2011), the failed encounter between overwhelming sensations and resources for containing entropy (Ferrari, 2004), the relation between pictorial or verbal symbolism and sub-symbolic levels (Bucci, 2007), deficits of maturational development (Gaddini, 1992), the incompatibility of subjective and objective thinking (Bach, 1998), etc.; but it presents implications that are consistent with various clinical situations, such as the integration of autistic nuclei (Tustin, 1981), psychic retreat (Steiner, 1993), and the inaccessibility of patients in the analytic setting (Joseph, 1975) – quite apart from points of contact with the neurosciences and philosophy (Damasio, 1994; Garroni, 1992; Nagel, 1981).

The body–mind relationship also inevitably brings up the possibility of body–mind dissociation. This subject was discerned quite early in psychoanalysis by Victor Tausk (1933) and was developed later on by Clifford Scott (1948) and Donald Winnicott (1958c [1954]). The dissociation described by these authors is particularly apposite in early catastrophic situations connected to an absence or distortion of maternal *rêverie* (Bion, 1962) or to specific relational traumas of various kinds (Seligman, 1999), which can cause a break in the body-affect-thought continuum (Lombardi, 2009b). It is a topic in some ways very close to those of dissociation and dissociative identity disorder, which have been explored in the North American literature (Loewenstein and Ross, 1992): situations in which the subject is well aware of being made up of different personalities with very different characteristics, or in which there is a lack of connection between different intrasubjective functions, such as thought and action. Subjects who suffer from varying degrees of body–mind dissociation can manage, in advanced stages of analysis, to have a clear perception of the internal disjunction that afflicts them: they can, for example, dream of being cut in two as if a saw had bisected their bodies, and the upper and lower parts no longer had anything to do with each other or had trouble getting together and being glued into one piece.

A vertex centered on body–mind dissociation supplements the classic psychoanalytic vertex, which tends to envisage a continuum and integration of the somatic and the psychic, which is the basis, for instance, of the empathic processes. As a consequence of his disagreement with Janet about dissociation, Freud became convinced that the dissociative manifestations Janet described should be viewed as manifestations of the unconscious (Ellenberger, 1976). More recently, Freud's perspective has been enhanced by a revalorization of dissociative phenomena, particularly in relation to different kinds of traumatic experiences (Bromberg, 2001; Davies and Frawley, 1994).

The body–mind dissociation to which I refer in this book should not, however, be confused with dissociation of a traumatic nature, nor indeed with the psychiatric conception of dissociation, whether at the psychotic or the hysterical level; it is to be understood as a discord that takes shape in a pre-mental period and cannot be identified with any known classified disease, but is analyzable – as we shall see – from a standpoint that focuses on the ways and forms of internal functioning, even if it does not take advantage of a reconstructive approach.

> If one regards the dual concept body/mind as a dynamic whole, the concept of illness/health becomes unsuitable, as well as reductive. More appropriate, instead ... that of psychophysical situations which display at one moment the domination of the physical, and at the next that of the mental, situations which can turn out to be more or less in harmony or in disharmony with the individual's needs.
> (Ferrari, 2005: 200)

The levels of functioning involved here are more primitive than the schizoid forms explored by Melanie Klein (1975f [1946]): when these discords are present in patients who are otherwise well integrated with reality, the distance found between external adaptation supported by rational abilities and the paucity or absence of contact with the sensory levels can be quite remarkable, as clearly emerges in the observational context of the analytical setting.

The discordant condition of the body–mind relationship can bring us uncomfortably face-to-face with the curative limitations of psychoanalytic work, even when it plumbs the depths. This means that certain patients, even after a long and engaged analysis, may not achieve a complete reconstruction of the body–mind connection. On the other hand, they may learn to make up for this deficit by constructing compensatory circuits of communication between body and mind. Somewhat like what happens in Oscar Wilde's *The Picture of Dorian Gray*, it is as if these patients could become aware of their impasse by means of analysis, developing an approach to their physical center through some sort of representation of their bodily phenomena: referring, for example, to their own image reflected in a mirror; or approaching the sensory perception of their bodies through physical treatments like massage, curative spas, or various physical experiences, including sexual relations in the broader sense of neosexuality (McDougall, 1995); thus restraining their tendency towards a complete distancing from their own physical nucleus.

Very insightful analysts (including Donald Winnicott, Thomas Ogden, Joseph Lichtenberg, etc.) have variously explored the body–mind relationship. I do not, with my own focus, pretend to exhaust the complexity of this clinical area, but would ideally contribute to its revalorization, recognizing in it the source of the most primitive conflict, which can give rise to serious manifestations, as well as to less evident disturbances that are often masked by "good functioning."

Bion and the theoretical simplification of thinking in the presence of emotions

Since every clinical contribution inevitably involves the role of theory, I shall dedicate a few lines to the latter, in an attempt to shift the emphasis to a vaster epistemological problem oriented towards stimulating awareness and inquiry in the analyst.

Bion (1962) was the first to bind thought to the presence of emotion – so that, as he saw it, if there is no emotion, there is no thought either – and he called for an epistemological approach in psychoanalysis that would require – absolutely – coming to terms with the need for *theoretical simplification*. This simplification should arise from the problems posed by listening to the difficult patient in the psychoanalytic session, and from the continuous series of personal choices that the analyst is called on to make in regard to the established parameters of the psychoanalytic tradition. In other words, the analyst needs general parameters pared down to their essentials, which they can then manage in their own way – "a theoretical framework of psychoanalysis which is yet capable of flexibility in action," as Bion describes it (1962: 40) – in order to remain in control of and responsible for his own choices.

With the increase in the number of theories to be found comes an increase in the margin of arbitrariness to which the analyst is exposed as regards the theories. There is a greater risk of intellectualization, as well as of a defensive use of the theories themselves, to the dangerous point of "pasting" theories onto the clinical context, so as to avoid the anxiety of the unknown or the travail of an authentic emotional transformation.

The logical and scientific thinking that the western tradition has built up, starting with Aristotle, forms a necessary but not sufficient condition for realizing a mental functioning with its roots in the unconscious: "Confronted with the complexities of the human mind, the analyst must be circumspect in following even accepted scientific method; its weakness may be closer to the weakness of psychotic thinking than superficial scrutiny would admit" (Bion, 1962: 14).

The analyst needs a personal list of the theories he most often makes use of (Bion, 1962: 39), so as to remain connected to the discoveries of his predecessors. This is a "theoretical" necessity that must perforce take account of the analyst's "clinical" need to keep his mind unsaturated and available for the reception of what the analysand is communicating. Bion (1955), in his essay on the development of schizophrenic thinking, provides a rigorously concise list of psychoanalytic theories that is still decidedly up-to-date:

(1) the importance of the *reality principle* in setting the psychic apparatus in motion, i.e., the theory that consciousness is connected to the sense organs (Freud, 1911a);
(2) the radical conflict between life instincts and death instincts (Freud, 1920; Klein, 1975g [1952]), a concept that has been abundantly criticized in psychoanalysis, but seems to me to be of great use in understanding the most severe clinical situations;
(3) the key importance of projective identification (Klein, 1975f), as well as of communicative projective identification (Bion, 1962), together with *rêverie*, identified by Bion as "that state of mind which is open to the reception of any 'objects' from the loved object and is therefore capable of reception of the infant's projective identifications whether they are felt by the infant to be good or bad" (1962: 36);
(4) Melanie Klein's clinical description of the sadistic attacks that the baby makes on the maternal breast (1975d [1935], 1975e [1936]), reinterpreted by Bion (1967c [1959]) as "attacks on linking," "hatred of thought," and "hatred of psychoanalysis";
(5) the distinction between the psychotic and the non-psychotic areas of the personality, which are present in everyone, from those who are phenomenologically psychotic to those who are considered generally sane and integrated with reality (Bion, 1967b [1957]).

"The dark night of the soul"

Bion was influenced by the ideas of poets and mystics such as Meister Eckhart and St. John of the Cross, so that the "dark night" – *Oh, night more lovely than the dawn* – became an essential guide to psychoanalytic experience, just as, in the mystical tradition, casting aside the light of the intellect allows one to draw nearer to or become one with God. Somewhat earlier, Thomas Aquinas reflected that too much information hindered the act of comprehension. Tolerance of the unknown and of mystery became, for Bion, the intimate essence of a psychoanalytic process conceived as a continuous "terrifying" evolution, which lends itself only at times to accessibility through consciousness. Bion borrowed his notion of *negative capability* from a letter by Keats, who defined it as being capable of "being in uncertainties, mysteries, doubts, without any irritable reaching after fact and reason."[2] Exercising the negative capability is, for the analyst, the definitive remedy for a "failure to observe" and an "inability to appreciate the significance of observation" (Bion, 1970).

For Bion, each session should be considered as a new session, oriented towards gathering new data: hence the analyst must protect himself against the risk of mental congestion by theories of uncertain reliability: ideally "the fact that any session is a new session and therefore an unknown situation that must be psycho-analytically investigated is not obscured by an already over-plentiful fund of pre- and mis-conceptions" (1962: 39). The negative capability thus turns out to be decisive for the analyst's being able to "relate to what is unknown both to him and the analysand" (1962: 124).

Mental models and abstraction are, for Bion, the mental tools that the analyst generally uses in his practice for organizing observed data. These are much more elementary and limited tools than psychoanalytic theories: their flexibility allows them to stand up to the impact of the analytic dialogue and helps to keep thought processes going in the course of the session: "the defect of the model as an instrument adds force to the need to produce abstractions" (Bion, 1962: 64). Models and abstractions are mediators in a system for which *experience is like scaffolding that is able to support a process of nourishment of the mind* that can generate mental growth, whereas psychoanalytic theories are simply too complex to be used in the practical context of analysis (cf. Lombardi, 2003c).

Bion underscores the constantly expanding subversive nature of psychoanalytic experience and the risk of forcing clinical reality to fit the Procrustean bed of what is considered an orthodox system.

> This is the characteristic of the mental domain: it cannot be contained within the framework of psycho-analytic theory. Is this the sign of defective theory, or a sign that psycho-analysts do not understand that psycho-analysis cannot be contained permanently within the definitions they use? It would be a valid observation to say that psycho-analysis cannot "contain" the mental domain because it is not a "container" but a "probe."
>
> (Bion, 1970: 72–73)

This problem becomes even more radical as one approaches a topic like the body, which by its very nature is like a constraint on the mind. The body plays a decisive generative role in terms of the mind, but is per se a "non-mental" object, which cannot be contained or consumed in any conceivable mental sphere. "There is ambiguity about the body," as Paul Valéry (1973) wrote, "It is what we see of ourselves. What we always feel attached to us. But also what we do not see and never will see."

This work is intended to place the body and the body–mind relationship in the rather exclusive company of those hypotheses, focused on the forms and functions of mental activity that can be considered orientative. All the same, this is an unknown with unexplored significance: even more so than the alpha, beta, etc. symbols that Bion considered "as unknowns whose value is to be determined" (1970: 73). It is this mysterious quality of what we wish to investigate that gives rise to the need to *favor an epistemological approach* – in which an unsaturated orientation is central – over a traditional approach focused on psychoanalytic theories. So the center of attention is the generative aspect of clinical experience, as well as finding such constants as there are in analytic communication.

Apart from epistemological problems, it should be noted that a choice that reappraises the role of psychoanalytic theories is not perhaps altogether alien to a certain personal limitation of the author, to the extent that I have found myself – as I made use in my clinical practice of the discipline of the absence of memory and desire proposed by Bion (1970) – increasingly, with the passage of time, favoring the virginal nature – the blank slate – of the clinical glance over the exigencies of erudition.

Thus, in the course of this book I shall not pursue the ambition of expanding my references to the various theories at large in psychoanalysis, hoping instead to draw the reader's attention to the details of what goes on in the analytic session, with the aim of providing some evidence of what has led me, over the years, to attribute central importance to the body–mind relationship and its dissociation. And so the reader will find here a series of largely clinical chapters – intended to arouse interest rather than to offer a dogmatic system of answers – although in some cases I shall seek to link clinical practice and theory within the limited context of the hypotheses that are favored here.

Sensory perception as the focus of the psychoanalytic gaze

Starting from Bion's observational standpoint, I shall move on to consider A. B. Ferrari's theory of the eclipse of the body, both because it derives from that standpoint, and might even be considered a sort of supplement to Bion's contribution or his own particular expansion of it on the body–mind level, and also because Ferrari's hypothesis forcefully puts the case for the importance of confronting the body in psychoanalysis, since it is constantly in danger of being dissociated, with the result that mental processes become abstract and impersonal. The re-emergence of the body with its related burden of concreteness creates atypical conditions for psychoanalytic working through, which can at times be confused with perversions or impasse. A psychoanalytic perspective that pays close attention to the presence of the body is, I find, particularly appropriate to today's increasing interest in the so-called primitive mental states, in which the containment of bodily experience does not necessarily coincide with the development of the verbal and representative levels of knowledge (cf. Korbivcher, 2014).

With the hypothesis of the eclipse of the body we witness an important *shift of perspective*: whereas Freud found that *sexuality* was the mainspring of mental functioning, and Bion had attributed a similarly definitive role to *emotion*, Ferrari focuses the psychoanalytic gaze on *sensation* – with all its disorganizing characteristics linked to primeval chaos – making it the driving force of the working through of the most primitive levels of the body–mind relationship. In contrast to the emphasis on auto-sensual states in autistic conditions and on primal anxieties about "falling, dissolving and spilling away" described by Tustin (1981, 1986), the eclipse of the body emphasizes *the organizing role of sensory perception* on the explosive levels dominated by primitive sensoriality, giving rise to sensory perceptual phenomena. The midnight of confrontation with the unconscious, evoked by Freud (1901) in the epigraph to his study of the parapraxis, reappears in the dark confrontation with the mysterious world of bodily sensations:

Um Mitternacht
Nahm ich in Acht
Die Schläge meines Herzens;

[Round midnight
I took notice of
The beating of my heart]
      F. Rückert (set by G. Mahler), "Um Mitternacht"

Many clinical phenomena that might at first glance seem essentially relational are used by the analyst – as we shall see in the course of the book – in aid of the *primary necessity of fostering body–mind communication*. The perceptional impact with sensory experience does not take place without conflict; indeed, it can be associated with a sense of catastrophe, or terror of a breakdown of the personality in the presence of bodily sensations – like what is evoked in Edgar Allan Poe's tale *The Fall of the House of Usher* – even when the impact is mediated by analytic *rêverie*.

This does not mean that the more developed levels of emotion (Bion) and of sexuality (Freud) disappear, but only that the analyst makes pragmatic use of a hierarchy devised on the basis of clinical urgency, in order to foster the growth of the analysand's personality and the analytic process.

Nonetheless, the emphasis on "sense" and "myth" on the primitive levels (Bion, 1963) does not exclude the contemporaneous presence there of the "passion" that derives only from a bi-personal context of confrontation and exchange. However, respecting the gradualness of the analysand's evolution, while keeping transference-based interpretations on one side, helps to provide a more rapid response to the serious symptomatic problems we have to face. Once the subject has taken on the resources of organization and dialogue on the body–mind level, the psychoanalytic process can benefit from having a more aware and reactive subject facing a specifically relational working-through.

Our analysands confront us more and more with the risk of loss of contact with the body, or even with its disappearance (Lombardi, 2009a, 2010). In contrast with the idea of the body that is present in psychoanalytic thought from its inception, the hypothesis of the eclipse of the body places *the body on the same level of importance as the mind*, resolutely assigning the ego–body relationship a significance beyond that of the more frequently explored ego–external object relationship, with the consequence that not only is development in the decisive direction of "minding the body" continually called into play, but so is the complementary challenge of "descending into the body." Whereas relational situations, both external and internalized, are generally at the center of psychoanalytic thought, the focus is shifted towards internal orientations, and towards the implicit theories the subject employs in relation to herself and to the relationship between body and mind. This is a choice that implies encouraging the analysand to take responsibility for her own intrasubjective functioning, and at the same time spurring the analyst towards a new creativity in the living substance of the analytic relationship.

"The essential experience is not the reading of this volume," Bion wrote (1970: 109), "but the matching of the real event in the psychoanalysis that approximates to these formulations." In the same way, *this* volume is meant to propose some formulations supported by a variety of examples that should bring the reader into contact with my clinical experience, giving him the chance, thereafter, to compare it with his own practice. Thus, I hope the reader can take this book as an occasion for confrontation that may inspire questions and further exploration, as suggested earlier, rather than as a system to adopt and apply, as is generally the case with traditional theories.

The model of "packing" and transference onto the body

Starting from his experience of psychoanalytic psychotherapy with autistic children, and profiting from the contributions of Hans Schilder, Esther Bick, Didier Anzieu, Françoise Dolto, and Gisela Pankow, Pierre Delion (2010) notes that *the great question about the transference in psychosis and on psychotic levels cannot be confronted without reference to the notion of the image of the body*, as a decisive spatial stage in the acquisition of a personal ego with a separate existence.

> The problem of determining limits seems to be the key problem in the psychotherapy of the psychoses. As long as no delimitation of the body has been achieved, it is not possible to engage in a therapy that calls upon the notion of the subject's actual history.
> (Jean Oury, quoted by Delion, 2010: 31)

In severe forms of autism and psychosis, there can emerge a disintegration of the boundaries of the self, with delusional colonization of the surrounding space, together with an impulse towards serious self-mutilation (tearing the eye from its socket, amputating the phalanges of the fingers, fracturing the forehead on the corner of a wall, etc.), as an expression of the patient's paradoxical attempt to take possession of a body of his own with its own boundaries. For these otherwise untreatable forms Delion bears witness to the utility of the technique of "packing": after preliminary psychological preparation of the patient, cold moist packs are closely applied, binding both legs and arms to the torso for 30 to 60 minutes, in the presence of two or more assistants who can help the patient whenever necessary and who, based on a technique first devised by Esther Bick, act as close observers of the session.

> Packing is a technique for making more present, and hence more real, the body of a severely disturbed patient who, in order to exist, attempts to regain contact with his body by means of an explosion of sensations, in some cases involving self-mutilation … Packing is one of the means of compensating for the missing representations of the organism … the bodily sensations created during the sessions offer material with which the child can construct some representational support that relieves the very profound anxieties connected to this fragile condition.
> (Delion, 2010: 105–108)

I have introduced the subject of *packing*, which, as such, is obviously not a possibility in the analytic session, as an illustrative *model*: it seems potentially instructive for the psychoanalyst in so far as it reveals the disorganization that takes place at the deepest levels in the absence of a system of bodily representation – which can exist even in apparently well-integrated patients – even as it also shows the organizing possibilities of a treatment aimed at potentiating the development of bodily representation. In the course of this book, the reader will be able to see how, even in a context quite different from the concrete one of *packing*, the analyst can attempt to construct a system of sensory representations of the patient's body, both through using *transference onto the body*, and by directing the communicational working-through in the session towards the *'vertical' axis* of the body–mind relationship. This orientation is not to be taken literally, but should, of course, be understood in the context of a flexible relational exchange typical of the psychoanalytic approach, in which the analyst makes it clear that she is in relational mode, even when that relationship is not in the foreground of a normal interpretation of the transference. When, in fact, we do not intervene with the classic system of interpretations of the transference, we find ourselves all the more involved in profound transferential dynamics that require the activation of the analyst's intense *rêverie* (Bion, 1962).

We might also in a sense speak of the need for *holding* (Winnicott, 1958b [1949]) – a conception that was, in its day, revolutionary in its approach to primitive states intersecting with the borderlines of the body (Winnicott, 1958c) – if clinical experience did not show the need to integrate *holding* with constant attention to the movements of the analysand's internal disposition, to the importance of the analysand's taking on responsibility about his relationship with his body, and about his use of thought, as well as other aspects which we shall see later on, that derive from the impact that Bion's contributions made on the psychoanalysis of primitive mental states.

Empirical research and the body–mind relationship

Recent neuroscientific research has led to the discovery of the anatomic/functional bases of intersubjectivity, thanks specifically to research into mirror neurons (Gallese *et al.*, 2007), so that we now know that evolution has led to the construction of neural mechanisms like a " 'we-centric space' ... grounding our identification and connectedness to others" (Vittorio Gallese, quoted by Emde, 2009: 556). These relational mechanisms turn out to be "the basic ground of our development and being" (Emde, 2009: 556). Recognition of oneself is thus connected to experiencing the other, so that, in a healthy person, the development of awareness of self and of the other seem like two sides of the same coin. The study, in infant research, of early relationality has also led to the concept of "we-ness" – which starts up after birth with early imitations of parental expressions and actions (Ammaniti and Trentini, 2009) – and ultimately to the theory of "we-go," according to which an intentional action is seen to have a relational basis, which could be considered a supplement, if not an alternative, to the theory of the ego, considered by some to be the expression of an obsolete "one-person psychology" (Emde, 2009).

What we learn from experimental research helps us to understand how the construction of the body–mind link develops in the context of early interaction, so that a harmonious horizontal mother–child relationship is crucial to creating a harmonious exchange and interaction between body and mind. In contrast, a discordant development of early relationality can give rise – bearing in mind how vulnerability varies from person to person, just as basic constitution does – to a disconnectedness in the internal relationship between body and mind, which we then see in our clinical practice in the form of dissociation or discord of the body–mind relationship.

Stanley Greenspan (1989) proposed a "developmental structuralist approach," integrating psychoanalysis with Piagetian psychology and experimental data, that recognizes *the existence of a very early developmental stage of the ego – characterized by the absence of differentiation between oneself*, the object *and the physical world* – whose main function is processing the sensory/affective area, i.e., working through stimuli and integrating them with other sensory experiences and with the motor apparatus. These phenomena, although they appear very early, can also be encountered in older children. In the latter stage, we can find notable differences from the sensory responses of newborns, and each subject reveals a specific sensibility of specific sense organs (affecting sight, hearing, touch, proprioception, etc.). The children who show signs of bad parenting also show a seriously compromised sensory integration (Greenspan, 1981). These early problems of the sensory area seem very similar to what we analysts encounter in certain patients: problems that require that we modify our psychoanalytic technique in keeping with the imperative – at early stages of relational non-differentiation – of stimulating a greater awareness of the proto-sensory levels.

Putting off the interpretation of the transference is thus not the same as repudiating the primary role of intersubjectivity, but is instead a practical way of getting at the fracture in the patient's body–mind relationship by orienting the intersubjective exchange during the session, in the first instance, towards facilitating the sensory integration and body–mind dialogue that presumably could not be constructed in the subject's earliest phases because of such circumstances as a distortion or absence of maternal *rêverie* (Bion, 1962). Thus, it must not be imagined that failing to interpret the transference corresponds to a neglect of the relational sphere. In reality, it is precisely reasons of a relational nature that lead to the clinical decision to favor the patient's most urgent body–mind problems.

Grappling clinically with the internal discords of the body–mind relationship requires the analyst's tolerating a paradox that involves renouncing a systematic emphasis on the psychoanalytic relationship at the same time as he makes a relational effort to tune into the patient's most urgent needs, trying to adopt his standpoint not only empathically, but also by using all of his *own* tools of cognitive attention: *a much greater relational effort than what is required for clinical work in which recognition of intersubjectivity is in the foreground.* We find, in fact, that we are working at levels of functioning in which, as mentioned above, the child's – or patient's – body can hardly be distinguished from the mother's – or the analyst's (Freud, 1929) – and in which we analysts are called upon to operate first of all as mediators in the primary processes of the patient's internal communication: processes that we generally presume are already well established, but that in these cases most certainly are *not*.

Together with what infant research has revealed about the intersubjective origins of the self, we should also bear in mind that it is hard to believe that we can free ourselves, in psychoanalysis, of the concept of the ego, which considers the subject in his specific intentionality and separateness from others. The concept of the ego, according to which "The ego is first and foremost a bodily ego" (Freud, 1923: 26), highlights the body as the place whence derive external and internal perceptions, which contribute decisively to structuring the subjective sense of the personality. Not unlike Freud, who viewed emotional life as a direct expression of an internal state of the body, the neurosciences have shown how "the core of the self" is to be found in primitive bodily emotions, and that consciousness cannot exist without a self-consciousness (or self-awareness) that comes from the recognition of the internal states of one's own body (Damasio, 1999).

> In Damasio's account of the core self, the conscious you springs from primordial feeling ... which arises from the non-conscious proto-self as it is being changed by what happens; in the words of T. S. Eliot "you are the music while the music lasts."
>
> (Sletvold, 2013: 1028)[3]

Eliot's phrase, as used by Damasio, clearly indicates the dynamic role that the sensory flow plays in the body–mind relationship in establishing mental activity and self-awareness, with the result that "the mind is not conceivable without some sort of *embodiment*" (Damasio, 1994: 234; my italics), and hence that we, as sentient beings, cannot ever leave out of consideration the music our bodies generate, or the "unheard melodies" of our proto-sensory states (Lombardi, 2008b).

The subject of the connection among psychoanalysis, infant research, and the neurosciences is complex and growing, and really needs a book of its own, and not one with a clinical approach. I would, however, like to mention that, in discussing one of the chapters in this volume,[4] Mark Blechner drew on his expertise in neuropsychoanalysis when he considered various elements of connection between body and mind in experimental research – such as the influence of temperature on the emotions (IJzerman and Semin, 2009; Zhong and Leonardelli 2008) and the connection among figures of speech, time, and bodily experience (Miles *et al.*, 2010) – and stated:

> There has been extensive research by cognitive neuroscientists, especially in the last 25 years, that explains how much our bodily experience interacts with our psychological perceptions, mostly unconsciously ... These findings give an empirical objective basis to Lombardi's clinical observations.
>
> (Blechner, 2011: 26–27)

Conclusion

What space for growth could there be today for interiority in a world dominated by artificial intelligence and social networks, and in which *seeming* is increasingly breathing down the neck of *being*, ready to take its place? The interest in the body–mind relationship recalls us to a subjective dimension of intimacy and interiority. Not only is relational intimacy difficult to achieve, but, most importantly, there is a danger that the intimacy whose confines are those of our own bodies and our particular sensibilities will become almost unattainable, because it is even more mysterious and ineffable through being rooted in the pre-verbal levels, as well as being the utmost challenge for our symbolic and cognitive tools. Hence we should not be surprised by the difficulty of gaining access to this area, even with a refined instrument such as the psychoanalytic approach. I believe that the new horizons of the body–mind relationship can spur new forms of self-awareness in dealing with the inner world and with an outer world that is ever more complex and unstable.

Notes

1 "And there is no new thing under the sun": Ecclesiastes 1:9.
2 John Keats, letter to his brother, December 21, 1817, quoted in Bion (1970: 125).
3 The quotation is taken from T. S. Eliot, *The Dry Salvages*, Part V.
4 Chapter 8. A first version was read at the Thirteenth Symposium of the Massachusetts Institute for Psychoanalysis: "Minding the Body: Clinical Conversations about the Somatic Unconscious," Boston, MA, May 1, 2010.

Chapter 1

Body–mind dissociation and transference onto the body

According to the Presocratic philosopher Heraclitus, conflict is the source of everything. Conflict was immortalized by the sculptor Phidias in the metopes of the Parthenon at the dawn of western civilization: he portrayed conflict between humans and beasts, and the barbarians and the civilized Greeks, or what finally comes down to conflict between the body and the mind. Freud placed conflict at the root of his notion of depth psychology. In our practice today we are facing new horizons of such a kind that the repressed unconscious is considered together with the unrepressed unconscious and its more pervasive role (Bion, 1970; Matte Blanco, 1975; Lombardi, 2015), with the result that *conflict reveals deeper implications, regarding, first of all, the body–mind relationship.*

Plato, in his dialogue *Phaedo*, expresses a conflictual concept of the body–mind relationship, a potential source of dissociation: "we make the nearest approach to knowledge when we have the least possible intercourse or communion with the body, and are not surfeited with the bodily nature, but keep ourselves pure."[1] Although Plato's position is not without provocative implications – not least because of his worry about the danger that man may sell his soul for "the gold of pleasure"[2] – Plato nonetheless introduces a dissociative supposition between body and mind when he speaks of "keep[ing] ourselves pure" – i.e., separate from the body – and of not being "contaminated" by its nature. This dissociative supposition was to become a constant throughout the history of western intellectual development.

A first draft of this chapter was read at the Alanson White Institute, New York, in April 2014. Translated by Karen Christenfeld.

At its inception, psychoanalysis had a revolutionary view of the individual as grounded in her body and its instinctual nature, thus granting the connection with the actual body much more prominence than it was to have later on with the development of object relations theory. Bion provides a lapidary summary of the initial psychoanalytic revolution when he states "The inescapable bestiality of the human animal is the quality from which our cherished and admired characteristics spring" (1970: 65–66).

The attention paid to reality –which is compromised in the major forms of mental illness such as psychosis – led Freud (1911a) to conceive of *the organizational role of consciousness in correlation to the sense organs* and also of *thought as a function with the task of containing motor discharge*. In this Freudian model of the origin of consciousness, a principal matrix of physicality, consisting of the sense organs, becomes capable of generating a perceptional flow from inside towards the outside world, and hence mental activity capable of recognizing reality and of delaying instinctual gratification, which to some extent reconciles the subject to the exigencies and limitations of reality.

From this same viewpoint of the continuity between the somatic and the psychic, Freud (1915b) underlined the need for continuity between the concrete and the abstract, distinguishing between "thing presentation" (*Dingvorstellung*) and "word presentation" (*Wortvorstellung*): "When we think in abstractions," he writes,

> there is a danger that we may neglect the relations of words to unconscious thing-presentations, and it must be confessed that the expression and content of our philosophizing then begins to acquire an unwelcome resemblance to the mode of operation of schizophrenics.
>
> (1915b: 204)

Freud thus maintains that the dissociation of the verbal sign from its "thingy" matrix can reduce a word to an abstraction shorn of its actual referent, hence confining the "thingy" nature of the world to an independent existence, extraneous and unrelated to representation.

Psychoanalytic practice now involves a much broader range of illnesses than what Freud contemplated in his day, so these hypotheses spanning body and mind can be seen to have a renewed timeliness and a potential for expansion in the context of a new clinical epistemology, which could release psychoanalysis from excessive abstraction and from the awkward straits of a systematic concept, and place it at the source of experience. The problem of conflict is now increasingly encountered in extremely radical forms, in which the body and the mind assume absolute roles, excluding each other entirely: when the body–mind conflict becomes intolerable, body–mind dissociation takes the upper hand. A psychoanalysis that takes the most primitive levels of inner integration for granted, concentrating too early on developed mental dynamics and object relations, is in danger of becoming anti-developmental and anti-therapeutic, and of turning into another of the many varieties of body–mind dissociation that are characteristic of contemporary life.

Insufficient maternal *rêverie* and loss of contact with the body

Freud's theories originated in empirical research: he always defended the experiential basis of his hypotheses, underlining the distinction between scientific theories that are the fruit of empirical research into real data and purely speculative notions. We should not, however, disregard the context in which Freud conducted his investigations, the Vienna of the *Finis Austriae*, pullulating with positivist yearnings and late Romantic affinities. The world we live in today is radically different from Freud's, and so is our phenomenology of mental illness. The agreeable patients who paved the way for Freud's discovery of the unconscious were part of a culture that guaranteed the continuance of the care that is given in the earliest phases of individual development. The modern world, instead, presents us with problems that increasingly express a very primitive complaint, traceable to one's earliest post-natal experiences – marked by the impact between the newborn and maternal *rêverie*– if not actually to the period of intrauterine gestation. The scarcity, deformation, or absence of maternal care has as its result such a distortion of development that it undermines a harmonious body–mind relationship, i.e., what Freud considered the instinctual and affective matrix from which the individual personality springs: a distortion so radical as to involve a dissociation from the body.

When I speak of *body–mind dissociation*, I mean a situation in which the body in itself continues to exist concretely, but disappears from the mind's horizon, just as the actual baby, originally pure physicality, may not feel accepted onto the horizon of the person looking after it: a reaction that obviously intersects with constitutional factors, so that certain babies are more liable to it than others. Deficient maternal care implies the baby's being required to adapt to external reality at a moment of its development in which it has not yet evolved sufficient resources to reconcile internal instinctual demands with external exigencies. This precocious adaptation causes a distorted development of ego functions (James, 1960; Winnicott, 1958c) such that the connection between the perception–consciousness axis and the emotion–instinct axis is particularly disturbed. Given how early this sort of problem appears, it is outside the conscious purview of historic reconstruction that characterizes the traditional psychoanalytic vertex. It requires instead *a working-through focused on the present*, on the heart of the analytic relationship, and on the activation of an awareness of one's own inner mode of functioning.

Bion (1970: 71ff.) was the first to call attention to the fact that a psychoanalysis that is up to evolving needs a container and a functioning *container–contained relationship*: a disorganized container–contained relationship makes the ordinary phenomena of psychoanalytic observation impossible, as well as preventing growth and personal development. Even though Bion never formalized a vertex centered on the body–mind relationship and the damage resulting from body–mind dissociation, his hypotheses about the container–contained relationship clearly refer to such a vertex, at a higher level of abstraction. When, for example, Bion (1970: 71) asserts that he is not in a position to "observe Mr. X because he will not remain 'inside' the analytic situation or even 'within' Mr. X himself," he is, without explicitly saying so, focusing on the implications of a body–mind dissociation such that the analysand can seem to be, as it were, *not inside himself*, or dissociated from the bodily reality that would be able to contain him, and is keeping himself similarly outside or unrelated to the psychoanalytic situation. This brings us back to the importance of the *body as the container of subjective experience*. The concept of the container likewise refers back to the importance of the setting, so that "the analysis has a location in time and space ... the hours arranged for the sessions and the four walls of the consulting room" (Bion, 1970: 71). If the field of analysis does not have these limits, Bion maintains, all psychoanalytic observations and any development of the analysand become impossible.

Body–mind dissociation, body–mind dialogue, and creativity

If we posit that the reception and the reflection that the mind accords the body form the indispensable starting-point of any form of thinking – Damasio (1994) would say that it was only through the body's need for it that the mind arose – then the absence of reference to the actual body inevitably implies the absence of a functioning mind as well. When I speak of body and mind, I do not mean to promote a Cartesian-style body–mind dualism: instead I intend to underline *the operational divergence effected by the body and the mind in the course of human functioning* – what Damasio (1994) calls *functional dualism* in the context of a position that recognizes a significant continuity between body and mind.

Even if we start from a unitary conception of the human being, we must take note of the existence in psychoanalytic practice of forms of profound dissonance in the body–mind relationship, justifying the term *body–mind dissociation*, a dissociation that is not about to take the place we are used to recognizing as belonging to the role of the unconscious. At the dawn of psychoanalysis, when Freud and Janet had their controversy about dissociation (cf. Ellenberger, 1970), they were both dealing with much more superficial phenomena than what we face in our practice today.

The conditions we shall seek to describe in the course of this book show a distinct tendency towards impasse in analysis because, as we shall see, the preconditions for internal working through, rooted in the body, have been compromised. In addition, the absence of bodily participation can easily lead to the ascendancy of unconscious falsehood (Bion, 1970), or to a condition of pseudo-existence characterized by imitative mechanisms that do not correspond to a solid personality basis. We find ourselves not only in a realm where outright psychopathology holds sway, but also faced with a *profound anthropological conflict* that is exacerbated by particular aspects of our contemporary world, so that we now feel as if we were taking part in the drama of the replicants in *Blade Runner* (dir. Ridley Scott, 1982), who are indistinguishable from us, although they are not human, or as if we lived in the condition shown in Spike Jonze's *Her* (2013), where the virtual reality of an operating system has taken the place of a flesh-and-blood partner. Being is under pressure from Seeming, causing an inner tension whereby the Freudian duality of thing-presentation and word-presentation is in danger of internal fracture and the whole representative system may be replaced by baseless abstractions. The presence of the body then seems relegated to a lost world, in which its needs and instincts are similar to a sort of *Jurassic Park* (dir. Steven Spielberg, 1993): simultaneously desired, feared, and denied. The only option left for the denied body may be just going its own way: rebellion and revenge by means of the violence of psychotic explosions, or the degeneration that takes place when the body resurfaces threateningly with somatic illness.

So we are increasingly faced with the mind's need to discover human limits by means of a direct confrontation with our bodily nature. Both analysand and analyst are called to the challenge of discovering our own tragic *conflict of substances*, the result of the bodily and mental dichotomy that inhabits us, and to find that each of us is – as Paul Klee sensed, at the dawn of the modern movements of the twentieth century – "half prisoner and half winged being" ("Halb Gefangener und halb Beflügelter"): only the toleration of the sense of powerlessness that comes from letting ourselves down into our bodily nature can give a non-mechanistic sense to our thinking and become a decisive stimulus to life and to personal creativity.

A shift of vertex

Assuming the existence of a basic primitive conflict between body and mind, which I shall be describing, together with its various implications, further on, I inevitably find myself shifting away from the standpoint from which Freud regarded it. Whereas the father of psychoanalysis emphasized the instinctual body that aspires to unbounded gratification, I, by contrast, am inclined to stress a condition of dissociation of the body, or the body's disappearance from the mind's horizon. In contemporary psychoanalytic practice we are faced with the explosion of an intolerance that asserts itself, first of all, through the blotting out of the body, which is felt to be the prime representative of our limits as human beings. While the Freudian vision and psychoanalytic tradition have familiarized us with the absolutization of the instinctual body, we find ourselves ever more often facing dissonant situations in which the mind has made itself independent of the body. Human beings, by structural and existential constitution, are placed between the two poles of body and mind: these are conflicting poles that draw us towards body–mind dissociation.

I should like, at this point, to insert a fragment of psychoanalytic experience, so as to begin to illustrate the theme of body–mind dissociation and its working-through – a theme that reappears, variously manifested, throughout the book. I feel I should point out beforehand that the reader will find, in these clinical examples, a rather different perspective: while in the first part of this chapter I limited myself essentially to description, in line with an etiological viewpoint – and hence I referred to dysfunctions of the mother–child relationship, which can foster a tendency to have the mind function in the absence of awareness of sensory data – the standpoint changes when we get right into actual analytic practice. In fact, we work with the current consequences of certain early dysfunctions, which have, with the passage of time, settled into a more or less stable personality order, to the point of forming an actual internal system based on organized theories of the mind, life, and relationships. The analyst thus faces the need to consider, first of all, the analysand's working arrangement for relating to herself. This arrangement is regarded as a working one – even when it is prompted by factors that are to a great extent unconscious – so as to emphasize that the analysand is responsible for herself and for the criteria she uses. This concept of responsibility as a distinguishing feature of the analytic project is a spur to opening up to change, which the analysand can introduce into the modes and forms of her internal functioning.

Underlining – as we did earlier – the shortcomings to which the analysand has been exposed in her surroundings spotlights the deficit dimension. Without in any way denying this dimension, I would add, indeed even favor, observing the internal arrangements the analysand uses in relating to the body, the mind, and the relations between the two. Thus we can view the theme of deficit together with that of conflict, and the inexhaustible problem of the destructive and constructive pressures to which human beings are subject, as basic characteristic elements of human functioning. As I see it, the perpetual to-and-fro from the body to the mind and vice versa is actually the basis of thinking operations. Experience is built up through continual interaction between the body and the mind, and between emotion and thought, in the intimate exchange between waves of sensations and the subject's perceptual and mental resources. When the subject chooses to avoid the often arduous work of transforming emotions into thought, he manages only to paralyze his mental functions.

In the context of our hypotheses, the pressure to dissociate from the body should be considered not only in relation to pathological distortions, but also as an expression of an *existential conflict* that is distinctly characteristic of man the animal. Indeed, emancipation from the body is an attempt to resolve, however factitiously, the essential conflict between sensation and thought that is structurally integral to *Homo sapiens*: just where concreteness and thought tend to establish themselves as independent substances, the human is faced by his own being, made up of an unhomogeneous medley of the physical and the mental (Garroni, 1992). From this viewpoint, the topic under discussion here should not be considered the expression of a merely episodic defect of thinking (Bion, 1962); instead it is actually the mind–body conflict, which has profound anthropological and philosophical roots in western culture (Finelli, 1995).

Slavery of the body and bodily claustrophobia

We shall now turn to a few brief clinical passages taken from the psychoanalytic sessions of Antonio. He was prey to continual anxious thoughts, including the idea that his apartment was being taken away from him, and he felt persecuted in various ways, particularly by the people in his office, from the managers to the secretaries, towards all of whom indiscriminately he adopted a subordinate and servile attitude. He suffered from psychosomatic digestive troubles, and had chronic respiratory infections. I feel that the nature of his problems makes him an interesting embodiment, as it were, of our theme.

> Antonio begins a session one summer by saying that he is struck by the fact that his analyst is wearing sandals that reveal his bare feet.

He is scandalized by the lack of propriety thus manifested. "These are the sandals of a slave!," he comments. He then recounts that on his way to my office he met someone in a gray business suit with a tie: he thought that that man must also be going to a psychoanalytic session. He adds that it could be his double.

In this start of a session one is struck by the attention he paid to a body peeking out and thus summoning his scandalized reaction. Antonio himself seemed to introduce the subject of dissociation when he revealed that he had an almost hallucinatory perception of himself in the man in a gray business suit, placing his double outside himself. So I might hypothesize that when Antonio set his dissociative mechanisms in motion, he was denying his own physical reality: a physical reality that had to remain hidden from his eyes, disguised under the gray of a business suit, as also under the gray of his feelings and his life. This can explain why the body that the analyst displayed with his uncovered feet was taken as a cause for scandal. We also see from his communication that the presence of his body had become for Antonio like the condition of slavery: evidently a condition he was attempting to avoid, by means of body–mind dissociation and the blotting out of the body.

More concisely, the theory behind the patient's internal arrangement is the assumption that the body makes slaves of us, whereas he wanted to be free of every form of "slavery," to the extent that he was willing to "do without" his body. This theory, in all its simplicity, can justify the anxieties the analysand reported. If by giving up his body he was giving up his first real home, his anxiety that his home was going to be taken away from him should not come as a surprise: it is just that his anxiety actually referred to his body-home, which he himself was taking away from himself, and not to the loss of his apartment-home – a threat that, moreover, he had good reason to know was not about to be fulfilled. We could also hypothesize that his refusal to seek a personal frame of reference in his body contributed significantly to his sense of precariousness as regards external reality: the quest for confirmation of his identity outside himself, instead of in the raw fact of his physical nature as the incontestable proof of his existence, led him to seek continuous approval and confirmation from others, from his professional role and from the advancement of his career. In addition, since he did not refer to an internal bodily referent, he was defenseless before the continual shifting of external referents, doomed to the constant instability that could be caused even by unimportant events, such as a variation in company policy, the transfer of managers or vice-managers, or even just secretaries' changes of mood.

We'll have a look now at another excerpt from a session, to enlarge our field of vision.

> Antonio relates that he was having a conversation with the manager and the assistant manager. The assistant manager failed to understand a reference made by the manager, at which point Antonio let slip an ironic comment, saying "Hello?," as when your interlocutor on the telephone seems not to have heard you, thus underlining his superior's obtuseness. At this point Antonio went into a state of panic, fearing that he had compromised his career forever. He told me he would rather have been the boxer whose ear Mike Tyson had bitten off a few days earlier than have possibly offended the assistant manager. And he added "Better to lose an ear than to ruin your career."

I was struck by the fact that the punishment Antonio wanted to inflict on himself for his presumed lack of respect was the amputation of a part of his body, a sense organ, and specifically the organ of *hearing*, in Italian *sentire*, which is also the word we use for feeling, both tactile and emotional, and hence reminiscent of one's emotional life as well, and one's own feelings. So I tried to introduce a comment that might draw his attention to his capacity for internal functioning, which he generally tended to forgo: that is, his capacity to be present, vis-à-vis himself and others, with the physical equipment of his sense organs and the attendant emotional resonance (the ear, hearing, feeling). Let's have a look at the dialogue that ensued.

L[ombardi]: You would like not to feel, not to be aware of the hatred that leads you to speak ironically.
A[ntonio]: That sort of comment was out of place.
L: It wasn't out of place in terms of your feelings. If you recognize your feelings, you can also find an acceptable way of expressing

them. As, by the way, with your use of irony, you seem quite able to do.
A: My foot is burning where the sole presses against the inside of the shoe. I'm just about ready to get mad. *(Pause)* It's odd how I don't feel the pressure of the couch on my calves today. It's as if everything were circulating properly. I feel relaxed.
L: It's your feelings that are circulating, your hatred that's circulating, when you're willing to accept it and express it. It burns, but not so much as you tend to fear it will. An acceptable burning.
A: I felt imprisoned when you connected the ear with feeling, imprisoned within my body. I prefer to escape from my body; for me it's a prison.

One sees from this sequence of dialogue that the analyst's positive evaluation of the analysand's ego resources, which the latter had generally tended to attack just as he did his physical functions (Bion, 1967c [1959]), had the effect of placing Antonio back within his bodily self. The sensory perceptions that originated with his foot affirmed the existence of his body. And the foot was precisely the part of the body that, in the course of that earlier session, was disdainfully associated with the analyst, who became "a slave." The sensation felt by the foot was a burning, which then opened the door to the perception of hatred. The reuniting of the patient and his body, together with the consequent limitations (the pressure on his sole) and the feelings of hatred, reveal a constructive value: Antonio had the impression that things were circulating well, both internally and externally. Not only could he now discover that he felt relaxed, instead of being prey to panic, but he had lost his habitual sense of being persecuted: the pressure of the couch disappeared together with the sense of pressure conveyed to him by the presence of his analyst, who was usually felt to be yet another of his external persecutors.

At this point in the session, assigning a place for feelings of hatred led to another important perception. Antonio revealed that when he placed himself inside his body he felt as though he were in prison, a prison from which he would usually escape ("I prefer to escape") by activating an internal mechanism that excluded every form of recognition of his body. Antonio's experience seems highly claustrophobic: being located within his body was felt to be inseparable from the acceptance of limitation, which Antonio instead erased in order to move towards the undifferentiated condition of limitlessness. This connection of the body with limitation and differentiation particularly emphasizes the continuity that exists between the recognition of the body and thinking functions, which would be unrealizable in the absence of respect for limitation and differentiation.

The tendency towards dissociation from the body, which is experienced as a prison, was actually leading Antonio not to achieve the freedom he would have liked, and not to escape from his prison or from "slavery," but only to inflict on himself the very "slavery" he wished to avoid, depriving himself of the sense of identity that comes with belonging to one's own body. By eliminating all reference to his body he not only failed to elude limitations, but he also found himself subject to external situations that were invested with all the criteria of aggression and intolerance that he regularly set up against himself. The freedom he longed for could thus be actually realized only within the limitations that the body provides: this is confirmed by the sense of well-being, relaxation, and internal circulation that he felt at the end of the session, which we could interpret as the acquisition of freedom that Antonio was finally experiencing when he was willing to place himself within his physical frame, and willing as well to pay the emotional price of the burning hatred that came from recognizing the limits of the human condition.

Antonio's condition commands our attention in part because it lends itself to a generalization that, as we mentioned at the outset, brings us back to certain characteristics of human beings that are particularly relevant to our time, such as a tendency towards dissociation of the mind from the material bodily foundation in which it is located.

Transference onto the body

"My foot is burning": when Antonio becomes aware of the sensation in his body, he is performing transference onto the body. And just a bit later this serves to reveal an important experience of bodily claustrophobia: "I felt imprisoned ... for me [the body] is a prison." Antonio generally uses thought in a way that contrasts with the experience of the body, so that thought is not the expression of the progression *body, affect, thought* (Lombardi, 2009a), but is instead the expression of a state of dissociation, in which, as Freud would have said, *words lose their connection with the world of concrete things*. To put it another way, the subject tends to use a symbolic system to avoid the experience of sensations, which are feared to be catastrophic and intolerable. In clinical conditions of body–mind dissociation, the activation in analysis of a transference by the analysand onto his own body can stimulate his integrated experience of himself, in which thought can intersect with internal sensations: a condition in which he can discover a point of contact and a possible consonance between his thinking and his feeling.

When we speak of transference in psychoanalysis, we generally mean the *transference onto the analyst*. The interpretation of this transference is generally regarded as central to psychoanalytic technique, to the point where it is considered the evidence of the psychoanalytic authenticity of the working-through. Authors like André Green have sought to resist this limitation of the concept of transference to the relationship with the analyst, emphasizing a double transference whereby the transference onto the analyst as an external object coexists with a *transference onto the word* (Green, 1984b: 181; 2002, 59). This expression refers to the flow of affective traces towards the quest for representations, a flow of feelings at the border of the unconscious directed towards the words of the analysand and the analyst. And in fact the first time that Freud used the word transference (*Übertragung*) was in *The Interpretation of Dreams* (1900), to indicate the transfer of unconscious traces onto the representative material of the day's residues. So Freud had a much broader concept of this word than the restricted sense of transference onto the analyst that it acquired with the subsequent development of psychoanalysis. Significantly, the transference that apparently most interested Freud, to judge from some clinical evidence, was that onto material that might set up a connection with the unconscious (Pohlen, 2009). And the fact that Freud regarded the unconscious as a sort of relay station between the body and the mind clearly emerges from his letter of June 5, 1917 to Georg Groddeck, in which he declares that the unconscious is the point of connection between body and mind, precisely the *missing link* that was for a long time sought (Freud and Groddeck, 1973). Hence it should not come as a surprise that what the analyst finds in her search through the material of the analytic session for a link with the body can become a means for the analysand to reach levels in which even the functioning of the unconscious is involved!

In the course of the book we shall see in various ways how, at primitive levels, a working-through constantly focused on the analyst can be anti-developmental and anti-therapeutic, distancing the subject from himself in all those states in which he has trouble relating to his own body and his own primary emotional levels. He is thus exposed to the risk of the paralyzing regressive dynamics of compliance and imitation. When we work with primitive mental states, the transference onto the analyst cohabits with *transference onto the body*: concentrating on the latter as the driving force of the working-through makes it possible to construct, in the midst of the analytic session, a fabric of body–mind connections, to which the patient would otherwise not have access. Ferrari (1992) conceptualized the contemporaneous progression of the *body–mind relationship* and the *analysand–analyst relationship* as a vertical axis and a horizontal axis respectively. This "vertical" transference of the analysand onto his own body could not take place without a *rêverie* (Bion, 1962) based on the analyst's capacity for "listening" to her own sensory world: thus there comes about in the session a *double and parallel transference on the part of the participants each onto his or her own corporality*. This focusing on bodily participation decisively facilitates the processes of empathy and emotional communication within the analytic couple, since a connection with sensations and sensitivity in general is a precondition for the emotional life.

The focus on the transference to the body is of essence particularly when the analysand shows an absence of emotional resonance, together with clear manifestations of estrangement from or indifference towards himself and his own physicality. I would emphasize that transference onto the body makes it possible to reach a level of experience that cannot necessarily be reduced to terms of particular mental contents. In fact, exploring feeling as a general human category brings up our vaster original condition – which itself cannot be directly reduced to symbolic terms, and which is ingrained in our identity as *Homo sapiens* – in which *the duality of knowing and feeling coexists with that of mind and body, as identity*: our awareness of bodily feeling can be the source of "the very sense of being, which is in continuous opposition to non-sense" (Garroni, 1992: 15).

Bodily counter-transference

The primacy of the sensory pressure that comes to light when the working-through creates a connection with bodily experience means that the analyst must operate on the same unorganized levels of fluid, untranslatable, and potentially explosive sensations that the analysand is living through. Thus the patient's bodily pressures – even before they are understood – should be cooled down, principally by means of the resources of internal containment. At these primitive levels, the analyst is confronted not so much with specific mental content or clear-cut conflictual areas – like those one finds in the more integrated phenomena of the counter-transference – but instead with more radical and primitive manifestations – which I shall indicate here with the term *somatic counter-transference* – so that the analyst finds herself containing in her own body the pre-symbolic sensory manifestations that pre-date mental phenomena, thereby fostering the conditions for mental functioning at more evolved levels.

There is now a general agreement to regard the counter-transference primarily in its non-pathological and non-refractory aspects (Gabbard, 1995). When primitive levels connected with bodily experience are in play, one has experiences that are distinctly characterized by unconscious participation and in which anxiety can easily become oceanic (Freud, 1929). These archaic levels involve approaching non- and pre-symbolic areas marked by indifferentiation and concreteness. In the course of psychoanalysis, the progress of the working-through can include confronting extreme phenomena of body–mind dissociation, with the sudden and sometimes long involvement of various sorts of somatic reactions. *The somatic counter-transference is actually the analyst's transference onto his own body, which is a prerequisite for accompanying the analysand's working through the approach to his own body*, particularly in developmental conditions in which the patient's body–mind dissociation is no longer in control. Here one encounters the various sensory sensibilities of analysts, so that one might especially notice Freud's hearing faculty in relation to his patients, or the particular visual quality of Melanie Klein's clinical talent. At the most primitive levels, phenomena of more diffuse reactivity enter into play, so the analyst's body functions like a receptor organ for the analysand's unconscious communications. The whole body becomes a sort of tympanic membrane for receiving purposes.

The somatic counter-transference can appear in the most varied ways, including a particular sensitivity to internal movements. So certain sense experiences draw the attention of the mind, as if they were subjected to the mediation of a magnifying glass: for instance, the sensory acuity of particular areas of the body, and various subjective somatic phenomena such as sensations of heat, nausea, dizziness, changes in respiratory rhythm, etc., as well as transitory physical indispositions (pains, muscular contractions, cardiac arrhythmias, etc.). These somatic phenomena can be accompanied by a transitory limitation of the resources of abstraction: the analyst's cathectic energy directed towards sensory-emotional levels can facilitate a willingness to contain sensory-emotional experience, which is in the process of being organized within the analysand.

A psycho-sensory pentagram

Over the course of time I have noticed how my analytic listening is greatly conditioned by some of my internal sensory movements, such as the perception of the weight and heat of my body, especially in the lumbar region. My disposition for listening to a patient's communications could not include emotional participation, not to mention rational comprehension, without *my personal sensory focusing*, from which my affective resonance and my intellectual activity branch out. It forms a sensory background that functions, in organizational terms, as a sort of *psycho-sensory pentagram*, on which there gradually gather traces of communication, both emotional and rational, from the analysand.

Considerable attention and dedication are called for in receiving the phenomena of the so-called somatic counter-transference, since physical emotions can be violent and difficult to contain and their metabolization time must be patiently allowed for. This time is independent of the analyst's will and can enter into conflict with other aspects of his life. The emotional working-through of the deeper levels extends, in fact, well beyond the confines of the session and may also exclude the conscious levels: it is hardly an accident that Freud, in his last work (1938), tended to attribute to bodily sensations a close correspondence to unconscious phenomena. The analyst is thus called upon to be aware of his internal reactions even outside his office, bearing in mind that they can perfectly well show up when he least expects them. Well beyond our conscious will, the experience we have with our analysands accompanies us continuously, and the related emotional working-through is continuous, active, and intense.

I shall give a brief example of the problems that emerge from the need to respect our sensory-emotional bodily reactions and the specific time their working-through requires. The example is taken from a turbulent period of the treatment of one of the cases we shall encounter later in the book. After some very dramatic sessions with personal attacks and many sorts of insults from the patient, I had gotten into the habit of allowing myself time for working through the state of physical chaos in which the end of the session generally left me. I was indeed often completely exhausted, as if I had finished a race or some enormous physical task; my breathing was shallow and labored and I had palpitations, all in connection with the emotional violence that had emerged during the session. Only some time to rest – as when one catches one's breath after a long run – would bring about a gradual reduction in my somatic reactions and allow me to put my sensory world back in order. One day I had not succeeded in scheduling my dentist's appointment at a more convenient time and I had to leave my office without my habitual period of emotional decompression after these sessions. I had no time to lose, so I quickly grabbed the removable radio from my car, but I moved in such haste that the radio fell onto my foot, causing a serious contusion, as a result of which I later had to have the nail of my big toe surgically removed. This trivial episode becomes significant if we consider that, were these forms of loss of motor coordination to increase, they could well cause accidents of far from trifling importance to the analyst. It can perhaps give us an idea of the risks implicit in the micro- and macro-phenomena of body–mind dissociation to which an analyst who works with difficult cases can be exposed, and of the caution and care that his self-government requires, going far beyond the specific processes of comprehension that are involved for more developed and mentalized areas. While comprehension can be very swift, emotional digestion takes considerable time and one must allow the affects to follow their own tempo.

Because of the objective difficulty of describing the involvement of the various levels called upon in clinical experience I shall not always manage, in the course of the book, to represent faithfully the three-dimensionality of my subjective experience with all its somatic implications. Hence I leave it to the sensitivity and intuition of the reader to imagine the foreseeable sensory and emotional reactions that accompany the exploration of the most primitive levels of human experience.

Towards a new centrality of the analysand

In this book I propose *a radical shift of emphasis, such that the interest of the body is not limited to its symbolic meaning or to related unconscious phantasies*. In other words, all of psychoanalysis does not come down to a mere metaphorization – with all due respect to the undeniable value of metaphors – but does instead call for a confrontation with reality, and with that first expression of reality, the body. In many cases a working-through aimed at a relationship with one's own body is the groundwork for mental functioning, offering a concrete referent for what Freud called *thing-presentation*: thanks to the real referent introduced by the body, this presentation begins to make sense, together with a personal experience of one's own unconscious. In the absence of the concrete internal referent of one's own body, the work done on symbols is in danger of remaining abstractly self-referential, empty of personal substance and anti-developmental.

In the last few decades the body–mind relationship has been underestimated in our discipline, probably because it could involve a retrenchment of the interpretative and metaphorizing power of psychoanalysis, since it spotlights elements of evidence that might be felt to diminish the intellectual status of the analyst.

Some analysts are capable of taking as a sort of threat to their identity the increasing importance of concreteness and the limited ability to deal with metaphoric levels in so many people who now enter analysis. In fact, even in patients with apparently developed mentalization, it often happens that the evolution of the analytic process includes a valorization of the more concrete levels of experience, so that a link between thought and the actual physical person of the subject can be constructed.

The real and concrete body has been forgotten in psychoanalysis, perhaps also because it reduces the charismatic power of the psychoanalyst as the "expert" in terms of the analysand's situation: it is not fortuitous that recognizing the existence of an actual body implies the recognition of the *real barriers that pertain to bodies*, so that the analysand is the only one who can actually be an expert about herself – about what takes place within her own "borders" – and thus the analyst is structurally prevented from going beyond a hypothesis, a suggestion or an external catalysis of the phenomena that remain substantially internal to and primarily within the province of the analysand. It was with telling perspicacity that Bion noted that patients' problems "are due not to their failure to represent but to their failure to *be*" (1970: 18).

Placing the body in the foreground in psychoanalysis implies giving back to the analysand a territory where she has a genuine expertise and authority: an authority that has too often been overshadowed by an analytic culture that is maddeningly focused on the interpretation of the transference and the request for dependency. Valorizing the body in psychoanalysis can therefore have a decisive protective function in the face of unwitting operations of colonization and subjection of the patient to analytic knowledge. It can also militate against losing awareness of the decisive role of responsibility that the analysand continues to play towards herself, even in the intimately relational context of the analytic process. And I hope that what I have given a preview of in this chapter will become increasingly resonant and intelligible to the reader as he proceeds in the reading of the book.

Notes

1 Plato, *Phaedo* 67A, quoted by Reale (1999: 209), here translated by Benjamin Jowett.
2 Plato, *Republic* IX, 589, E590A, quoted by Reale (1999: 309).

Chapter 2

Visual power, emotions, and mental growth

A clinical essay on some of Bion's earliest psychosomatic intuitions

As an old proverb has it, *well begun is half done*. In this spirit I should like to go over some brief passages from one of Bion's first papers, "The imaginary twin" (Bion, 1967a), which he read to the British Psychoanalytical Society in 1950, and in which he set forth certain ideas that would come to characterize his approach. They appear here in inchoate form, just as they emerge from his consideration of clinical material. Hence these hypotheses, well grounded in the concreteness of his experience, are particularly relevant to clinical experience generally.

The increasingly wide-spread interest in Bion's thought is, I find, revealing the risk of the codification of his thinking as abstract psychologizing, whereas I believe his contribution is inconceivable without reference to clinical experience, where one is called upon to effect a dynamic fluctuation between concretization and abstraction, and to be open to new thoughts and different ways of thinking in one's dialogue with a patient. In other words, Bion's legacy can be seen as the antithesis of a self-absorbed system. He sets out from an awareness that the psychoanalytic exploration of the unconscious and its theorization have run up against a point of saturation, so that instead of contributing to the *escalation* of the number of psychoanalytic theories now in circulation, they require an *epistemological sensibility on the part of the analyst* as the foundation for the exercise of curiosity about an object that is in itself unknowable.

So let's enter the thick of Bion's early psychoanalytic contribution, regarding it in the context of his clinical work illuminated by some of

A first draft of this chapter was read at the University of Nantes in December 2013.

his comments. I shall try to focus the lens on a few micro-sequences of the session in which the body is highlighted, so as to get at Bion's clinical thinking at its origin in his own clinical experience. I'll begin with his description of a physical movement the patient makes after a comment: "[The] patient shifted uneasily on the couch and became tense." At this point the patient says:

> I feel curled up and I am afraid that if I stay like this I shall have cramp. If I stretch out I shall become rigid and touch the pillow and contaminate it and get contaminated back again. I feel as if I were in the womb.
>
> (Bion, 1967a: 10)

Bion interprets the hatred that, as he says, "a less cramped position would release" (11). This hatred is also understood in relation to the analyst, to the point that the patient fears the development of an analytic relationship because of the risk of coming up against mutual hatred. Let's have a look at how Bion spurs the patient to appropriate, in a responsible – non-regressive – way, his feelings and the actual situation of the intersubjective relation that analysis implies.

What seems even more important is the appearance in this clinical fragment of a physical experience the patient has during the session, together with his paranoid feeling of contamination, activated by an experience of physical contact. In this passage, the reference to the *concreteness of the experience of the body* is accompanied by an emphasis on *hatred* and on the patient's accepting *responsibility* in terms of his real ego resources.

In the following session the patient brings in a dream accompanied by great emotional violence:

> He said that a man had presented him with a bill and then left the house. The bill was far too large. He followed to expostulate but the man rapidly disappeared, disregarding my patient's attempts to arrest his attention by tapping him on the shoulder. My patient felt overwhelmed with rage such as he had never felt before and awoke in terror.
>
> (11)

Bion connects the dream with the experience of the previous session, noting that this evolution significantly improved the patient's relationship with reality.

The actual experience of sensory contact (muscular tension) and of the translation into words that the analyst proposes (the feeling of hatred) is transformed in the dream into the representation of a written document (a bill) and a sensory contact (tapping the man on his shoulder). The bodily element and the representational element are side-by-side. The dream in its turn opens the way to a violent emotional activation: a "rage" "never felt before," which passes from the dream to wakefulness. The bodily participation and the rage seem to contribute decisively to make real the patient's psychoanalytic participation.

At this point of the analytic development, the patient produces associations about eye infections and ophthalmologists ("eye men"). Bion associates the presence of eye men with various unconscious fantasies, which seems in line with a certain Kleinian tendency to plunge headlong into the interpretation of unconscious fantasies, lest the entire enterprise, from psychoanalysis to psychotherapy, be degraded. I should like to state at once that this "headlong plunge" of Bion's into unconscious fantasy does not seem very convincing as regards the patient's very primitive level of functioning. What appears to be more efficacious – in addition to fostering the development of an original perspective – is instead Bion's emphasizing that "The eye men ... also represented the reinforcement of the investigating weapons by something like intellect" (14).

This emergence of the eye as an expression of new resources connected with the external and internal worlds is associated with an interesting note of Bion's about an emerging need of the analysand's: i.e., that the analyst, although considered for various reasons important, ought "not to interfere." In other words, this clinical experience was showing Bion the need to put the brakes on his interpretative apparatus, with its tendency to keep the analyst constantly in the foreground through the systematic use of transference interpretations. And this discovery of his seems essential to being able to support the development, in a difficult patient, of a new and delicate internal functioning that fosters mental growth: the eye. What is apparently being questioned here is not only the pre-eminence of the transference, but also the pride of place regularly granted to reference to the external object and its organizing function, or the idea of the good breast as the first ego-nucleus. At the same time, however, Bion stresses the organizing and perceptual function of the body with its anatomic and physiological apparatus.

So what of the "eye men" then? If there is still some doubt, we can ask ourselves again if he's referring to an unconscious fantasy or to something more concrete and real. And then we can look at Bion's answer. He writes "I could consider the two eye men as parts of his body, possibly his two eyes that were to be harmonized into binocular vision." We know that *binocular vision* was to have an important place in Bion's work. Here we find this insight in its prototypical concrete reference to the reality of two eyes as parts of the patient's real body – part of his anatomic and physiological apparatus.

Further on in the patient's material there enters "an ear, nose and throat surgeon," together with some persecutory feelings towards that doctor. At this point Bion puts forward the hypothesis that progress was felt by the patient to be unendurable, since psychoanalysis involved examining his own problems "with all his senses, including sight and intellect," a "painful co-ordination" of these senses, and "the imposition of responsibilities which he could not shoulder" (15). Once again Bion avoids a confrontation with the element of unconscious fantasy in order to underline *the concreteness of the sense organs*, the *pain* – not only mental but also *psycho-physical* – that arises from the need to coordinate the sense organs, and the *responsibilities* inherent in functioning in the real world, which themselves arise from the subject's sensory perceptions.

We'll skip ahead now and have a look at the conclusions Bion draws from the three cases he presents in this very early article. He writes, correlating the eye and mental growth, that "*vision ...* seems to be linked with the development of intellect" and that "*visual power ...* represented the emergence of a new capacity for exploring the environment" (my emphasis). And he then adds:

> it has been possible to show that in this respect the analysis was being felt as an addition to the patient's armoury for investigation and was likely therefore to be reactivating emotions associated with very early advances in psychological development that had a similar effect in increasing capacity. The increase of power was felt to demand an increase in intellectual grasp.
>
> (21)

Visual power thus appears as a new capacity for exploring and learning, and this capacity implies an increase in mental capacity. It reactivates "emotions associated with very early advances in psychological development," thus preceding the very early Oedipal phase explored by Klein. This capacity has, however, a specific value in the patient's current life because it becomes inseparable – as Bion immediately makes clear – from the tendency to take responsibility for oneself, one's life, and one's relationships. Hence it is an instrument for taking note of pre-existing problems in the personality that are waiting to be revealed: in other words, the activation of visual power produces an "increased capacity for awareness" that offers the conditions for achieving new changes, or rather the conditions for a work-in-progress that is never finished.

In later works Bion was to develop this point more fully, emphasizing how *perception can be too powerful in relation to the sensitivity of the receiver apparatus*, so that an emotional catastrophe can become inevitable. In that case the catastrophe becomes the signal of the start of a new kind of perception and of the possibility of introducing change. This important conjuncture offers us a key to reading certain forms of psychotic decompensation – particularly during adolescence – in developmental terms (cf. Lombardi and Pola, 2010).

As regards relating to reality, if the process of perception fails to lead to assuming responsibility and to a real change, it means that the mental metabolism is not fully functioning and that there are interferences (that might be susceptible to analytic exploration). Reading between the lines we can glimpse what is involved in the relativity to which the analytic experience is exposed: if the subject does not make room for the emotional implications of a new way of perceiving there can be no metabolizing and growth, just as there can be no real growth if there is no room for the pragmatic implications of thought – that is, if there is no internal assumption of responsibility and willingness to change arising from the perception itself. Such evidence of the relativity of psychoanalysis meets with apparent obliviousness from many psychoanalytic societies that aspire, during the formative process, to the total control of their members.

In *The Imaginary Twin* Bion establishes a different priority from that of the analysts who preceded him: i.e., analysis does not deal so much, or not only, with examples of repression and splitting that must be resolved, but instead with the activation of mental resources whose prerequisite is the functioning physical and anatomical equipment connected to our specialized sense organs. Thus the analyst presents to the patient "problems of mastery of a new sense organ." And these problems reveal the characteristics of a psychosomatic problem.

"For myself," Bion writes, towards the end of his paper (21–22):

> *I have found it impossible to interpret the material presented to me by these patients as a manifestation of purely psychological development divorced from any concurrent physical development.* I have wondered whether the psychological development was bound up with the development of ocular control in the same way that problems of development linked with oral aggression co-exist with the eruption of teeth.
>
> (Bion, 1967a: 21–22; my emphasis)

Here we find a point that leads us to the reason I do not concur with those who consider psychosomatic problems as a specific category. If analysis calls into play "problems of mastery of a new sense organ" a psychoanalysis cannot fail to include somatic involvement, on the part of both the analysand and the analyst. More simply put, it's hard to believe that an analysis can result in any sort of change if it is conducted at a purely intellectual level – that is, if it does not expand to involve the body and concrete action in real life. In other words, I am saying that it seems improbable that psychoanalysis can actually be therapeutic in serious cases if it is not taken to the most primitive levels of the personality where, in the here and now of the analytic session, the bodily roots of the capacity to think are organized.

To recapitulate what we have seen so far, I think that this early work of Bion's shows us various interesting elements – developed by Bion in different ways over the course of his life – such as *the relationship of the sense organs with the actual body as regards the growth of the mind* (or something that could be interpreted as the expression of the body–mind relationship, a point that all but disappeared from Bion's subsequent work), *the cardinal importance of the relationship with external reality, the role of visual power and of coordination among the various senses, hatred as an instrument of internal and relational confrontation, the need for some tolerance of frustration and pain (connected to the use and coordination of the sense organs), the function of responsibility, and binocular vision*: an assortment of elements that gives us quite a good idea of the direction in which Bion would later move in his major works, starting with *Learning from Experience* (Bion, 1962).

It is an interdependent assortment of data that requires no particular theoretical equipment if one wishes to understand it: an indication of the importance that Bion attributes to common sense and empirical evidence as an alternative to the excessive use of psychoanalytic theories. For Bion, the number of basic psychoanalytic theories could be reduced to four or five: they are important to the extent that they can be used as a basis for comparison. And each individual analyst must accept responsibility for his choice of guiding theories. Bion himself referred particularly often to theories regarding mental functioning for the containment of motor discharge (Freud, 1911a), projective identification (Klein, 1975f), and the differentiation between the psychotic and the non-psychotic parts of the personality (Bion, 1967b). However, Bion maintains that psychoanalytic work is to be carried out not with psychoanalytic theories, but with the use of common sense: that is, by means of what he calls mental models (Bion, 1962), which allow one to hypothesize the internal disposition with which the patient relates to his thinking apparatus (cf. Lombardi, 2003c).

I shall now attempt to explore some of the clinical implications of the interpretation of Bion that I've presented, underlining the link between primitive mental functioning and certain aspects connected to the body, such as the sense organs. Thus, this reading of Bion is inevitably conditioned by my interest in phenomena connected to the body–mind relationship.

The discovery of visual power

We shall now consider some aspects of the clinical case of Mauro, in which we can see the developmental role of the visual capacity as a springboard to the construction of an ability to think. Mauro was at this point a 24-year-old patient with a psychiatric diagnosis of schizophrenia, agoraphobia, and erythrophobia, who saw three different specialists with his family for psychoanalysis, pharmacological treatment, and consultation respectively. I followed the case as a supervisor.[1] I find it significant because of its evolution from body to mind, i.e., from the concrete physical level of blushing to emotions that were recognized and considered, and formed the basis of his ability to think.

A turning-point in this clinical work came when the patient decided to forgo a surgical procedure to cut some nerves in order to eliminate blushing. In analysis he could see how the surgical solution corresponded to his seeking "not to feel anything," which he had regarded as the ideal condition.

It was in this developmental phase when Mauro rejected the "surgical solution" that the analyst had the impression that she was facing a person who was opening his eyes to the world for the first time. "I see all these people moving about: Where are they running to?," the patient remarked.

During a session, Mauro suddenly said:

M[auro]: I can't look at that plate, it's not respectful.
A[nalyst]: You feel that looking isn't respectful. For you, your eyes offend.

We see how the patient's conception of looking is characterized by paranoid fantasies of lacking respect and anxiety about retaliation. The analyst verbalizes the internal theory used by the patient in relation to eyes and looking, in order to foster his self-awareness and change.

Let's have a look at some other sequences.

M: When they look at me, they're stabbing me.
A: You attribute to a look all the hatred you fail to recognize, so that being looked at becomes being killed: instead of considering that looking is part of seeing.

And then, in a subsequent session:

M: I have to take my pills in front of the mirror because that way I can see myself; otherwise I can't trust my mouth.
A: If you learn to trust your ability to see you will also be able to grant your mouth an actual location: a way of seeing yourself and finding yourself.

On all these occasions the analyst stresses the value of the eye and of seeing, distinguishing between the realistic visual function of the eye and an instinctual orientation characterized by hatred, in which the eye is felt to be piercing and violent, and "looking" becomes equal to "killing."

This clinical material shows us how the border between the abstract visual function directed towards seeing, and the gaze as something concrete, intrusive, and violent, can become quite unstable in psychosis: a shifting shadowy line that has been an object of exploration in films, both as a *conflict between seeing and not seeing* – so that the eyes can be simultaneously open and closed, as in Stanley Kubrick's *Eyes Wide Shut* (1999) – and as *confusion between perceiving and killing* – for example in Michael Powell's *Peeping Tom* (1960), in which the gaze/movie camera very nearly becomes a lethal weapon.

Returning to the case at hand, Mauro observed on another occasion:

M: The weather has changed!
A: *(The analyst is surprised by his ability to detect change.) You're observing that something has changed.*
M: Yes! Because on Tuesday it was sunny and today it's raining.
A: Now you can see how Tuesday is different from Thursday.

The analyst's comments, in the treatment of serious cases with thinking defects, should be guided mainly by good sense, and should be directed towards helping the patient achieve a first perception of reality, when a perceptual orientation tends to be alien to a patient who is sealed off from the world in a dimension that knows neither space nor time. In this brief fragment, *time* occupies center stage in the patient's perception (and I should mention here that the word for weather in Italian is the same as a word for time: they are both called *tempo*, which I shall use where necessary) – and in a curious way, abstract *tempo* is perceived through the mediation of concrete, atmospheric *tempo* – indicating a confrontation with real space-time. Simple though it was, his perceiving with his eyes the difference of one day from another introduced an innovation in a universe that had been paralyzed, atemporal, and aspatial.

Some aspects linked to the sense organs then appeared.

M: In a dream I'm with my mother, and I can feel that my ear is dirty. First I try to clean it by myself, but I can't manage to, so then I ask my mother to have a look and to clean it for me.

A: You tend to look after your ears and your sense organs just as a mother looks after her baby. Now you keep your ears clean, in the sense that they're open to external stimuli, in the same way that you're learning to keep your eyes open.

The analyst does not interpret the maternal transference onto herself – although she is certainly present at a certain level in the patient's communication and in the effectiveness of the analytic relationship, but instead she underlines *the patient's transference onto himself*, or what I have called *the transference onto one's own body* (Lombardi, 2005a, 2010), and in particular his relationship to his sense organs as a starting-point for a *consciousness connected to the sense organs* (Freud, 1911a).

In an evolution in which *the analyst ascribed primary importance to the analysand's relationship with himself*, references to bodily sensations started to appear in the analytic material.

M: How odd ... My stomach is hard.

A: You are aware of the sensations in your stomach and are able to wonder what these sensations might be communicating.

So the hard stomach can be translated by the patient into communications with an emotional import, such as "I feel tense," "I feel a tension that starts at my stomach and spreads all over me," to the point where it becomes, as we shall see, "I'm frightened" – i.e., the explicit expression of a feeling. This is a very important development, considering the fact that the patient started this analysis with a condition of "feeling nothing," in which, moreover, the physiological and corporeal proto-manifestations (the vasomotor discharge of blushing) had been diagnosed as something to be eliminated by surgical excision.

One day, for the first time, Mauro connected his fear of blushing to something he could question himself about:

M: At a certain point I felt my face getting hot, and then I asked myself, "But why do I react like this when someone talks about the past?"

This simple passage was like a Copernican revolution in Mauro's internal cosmos: for the first time *blushing* was no longer considered a failing to be ignored or eliminated, but the *starting-point for questioning himself.* During this same period the analyst began to notice that Mauro took his time before answering her: as if the initiation of a *visual power* were leading him, after he had begun to be aware of the temporal dimension, to make a *pragmatic use of the concept of time so as to "give himself actual time."*

M: Before, when I heard a funny remark I would immediately blush. Now a funny remark is a sound that enters my ear and hits my brain: at this point I feel that there's *a pause*.

A: Thanks to this pause you are able to work mentally. During the pause you take in the effect of the words on you and you give them a meaning.

Thus the perceptual discovery of time was explicitly worked through by the patient with the discovery of an internal time that Mauro called a "pause." While previously an ironic quip was taken as an attack, now Mauro was introducing a temporal margin that allowed him to give the remark some representative and symbolic meaning. This passage seemed to be a crucial moment: it was as if a primitive stimulus–response reflex arc had been replaced by a broader reverberating circuit, in which a stimulus was followed by a temporal delay, a pause, out of which phenomena of self-observation and self-awareness could develop.

So the patient felt stimulated to carry out further observations of his way of functioning. One day he noted:

M: This is a period when I feel my face getting hot before I go out, whatever is going to happen outside.

A: You're noticing that anxiety attacks you before you go out. It's as if you were anticipating trouble even though you don't know what will take place, instead of waiting to see what happens.

In this way it became possible to point out to Mauro his decided tendency to function by "foreseeing" events, which was in line with his interest in control and the negative fantasy that things always go badly: a system in which the repetition of his expectations took the place of activating a perception of reality.

The consequence of this working-through was a distinct reduction of his persecutory anxieties, to the point where he stopped complaining about his blushing as a distressing symptom.

This phase at the same time paved the way for a new anxiety, because Mauro was faced with a paradox.

M: Now, just when I'm doing better, in a certain sense I feel worse, in the sense that before, when I didn't feel, I didn't have any problems. Now that I'm feeling, I'm aware that I'm better, but it also costs me a lot of effort.

A: It's like the gym. At the start your muscles aren't in shape and it takes more effort. Then, with the passage of time, you get into shape and it can become less tiring.

So Mauro was discovering that he could manage his mind from inside, and restrain his apprehensive anxiety. In this way respect for temporal limits and the analytic "gym" that helped him work out being in the present allowed him to reassess the negative fantasies associated with his anticipative tendency, and to activate real perceptions mediated by his eyes.

With experience Mauro began to understand that only a dialogue with his anxieties could make them tolerable.

M: Now, when I go out, things are changed. Before there was this "I don't feel." Now I don't think first and this frightens me.
A: What you call thinking was your way of controlling what might happen. Now instead you can tolerate fear and take care to keep yourself in the present.
M: I used to mind my own business and weigh everything beforehand. Now everything's becoming different and new: and it frightens me. *(With a more positive tone)* But it's nice, this simultaneousness with what's happening to me.

Mauro is here taking note of his former way of functioning, centered on anticipative control and "not feeling," with which he contrasts his willingness to live in the present and tolerate his "feeling" frightened.

This "simultaneousness" could give rise to genuine experience that might stimulate mental growth. If he respects the progress of time and the functioning of a visual power focused on the present, the word "thinking" can acquire a more realistic meaning for him, unlike what used to happen in the past when "thinking" for him was tinged with the omnipotent coloration of anticipation and control. Incidentally, this point might lead us to consider the defensive implications of detachment from actual experience that may derive, for all of us – psychoanalysts and psychiatrists – from a kind of thinking that is excessively anchored to preconceived theories and insufficiently synchronized with what is happening in the constantly changing process of clinical experience.

But let's return to the implications of Mauro's two different ways of orienting his mind – "anticipative control" and "thinking in the present" – by following the personal exploration that the patient started up in analysis.

M: I believe I've understood how it works. I was thinking about it the other day. I used to live like a baby who's frightened and who's totally paralyzed. But now I say to myself "I'm experiencing fear."

A: You can see how you've changed: from your paralysis you're moving on to an ability to feel and to a dialogue with yourself.

M: You know how it is when there's an earthquake? There are buildings that, even though they seem new, collapse, while others have been specifically built to be earthquake-proof: they totter but they don't fall. Before, I was paralyzed by the idea of a collapse; now, I feel the fear, I totter, but I don't collapse.

We can see how Mauro's internal theories about thought were shot through with concreteness, to the point where the feeling of *fear* seemed *distinctly corporeal*: "shaking with fear" reveals its concrete dimension in its link to physical manifestations such as palpitations, unrest, and muscular tremor: in other words, bodily earthquakes. (It should, incidentally, be noted that Mauro lived in a city that was completely destroyed by an earthquake many years ago, so that collapsing buildings have quite a concrete referent in his culture.) In the course of the analytic evolution, the awareness Mauro had developed of his ways of functioning led him to discover that *he could tremble without necessarily collapsing*, as is the case with earthquake-proof buildings. This evolution also applied to a further working-through of his erythrophobia, since the vasomotor tremor of emotion that had formerly exploded somatically could now be received in a different way in the context of a mind disposed to recognize and accept the "tremor" of emotion instead of rejecting it while waiting to do away with it altogether. We might describe this new form of interaction between the physical roots of emotion and the mind as another example of Bion's *container–contained relation* (1970).

So the case of Mauro has allowed us a look at the evolution of a blind and explosive corporeal-sensory reaction (blushing and erythrophobia) at the dawning of a visual capacity that would then pass on to perceptual functioning capable of coexisting with the disruptive thrust of emotional tremors: an evolution that accepts the role of the eye and the gaze in constructing progressive mental functions that lead to thinking in the presence of emotions (Bion, 1967d [1962]). In this evolution the creative interchange between perception and tremor contributes to the creation of a binocular vision, in which thought and emotion reveal their mutually complementary natures.

The lost eye

We can now proceed to a second case, which provides further evidence of the organizing role of the eye and of seeing, as well as the disruption and collapse to which the emotional eye may be exposed. Rosa started analysis when she was 24, after a serious psychotic crisis was followed, a few months later, by attempted suicide. Analytic work extended over fourteen years at four sessions a week, during which we confronted – thanks to a team effort with a psychiatrist-pharmacologist and an analyst who attended the family – four long acute psychotic episodes. Each of the episodes was followed by significant personal growth and constructive change in the patient's life.

At the start of the analysis Rosa's gaze seemed absent and passed over me as if I were transparent. The sessions were dominated by recurrent states of physical malaise (stomach ache, nausea, and various kinds of aches and pains) and by an extreme paucity of content.

After more than a year of this I happened upon her right before me in the street, but her look remained absolutely vacant, as though she couldn't see a thing. Only after a couple of years did Rosa give some signals of coming out of her serious state of non-differentiation by means of the activation of an ability to see.

Rather than exploring the moment in which Rosa discovered her visual capacity – having considered something similar in our first case – we shall be looking at some aspects of the subsequent development that show the implications of her visual power in terms of her identity generally, as well as the massive regression to which her visual capacity was subject when the emotions of pain and loss became intolerable, so that – as the patient herself put it – "an eye fell to the bottom of the sea" – i.e., into the undifferentiated depths of psychotic confusion. Whereas, during the first phase of her analysis, the acute psychotic episodes had shown a paradoxically positive value as an emancipating stimulus in terms of her paralytic and non-vital condition, in the course of the seventh-year crisis the acute explosion seemed instead connected to regressive phenomena of disavowal in the face of the mental pain of mourning.

In the course of the fourth-year crisis Rosa often referred to eyes, seeing, and sense organs. In a session that was devastated by screaming and beating at the walls, Rosa suddenly brought out a photo of herself and showed it to me, saying, "You were more handsome when I first came to you." I read this communication in terms of a reduction of her idealization of me, but even more as an index of her emerging differentiation, so that she could now see me and herself as people who were separate in space and time.

When I told her this, Rosa replied:

R[osa]: Exactly, now I'm alone, I'm separated from you. It's a great thing to be alone: I can make my own life, with a house of my own. I need a center of gravitation: ears, eyes, nose, feeling, taste. That's my center of gravitation.

I was greatly struck by her response, which referred to a whole constellation of "sensory powers" that she was beginning to discover she possessed: *ears, eyes, nose, feeling, taste.* In this constellation of sense organs and senses Rosa was starting to recognize a crucial *center of gravitation.*

On another occasion Rosa simply and directly communicated that she had acquired her own space and personal identity, which was specifically anchored to her *visual functioning and perception of colors*.

R: Before, everything was there, but not Rosa. Now Rosa's there. Before, red was green for me, and green was red. Not now! Red is red and green is green. See, this is what I've learned. I've learned that if I weigh 68 kilos I can't say that that isn't my weight. Things are what they are and that's it! That's what I've learned. The world is simple: everybody wants to make it complicated, but it's simple.

Thus Rosa's identity seemed to be forming itself on the basis of the activation of a perceptual faculty that favored the immediate perception of reality, in which every sense organ played its specific role and – as regards seeing – every color was unequivocally itself. And so everything she perceived would remain true to itself: *Things are what they are and that's it!*

After a further three years of analysis the theme of the eye re-emerged with the dramatic concreteness of an acute psychotic episode, this time with a regressive effect on the preceding development of her acquired perceptual faculty.

Entering my office for a session, Rosa presented a somnambulistic manner, walking like a ghost making its way through the clouds. After she had stretched out on the couch her first remark was:

R: The first dead person I saw was called Mario. *(Pause.)* I lost an eye.

I didn't know who Mario was, but this wasn't the first time that I was having to deal with mysterious communications. A few sessions later I would learn that this was Rosa's brother, who was drowned before she was born: a brother whom she had at this point never mentioned to me.

I attempted to establish some form of meaningful relation between the elements that she was naming. My attention was called to the correlation between perception ("The first dead person I saw") and the immediate defense by means of negation ("I lost an eye"). An extremely swift mental movement was being organized in an area at the border between the conscious and the unconscious that is loaded with concreteness. Thus, I thought that this blinding might reinforce her psychotic tendency towards negation, so I tried to verbalize her anxiety connected to suffering, stressing the value of "seeing" (which here was already a form of "thinking" of reality) as an organizing factor that could contain her anxiety. Hence I said:

A: Seeing death makes you suffer, but you can use your eyes to see it instead of blinding yourself. Otherwise you will suffer twice as much.
R: *(Twisting about uncomfortably on the couch, as if she has a snake in her belly, and then replying)* I'm very sick, I have to spit out the toad that's hurting me. Now I'm going to vomit.

I noted that her reply showed a certain tendency to approach her pain, even as she perceived it as something poisonous she had urgently to expel. As I listened to her I noticed some dizziness and a violent contraction of my stomach, as if it were I who was about to vomit. I had to start breathing very regularly to try to establish an internal coordination that seemed threatened by the imminent upset. From that point on the session took a positive turn towards clear feelings of loss and mourning that had to do both with her dead brother and with her unborn children, whom Rosa felt guilty for having destroyed. Allowing space for crying and for the feelings that accompany mourning permitted Rosa during the same session to reclaim the eye that she felt she had lost in the sea of psychosis.

A couple of weeks later the theme of the lost eye resurfaced in the more evolved context of a dream. The dream's creative activity signaled the restoration of a conscious/unconscious differentiation that the acute explosion had shattered: now the lost-eye theme could be contained within the representational confines of a dream. Nonetheless, it was still an area in urgent need of further work.

R: Today I dreamed I was a monster with just one eye. *(She suddenly changes the subject.)* Yesterday at the station I went and asked for a cappuccino. The guy looked at me and said "You're too beautiful." *(Adopting a resigned manner)* I'd gone the wrong way.
A: [I had the impression that the anxiety about losing an eye was supported by a sensual tendency towards gratification, "too beautiful," a means she would sometimes use to protect herself from

pain.] *You're seeking satisfaction only, so as to steer clear of hatred and see only beautiful things. That's why you have only one eye. At this point, though, you yourself realize that you've gone the wrong way, because you're left with just one eye and without the capacity for emotional digestion.*

R: *(With an anguished tone)* My father was ill, my boyfriend's mother was ill. This doesn't mean a thing to you, Doctor. You're another person. But it means something to me. *(She starts to cry.)*

I then pointed out to her that recognizing the value she attributed to her affective relationships gave her back both her eyes and her humanity, so that she ceased to be the inhuman, one-eyed monster of her dream.

In this brief sequence we can see how the dream was able to anticipate the risk of falling into acute psychosis, indicating the imminent risk of a further loss of the eye of thought. Indeed, in this context the eye of thought is exposed to the *earthquakes originating in the emotions* – as Mauro, our first patient, would have called them. The eye felt the direct effects of the psychotic defense of disavowal that the patient set in motion to avoid mental pain. We can also see the speed with which binocular vision became reintegrated into a more harmonious mental functioning when Rosa – supported by the analytic work we had done together – disposed her mind towards the tolerance of pain.

A bodily gravitation towards abstract thought

To recapitulate, starting from certain principal ideas that Bion set out in his early essay on the imaginary twin (1967a), I have explored – in two clinical cases – the cardinal role of the senses (*ears, eyes, nose, touch, taste*) in the development of an internal psycho-sensory center, from which there arises a capacity to think associated with being able to bear separateness and solitude. Along the way we have seen how the recognition of emotions, and the tolerance of hatred and mental pain, create the conditions for individual development based on a binocular vision that places the conscious and the unconscious, as well as thought and emotion, side-by-side.

The working-through that leads to the construction of an internal psycho-sensory center, or rather to an individual gravitation based on the body and the perceptual functions of the sense organs, would seem to be a crucial precondition for the development of a capacity for thought, and in particular for the working-through of the absence of an object, so that "the 'no-breast' inside becomes a thought," which Bion hypothesizes in his essay "A theory of thinking" (1967d: 112). While it is true that the capacity for abstract thinking is built up through a detachment/emancipation from the sensory/corporeal level through the mediation of the analytic *rêverie* (Bion, 1962) – a detachment by virtue of which the body and thought become like two discrete organizations, even though they are in direct and reciprocal continuity in the context of harmonious functioning conditions – I find it equally important to consider how the capability of abstraction is built up from a basis of experience organized around the perceptual capacity of the sense organs, which are bodily in nature, and hence in the context of the body–mind relationship.

In this chapter I have sought to describe this more primitive level of the first emergence of a capacity for thinking, which is connected to the body and to the sense organs. This passage allows us to position Bion's general theory of thinking more appropriately and can help us to save this part of his legacy from sliding towards a self-referential conception of thought, disconnected from the physical matrices where perception and emotion originate.

Note

1 I would like to thank Dr. Sandra Isgrò, who conducted this analysis.

Chapter 3

Intersubjectivity and the body

Jay Greenberg and Stephen Mitchell's *Object Relations in Psychoanalytic Theory* (1983) arrived in Italy in 1986, three years after its original publication in the United States. The book is immediately remarkable for its uncommon comprehensiveness in introducing a pluralistic vision of psychoanalysis, integrating at the same level of authority both orthodox thinkers, such as Melanie Klein, Donald Winnicott, and Heinz Hartmann, and more independent contributors, such as Harry Stack Sullivan, Erich Fromm, Ronald Fairbairn, Harry Guntrip, and so on. Psychoanalytic training as sanctioned by the Società Psicoanalitica Italiana, a component member of the International Psychoanalytical Association, is always clearly marked theoretically by the study of Freud, integrated to a lesser degree with British, French, and American contributors. In fact, Italian psychoanalytic culture has demonstrated little interest in external contributions to the official psychoanalytic milieu, there being almost no connection between the Freudian school and other theoretical lines. In that context, Greenberg and Mitchell's book has offered an open and dialectical panorama of intertwined psychoanalytic perspectives, unlimited by the sanctioned areas of political orthodoxy.

In the last thirty years, we have witnessed important changes in which the world we live in has become more complex, and the forms of mental disturbance more deeply rooted and archaic. A pervasive factor that is not without effect on mental functioning derives from the ever greater influence of computer science and artificial intelligence, which offer us great advantages, but also contribute to making the

A wider version of this chapter was published as Lombardi (2013b). Translated by Gina Atkinson, M.A.

body–mind relationship in present-day humanity more complicated and problematic. Increasingly less rooted in her body and in her self, the difficult patient of today has precarious object relations that are particularly prone to superficiality, bi-dimensionality, and profound dissociations. A discontinuity among the worlds of sensations, of emotions, and of thinking quickly comes to mean that a traditional working-through ends up being impossible.

Given these present-day clinical problems, it might be possible to look at the connection between relational levels and intrasubjective ones with new eyes. If, in fact, during the era of Greenberg and Mitchell's 1983 publication, there was a particular historical demand to keep the drive model and the relational model rigidly separate, today new demands to broaden the range of action of psychoanalysis are appearing on the horizon. We can look at the internal level, then, not so much through the lens of the old drive model as through a new sensitivity to the individuality of each patient's internal arrangement and to new horizons that have been opened up by problems pertaining to the body–mind relationship (Bion, 1962; Lombardi, 2002).

Various colleagues, to whom I am most grateful, have contributed in recent years to the debate about my clinical perspective focused on the problem of the body–mind relationship and its dissociation, starting with a discussion of a series of analytic sessions (Lombardi, 2004b) organized by Henry Smith in the *Psychoanalytic Quarterly*, in which Jay Greenberg (2004), Vincenzo Bonaminio (2004), and James Grotstein (2004) took part. Later, Paul Williams (2007) generously provided a detailed commentary for *Psychoanalytic Dialogues* on a clinical work of mine about a serious case of psychosis with a risk of suicide and of acting out a homicidal transference. Williams broadened my understanding of the case and enriched my perspective, in part by connecting it to the clinical work of other psychoanalysts from the Independent Tradition, such as Nina Coltart, Phil Mollon, and Donald Campbell. Elsewhere, Mark Blechner (2011) discussed my clinical approach in some detail, and included a few interesting connections with the most recent developments in the neurosciences.

At this point, I would like to discuss two very different clinical cases. These can provide some idea of the distinctive characteristics and paradoxes one may encounter in analytic working-through at the borders between mind and body.

The disappearing patient

Mary, a woman in her forties, has requested a consultation for problems following her divorce. The patient seems intelligent and motivated. The transition from our first consulting conversations to the analysis carries unexpected developments, however: already before her first session, Mary telephones to say that, because of an unexpected commitment, it is impossible for her to come. She manages to arrive only for her third scheduled session, towards the end of her hour, and her communications are so anxious that I am unable to address the subject of her presence in the session.

Starting in the middle of the second week, Mary stops notifying me by phone but continues not to come. I am forced to wait until the third week before I can reach her by phone, at which point Mary tells me she has overestimated her available time, and so she has decided that the project of analysis is not feasible at present. I propose to her that we talk in person about the situation that has come up, and I manage to arrange an appointment with her, even though she will not be available for another month.

I found myself asking internally why, despite my long clinical experience, I had not perceived a situation of attacks on linking (Bion, 1967c) as drastic as what had suddenly broken out in Mary. Could it be that I was such a blind and incompetent analyst?

When Mary finally arrived for her appointment, she initially displayed a distant attitude, which could scarcely be reconciled with her motivated demeanor during our first consultation. It was necessary to do all the work of re-establishing the analysand's motivational factors through which we had arrived at our agreement to begin analytic work. Mary explained this change by saying that, as she was drawn into the vortex of work commitments and other concrete things, all awareness of herself had disappeared. Apparently, I replied to the patient, this attitude of a disappearance of self-awareness could be placed along the same line as her concrete disappearances at the beginning of the analysis, even if – I added – in this latter case, an external person was also implicated, namely myself, with whom she had felt able to make a commitment.

Gradually, as the meeting progressed, I noted that Mary was again showing the characteristics she had displayed when I met her during our initial consultations; it was almost as though she were making a transformation before my eyes. With regard to the reactivation of her interest in a prospective analysis, I clearly articulated to her my impotence concerning the problems affecting her attendance at sessions; a problem could be discussed between us, but when she was not in a session, she would have to take responsibility for managing on her own. If she was interested in being helped by analytic means, I continued, it would be necessary for her to commit to being present at agreed-upon sessions, in order to discuss and together deal with the difficulties and problems that she must be noticing inside herself. From then on, she decided to commit to the experience of an analytic journey, and the resumption of sessions yielded some interesting observations.

"I constantly pull out my phone to see if there have been any calls," Mary commented in one of her early sessions. "But the ring would be enough to let me know if there were a need to reply to someone. I'm always clinging to my cell phone!" Starting with this simple observation, we could discuss her tendency to keep on clinging to an external mechanical object at all costs, and thus to avoid the possibility of being inside herself and listening to herself. The cell phone seemed to be set up as an alternative to an axis of internal communication that would allow her to feel something of what was happening inside her.

From then on, a phase developed in which Mary began to suffer from physical ailments of various types. In parallel to these illnesses, an impression of Mary emerged in which she seemed to feel less lost in space and more in contact with herself, though perhaps less brilliant and efficient at her work. To myself, I explained this correlation between the patient's physical illness and a subjective improvement of her mental state by noting that her body, in coming to the foreground through physical symptoms, formed a sort of presence that could now direct her mental attention towards her real person.

A little while later, Mary had a sinusitis and a catarrhal otitis that required vigorous medical treatment; the otitis significantly impaired her hearing and her ability to localize external sounds. "Since I've been sick," she said,

> I hear few external noises, and so I'm discovering a whole series of internal sensations that I've never taken into account. It's as though I have a whole series of internal messages, and before it was like they

didn't exist. It's shocking to discover that certain things create an attraction in me and yet in others, in contrast, rejection and unpleasantness. For me it was as though they were all the same, and any thing or person could go well. It's as though I've never had my own personal response, as though I never felt anything inside myself!

The analytic work thus gradually permitted Mary to carry out an internal sensorial registration and to accept her own sensorial and emotional reactions to various external and relational contexts.

This clinical vignette shows us how the patient's initial problem of not connecting with herself emerged in the analytic relationship with explosive force – that is, with an instance of acting out that made the analysis itself disappear, causing the disappearance of the very tool that would have helped her. Considering the close correlation between intrasubjective and intersubjective relations we could hypothesize that the start of the analysis had permitted an exteriorization – on the level of the analytic relationship – of Mary's extreme body–mind dissociation. The impulse to cancel the analysis paralleled the impetus towards cancellation that the patient exerted in relation to herself, towards her own body and its sensorial derivatives – a very deep conflict with strong pre-mental and pre-representational elements.

Perhaps not by chance, in my first meetings with Mary I did not have any inkling of this drastic internal dissociation of hers. When the body–mind conflict played out in the analytic relationship, it could be identified in acting out – that is, in the concreteness of the cancellation of sessions. The possibility of coming closer to Mary's problems created at this point a new basis on which to develop an analytic exploration; from here onwards, the process of working-through enabled the patient's gradual approach to her own body, at first apparently absent and dissociated. The presence of the body seemed to emerge from a very deep abyss through an outbreak of bodily illnesses, which in turn contributed to a process of working-through aimed at listening to the self.

The disappearing analyst

At this point, I would like to consider a case in which enactment fulfilled an important relay function in the development of the analytic relationship.

Ferdinando is a young man in his twenties with a meek air about him; he requests analysis because he is haunted by violent suicidal impulses. He presents with an addiction to hashish and a tendency to involve himself in dangerous episodes of brawling and violence, for which he has even been arrested. This proclivity for violence contrasts markedly with his harmless and defenseless air.

After our initial period of work, the memory of a serious, traumatic event emerged, in which Ferdinando, at the age of 13, had used violence towards his eight-year-old neighbor, involving her in certain sexual games and making her touch his penis, with masturbatory intentions. His childhood had been very difficult; he felt imprisoned in a very closed family that was dominated by a friend of his father's, who was a Mafia boss.

Notwithstanding a reconstruction of the influence of his childhood past, Ferdinando's working-through proceeded in a laborious manner, with long periods of silence that he only rarely managed to come out of, despite my constant effort to keep some degree of verbal communication going. For me it was a particularly painful situation, both because of the sense of paralysis and impotence communicated to me by the analysand, and because of the almost total absence of verbal and mental content in his analysis. I found myself experiencing a strange sense of physical exhaustion, at times like a heavy anvil on my head and an almost unbearable somnolence, and a feeling as though I were sinking into a stupefying coma. I noticed a pronounced physical strain even in carrying out the normal motions of breathing. During interruptions of the analysis for vacations, the situation became more complex owing to an exacerbation of the patient's sense of futility, continuing suicidal impulses, and his desire to end the analysis, which was felt to be part of the general uselessness of everything. In these situations, there was some utility in my clearly articulating the pressure to destroy both himself and his analytic project according to the criterion of "Samson dies with the Philistines";[1] thus we were able to hold back the push towards action, protecting the analytic continuity.

In this precarious state, one day it happened that I completely erased Ferdinando's appointment from my mind, arriving at my office only to see my next patient, as though Ferdinando did not even exist in my schedule or in my mind. I had to excuse myself to Ferdinando for the mishap to which I had fallen victim, assuming full responsibility, and

I assured him that the missed session would be made up at my expense; thus I put him off until the next session, offering him a chance to talk again about what had happened.

Having become "a disappearing analyst" increased my disorientation and my exhaustion, causing me to feel afflicted by a deep sense of unreliability and professional incompetence. Was it possible that this difficult situation had induced me to rid myself of the analysand in so extreme a manner, after I had gone to such trouble and struggled to make his analysis succeed? Could it be that I had added my negation and rejection to the patient's difficulties?

In the next session, Ferdinando and I discussed the event, noting the paradoxical fact that an interruption of the analysis, which we had seen in the foreground of his intentions, had in fact been acted out by me, as though the combination of impulses towards hatred and cancellation pertained to me and not to Ferdinando himself. Was it simply a reaction of exasperation on my part in the face of Ferdinando's threats to end the analysis? Or was there something more that could pertain not only directly to me, but also to the patient himself, and thus a situation that involved both of us?

The analysand associated this episode with the memory of a past situation in which he had carried out an identity switch with someone else, whereby one person had acted out the impulses and fantasies of the other. Against this backdrop, the hypothesis began to appear in Ferdinando's mind that one could act out as a consequence of influential external factors, whose importance it was not always easy to recognize clearly. This information now made him think about how his violent family situation, both implicit and explicit, had been acted out on him – a situation he had continually been forced to confront.

From that moment on, we witnessed an unexpected turning-point in the analysis; in fact, from that moment it became possible to work through the patient's gesture of adolescent violence against his younger neighbor. We could place this situation in the context of an absence of thinking, in addition to the context of family relationships that were marked by violence and control, rather than seeing it as merely a personal act, one he experienced in retrospect as an unpardonable offense for which he suffered a crushing sense of blame. The readjustment of his role according to a broader relational context permitted Ferdinando to assume a more realistic sense of responsibility – that is, one without the sense of being persecuted that had characterized him from that time. Among other reactions, he took the initiative of contacting the girl who had been the object of his violence in order finally to talk with her. After doing so he was able to forgive himself for an episode that, until that moment, had been completely unspoken about.

From then on, Ferdinando demonstrated clear signs of improvement, including a positive change on the level of his collaborative participation in sessions. In addition, he initiated an affective relationship with a young woman who, after he had completed his academic program, became his wife.

This episode shows the analyst involved in a clinical situation complicated by a paralysis of symbolic working-through: the exchange of words between Ferdinando and me had become practically nonexistent, and the analytic relationship was paralyzed in a situation saturated with anxiety and death threats. This is not a matter of a repetition in the transference characterized by unconscious fantasy; in other words, it relates to the confrontation with a disharmony in the body–mind relationship (Ferrari, 2004; see also Chapter 4 of the present volume), in which the body ends up being unreachable by the mind, and the normal working-through resources of the analytic couple are put in check. The appearance of an enactment that involved both analysand and analyst, in which it was the latter who acted out the cancellation of the analytic relationship that was wished for by the analysand, opened the way to a tolerance of not thinking and to a recognition of the paralyzing force of emotions. In addition to this, it was possible to come to a recognition of the relational component that lay behind thoughts and actions, without this implying a form of not being responsible or of delegation.

Conclusion

In this chapter, I have explored two clinical cases that illustrate, at different levels, the role of the body–mind relationship in the context of object relations. I have observed that the development of certain archaic levels of the object relationship is not supported by symbolic or reconstructive interpretations, but rather proceeds through the work of recovery of a body–mind connection that is sometimes realized at the cost of acting out that involves both participants in the analytic relationship. The analyst's unsaturated orientation (Bion, 1970) permits the emergence of experiences that have not yet been woven into the system of representations, and enables them to evolve in a meaningful way towards change.

I hope I was able to show something about the lesson I personally learned from Greenberg and Mitchell (1983): that patient and analyst influence each other in a way that is beyond knowledge and understanding, and that the specific nature of the analytic relationship is a determinant therapeutic factor. I hope that this brief clinical material can also give an idea of the complexity of the clinical phenomena that confront today's analyst who works with difficult patients: in particular, we have seen how the object relationship can be invested with the conflicts, discontinuity, and deep chasms that characterize the internal body–mind relationship. And this is a point I presume would merit further attention and exploration by psychoanalytic research.

It is the impact of the ineffability of the body that, today more than ever, drives the authenticity of object relations.

Note

1 Samson was a biblical figure who was granted supernatural strength by God in order to combat his enemies. After having lost his strength, which had been connected to his long hair, he was captured and blinded by the Philistines. When he was brought inside the temple for the Philistines' religious sacrifice, Samson, his hair having grown long again, asked a servant to place him close to the temple's central pillars. "Samson said, 'Let me die with the Philistines!' Then he pushed [the two pillars apart] with all his might, and down came the temple on the rulers and all the people in it. Thus he killed many more as he died than while he lived" (Judges 16:30).

Chapter 4

Primitive mental states and the body
A personal view of A. B. Ferrari's concrete original object

This chapter discusses an approach in which psychoanalytic observation is concentrated on events lying between the bodily and the psychic fact, and my argument will be based primarily on Freud's (1915c) conception of affects as the link between the somatic and the psychic. Some of Freud's (1911a) most significant intuitions are reformulated by Bion (1963) in his grid, a condensed model in which the pure abstraction of mathematical calculation appears as a direct development of the beta and alpha sensory levels. In his last years Bion explored some new possibilities for expanding the grid:

> Suppose the analyst wants to investigate more deeply this very area that lies between corporeal fact and psychic fact. He can interpose between the Grid rows A and B the entire Grid as if within the Grid itself could be seen in depth further Grids. In this way he could amplify the Grid indefinitely to suit himself, provided he explained what he had done by some phrase such as "second cycle," as contrasted with "first cycle."
>
> (Bion, 1990: 67; my italics)

The route that in the ideal case leads from sensation to thought is in reality susceptible to accidents resulting in fractures of greater or lesser depth in internal integration. Bion's approach to these forms, which was well ahead of its time, was based on a neurophysiological model:

> let us suppose that the central nervous system does not develop further than the thalamus, and that there is a world which can

---

This chapter was previously published as Lombardi (2002).

be contacted by the parasympathetic or the autonomic nervous system which has the thalamus as its brain ... I suggest that the patient who can mobilize his thalamus can have dreams and can have experiences analogous to seeing or hearing things, but is not hearing or seeing anything because no system of sensory organs is developed.

(1990: 43)

Bion here seems to be glimpsing a precursor of the apparatus for thinking thoughts, closely resembling apparatuses of a concretely bodily kind, replete with sensory elements that are unable to be transformed into experience for lack of connection with the cortical areas of the brain or with conscious levels of mentalization.

A number of authors (Meissner, 1997, 1998a, 1998b, 1998c; Solms and Nersessian, 1999; Mathis, 2000) have recently drawn attention to the body's contribution to psychic reality – an idea also reflected in the growing interest currently being shown in the dialogue between the neurosciences and psychoanalysis (Bucci, 2000). Indeed, to borrow a phrase from Damasio (1994), the mind had to be there for the body first or it could not have been there at all, and this applies to several of Freud's most important models (1893–1895, 1911a, 1938) too.

In my discussion of primitive mental states and corporeity, I shall refer, albeit within the limits of a chapter, to the contributions of certain authors who have attempted the treatment of particularly difficult patients: the reference to corporeity is not always obvious in the chosen theories, but I considered it implicit in the involvement of very archaic areas of mentalization. I felt that this bringing together of authors writing from sometimes widely differing standpoints could throw light on different levels of internal and relational functioning observable in similar, or indeed in some cases positively overlapping, clinical realities. I shall go on to illustrate some little-known hypotheses of Ferrari (1992, 1994, 2004) that take the body as the starting-point of mental functioning. These postulates further develop Bion's approach and use the body–mind relationship to promote emotional experience and growth within the psychoanalytic session. My view of Ferrari's contribution will be a personal one, molded by my clinical experience and by connections suggested by my reading of other authors. It has been pointed out that the accessibility of Ferrari's ideas is limited by his "densely self-referential style" (Ginzburg, 1999) and by his lack of references to the current psychoanalytic literature. As a result, one may fail to make the acquaintance of some hypotheses whose interest centers on their author's choosing to place corporeity in the foreground – an approach that, as stated, brings together the psychoanalytic and neuroscientific standpoints and, as it were, recapitulates in a new key the one-person level of functioning in a present-day context in which "some important and hitherto underdeveloped aspects of the one-person model are in danger of becoming lost" (Grotstein, 1997: 404).

The chapter ends with some clinical fragments from a case in which the body emerges as a central element in the elaborative process.

Aspects of psychoanalytic research on primitive mental states

This section deals with the most archaic aspects of mental functioning involved in the origins of affective life and the birth of thought. I am not, of course, claiming to treat these matters exhaustively, but shall attempt to describe an area of hypotheses and clinical manifestations that, as stated, concerns phenomena recalcitrant to the traditional approach, and that therefore justifies the opening up of new fields of research. Psychoanalytic research on the earliest phases of individual development reveals a child dominated by motor and sensory bodily functions (Bick, 1968; Mahler and McDevitt, 1982); in particular, Gaddini (1992) describes a basic mental organization (BMO) that embraces the "phenomena, which are as elementary as they are complex," of the first organization of the mind. This precedes both the structural organization of the mind described by Freud, and object-relational dynamics; it is a level on which imitation comes before introjection.

Although the central importance of work on the transference is one of the main areas of common ground in present-day psychoanalysis (Kernberg, 1993), a number of authors report experiences with particularly difficult patients with whom the timing and manner of introduction of a clear reference to the analytic relationship calls for careful choice – using, for example, transference onto internal objects rather than onto the analyst as a way of achieving communication with the patient. Ronald Baker, for instance, writes "In this way the risk of being experienced by the patient as a rejecting or retaliating transference object was substantially reduced" (1994: 748). Difficulties with the focus of interpretations are experienced, too, by the British post-Kleinian analysts, who "are exercising greater caution in their interpretation of the transference ... and stress interpretation at the most active – not deepest – level of anxiety, and with the patient's current level of mental functioning" (Hanna Segal, quoted by Kernberg, 1993: 660f.). Some of the post-Kleinian authors describe patients in whom the sensory-emotional dimension is either excluded or so predominant that it presents a dramatic obstacle to communication in analysis, thus posing enormous technical problems. For example, Joseph (1975) discusses in detail a violently schizoid type of personality, which remains split off and inaccessible to the analyst's communications: although such personalities appear to cooperate and communicate on a mature level, they in fact act out in the transference of an opposition to real contact with the parts capable of loving and becoming involved in a relationship with others. Steiner (1993) postulates the existence of a position on the borderline between the paranoid-schizoid and depressive positions; he calls this a "psychic retreat," which blocks the relationship with the analyst and with internal objects, paralyzing any possibility of development and growth. The author links this disposition to a pathological organization of the personality dominated by perverse aspects of destructive narcissism (Rosenfeld, 1971). Henri Rey (quoted by Steiner, 1993) describes a "claustro-agora-phobic" dilemma in which the patient alternates between searching for a refuge where he can feel safe, feeling himself trapped in it, and a fresh panic when confronted with open space.

These various hypotheses converge in the patient's difficulty in finding an internal space that will allow the functioning of internal and external relationships. The problems presented by the "difficult patient" have led some analysts to concern themselves with patients' pain in integrating the sensory and bodily levels of experience, rather than only with the opposition to contact in the transference or with perverse aspects. An original interpretation of the Kleinian approach in which corporeity plays an important part is given by Salomon Resnik, who was led by his clinical experience of psychosis to take account of the role of the body in the constitution of narcissism and of ego structure; here he is in part following another Kleinian, namely Scott (1948). A female patient of Resnik says "A person is something which is somewhere, which people can see, by which one can be seen, and which has a body. And having a body means looking and seeing oneself" (Resnik, 1976: 61; my translation). So if owning the body leads to the birth of the "person" together with the first expressions of mental functioning correlated with the sense organs, then conversely the negation of the body in psychosis gives rise to depersonalization. Resnik deciphers the language of the body through verbal expression and explores the various manifestations of the mental space: "I have no body." Another of his female patients says, making a lapidary negative correlation between corporeity and claustrophobia, "my clothes torment me; I am inside something that enwraps me and will not let me out ... I am very small ... the walls hem me in" (2001: 56). For this author, moreover, dreams in particular, together with the imaginative aspects of delusion, allow the analyst to enter into the expressive forms of the primitive psyche, where she may find "a language that could serve as a mediation between the 'biological stage' [and] the 'psychical stage' of the body" (Resnik, 1987: 53).

A shift of focus onto the centrality of the body in primitive mental states is embodied in a well-structured theory in which Ogden (1989) postulates the existence of an "autistic-contiguous position" as a way of generating experience on a pre-symbolic sensory level preceding or coexisting with the paranoid-schizoid and depressive positions. The author's starting-point is Freud's proposition that the ego arises first and foremost from bodily sensations (Freud, 1923: 26), a notion he integrates with Donald Winnicott's thought and with research on autism by authors such as Frances Tustin, who posits an "autosensual" phase of development even in the normal situation. Ogden thus describes a number of clinical situations in which the presence of the body imposes itself, making it possible "to create a place in which [the patient] could feel (through his bodily sensations) that he exists" (1989: 130). For instance, a male schizophrenic adolescent can gain access to existence through the strong smell of his unwashed body, and a female obsessional patient can overcome paralysis through the sensations aroused by a cold glass of wine, significantly described as "getting a thought right." In these cases the sensory level imposes itself as the sole condition for gaining access to existence. "In a psychological field in which the individual has little if any sense of internal space, the concept of internalisation becomes virtually meaningless" (1989: 135).

One of the most important contributions to the exploration of the mind–body boundary areas was made by McDougall (1989, 1995), who writes:

> The concept of mind–body duality, a legacy of Cartesian philosophy, can cloud our perception, skew our clinical work. Likewise, the assumption that the body has no "language," as some theoreticians claim, is also dangerously biasing for a psychoanalyst. Perhaps body-language is the only language that cannot lie!
> (1995: 157)

Hence the main function of the psychoanalytic relationship is to compile a dictionary that will enable the anarchic body to express itself symbolically; the neosexual solutions in which the body exerts itself by dragging the subject towards psychological birth assume importance in this context as attempts at self-therapy and reparation in the face of an otherwise irremediable internal void.

Again in France, Marty (1976, 1980) discusses the mind–body relationship in the context of the re-emergence of the body in somatic pathology; he places this re-emergence in the framework of progressive disorganizations and essential depression in which mental mechanisms tend to disappear. Marty (1985) also constructs a psychoanalytically derived model of psychotherapy, based on the view that the classical psychoanalytic setting is unsuitable for these patients' *pensée opératoire*.

Serge Lecours and Marc-André Bouchard, drawing upon the contributions of Marty, André Lussier, and Bion, systematize the various modalities (somatic, motor, imaginative, and verbal) of the development of thought and the various elaborative levels that characterize them ("disruptive impulsion," "modulated impulsion," "externalization," "appropriation," "meaning association") on the assumption that "the greater part of transference manifestations first emerge through disruptive and modulated impulsion" (Lecours and Bouchard, 1997: 865). The authors consider the study of the various forms of mental elaboration important because "contemporary experience with border-line and other difficult patients is not adequately rendered by the sole use of the structural model. For instance, mentalisation deficits or failures are not satisfactorily explained by intersystemic conflicts [and by] intrasystemic conflicts" (1997: 872). The authors give the example of the development of a borderline patient on the various levels of mentalization, which paralleled that of the transference. This case began on the highly concrete level of "burning sensations" that lacked associations with other images and impressions, but in time developed towards metaphorical expressions such as "exploring a volcano and still surviving"; much later, the patient achieved an integration (which the authors equate with the Kleinian depressive position) of images endowed with reflective distance, such as a "protective fence" and "weeping willows near a river." This clinical fragment in my view suggests an attempt to describe patients' clinical development by focusing on their internal functioning, rather than on the more generally explored level of the transference.

This interest in the functional characteristics of mentalization is represented in the literature from a variety of observational viewpoints. For example, in their study of the role of trauma in the psychogenesis of mental disorders, Peter Fonagy and Mary Target draw attention to the process, in borderline states, of "hyperactive mentalising," associated with other important correlates of the mental situation such as "the psychic correspondence between internal state and external reality" or "the propensity to continue to shift into a pretend mode and a partial inability to reflect on one's own mental states and those of one's object" (Fonagy and Target, 2000: 857). These patients appear so overwhelmed by their instinctual impulses that, like very small children, they drastically equate external reality and the external object with their internal emotional states; or else they may adopt the opposite form of internal functioning, involving a distorted type of mentalization that marginalizes or precludes any link with internal sensory and affective states. Within their own theoretical reference framework, these authors thus describe a type of disorder that powerfully impedes the transformation of the disruptive impulsion emerging from corporeity into reflective thought. In their case of Mrs. A., the disturbance of thought is associated with explicit attacks on the body in a twenty-year history of self-mutilation and suicide attempts:

> Mrs. A. habitually perverted her reflective function, deflecting attention from her own mental states, and distorting or negating those of other people. Her compulsive abuse of mentalisation protected her from actual insight or intimacy ... An illustration of this was

that, after a night of self-cutting and getting her 9-year-old son to help her write a suicide note, Mrs. A. came to her session excitedly trying to understand the stinginess of her brother's new wife, only mentioning her own outbursts the previous day in passing.

(Fonagy and Target, 2000: 858)

A compulsive mentalization is thus associated with the patient's alienness to emotions, while at the same time emotional experience appears almost inaccessible to the instruments of representation used by the subject for communication in analysis – as if the vectors from the mental and bodily levels are so dissociated as to describe virtually non-intersecting parabolas, with the consequent risk of seriously paralyzing the elaborative resources furnished by the analytic context.

The eclipse of the body

Ferrari's approach places the analysand's internal functioning in the foreground; he concentrates on the oscillations that cause bodily manifestations to assume mental characteristics, as well as on the obstacles and conflicts in the way of the progressive development of mentalization from the concreteness of the body to the abstraction of thought. He sees the body as primary and refers to it as the "concrete original object" (COO); this is not the body in a phenomenological or medical sense, but a living object able to emit sensations and endowed with specialized structures, such as the sense organs, having perceptual capacities. He writes:

> Let us assume that mental functioning commences with the first registration of a sensory perception, so that the operations of perceiving a sensation and of registering it take on different meanings ... The registration is presumably due to the need to place the sensory perception, which would otherwise be completely invasive, at a distance and, at the same time, to confer meaning on it.
>
> (Ferrari, 1992: 35)

The onset of sensory registration coincides with the beginning of the eclipse of the body, and the first mental phenomena are born at the same time.

Ferrari's clinical attention and research focus on the relationship of the sensory component to the mind or, conversely, on the relationship of thoughts to emotions and sensations, this being deemed the central point at which the failure of thought is structured. This approach seems to constitute a further development of the oscillation between the concrete and the abstract in Freudian metapsychology (Freud, 1915b), the emphasis being placed on the presence of the body as the first and founding entity upon which the subject's identity is based. This view of the body takes on particular significance in the increasingly common situations defined as distortions of development, and variously described as borderline or false-self pathologies (Winnicott, 1958b, 1965 [1960]), in which the subject loses the continuity between the physical and emotional nuclei of identity.

The notion of the eclipse of the body thus differs from the Kleinian conception, in which the relationship to the mother's breast and its subsequent introjection are seen as the structuring nucleus of the subject's ego (Klein, 1975g [1952]), and more closely resembles – albeit in a different context – the Freudian hypotheses according to which the autoerotic cathexis of the bodily organs precedes any other source of object cathexis (Freud, 1914b). The function of the mother figure, or, later, that of the analyst, is to filter and detoxify the contact with the physico-emotional elements, so that they become progressively more tolerable to the child (or analysand), thus helping to set in train the eclipse of physicality and the consequent construction of a mental space. Ferrari sees the constitutive *rêverie* of the maternal function, already recognized as decisive by Bion (1962), as involved first in the elaboration of the specific area to which the COO belongs and only at a second stage in the projective–introjective dynamics inherent in communication with the outside world. An approach of this kind, in which the ego–body relationship takes priority over the more commonly explored relationship between ego and external object, has sometimes seemed atypical and even "provocative ... because it forces us to see things from unusual perspectives" (Mancia, 1994: 1286).

Whereas Bion postulated an antithesis between beta and alpha elements, only the latter being manipulable for thinking purposes, Ferrari, it seems, considers that sensory elements are rendered unthinkable or toxic only by a lack of internal dialogue or by a misunderstanding in the mind–body relationship. Such forms of internal misunderstanding have been described, for example, by Ana-Maria Rizzuto in eating disorders: "Stimuli which in ordinary circumstances should evoke affect do not find in the internal representations the necessary safety to become aviailable for conscious awareness of feeling or for inner speech" (Rizzuto, 1988: 386).

Bion's conception of psychotic and non-psychotic areas (1967b) is thus revised, and Ferrari hypothesizes instead that the personality contains two distinct areas, an entropic area and a negentropic area. The first term is taken from Ilya Prigogine, who defines it as a "disorder which may, through the interaction of elements and forces, lead to a certain order, and hence to an unstable equilibrium" (quoted by Ferrari, 1992: 44). The term "negentropic," on the other hand, is understood as the life-preserving principle and refers to the mental noting and registering apparatus, in which it performs a function of "cooling" and stabilization of the "violence of the primitive functions" (Bion, 1965) that is characteristic of the entropic area. In this way, theories of the psychotic area are stripped of their sadistic and destructive connotations, and the interaction between the psychotic and non-psychotic areas is, as it were, restated in a new key that emphasizes the vital disorganizing–organizing alternation of emotion and thought.

Even given a continuity between some of Bion's hypotheses and those of Ferrari, it should be noted that Ferrari's construction does not follow unequivocally from Bion. Significantly, in the context of a Bion-derived psychosomatic theory, Meltzer (1983), for example, appears concerned to stress the expulsive aspect of the discharge of beta elements onto the body, rather than the propulsive aspect from the body in the direction of a development towards thought. Conversely, an author whose position may be said to be closer to Ferrari's is Tustin (1981), who holds that an essential element in the psychoanalysis of child psychoses is an active attitude on the part of the analyst in supporting the child and encouraging her to make distinctions within sensory experience and to integrate contrasting sensory inputs.

Utilizing the hypothesis of a conflict between the entropic and negentropic areas, we are led to consider personality in terms of a harmonic/disharmonic functioning of the mind–body relationship. A disharmonic condition results in a slide into opposing polarities: for example, sensory phenomena may predominate marasmically to such an extent as to jeopardize the reflective capacities, as conspicuously occurs in acute psychoses.[1] Conversely, there may be a distorted prevalence of intellectual abstractions, while any interest in sensations, emotions, and feelings is reduced or even disappears almost entirely: in the most extreme cases, the body may be experienced as a kind of "imaginary twin" (Bion, 1967a), which is very difficult to reach by mental representation and is therefore sometimes even concretely attacked. The hypothesis of such disharmonic situations leads to the constitution of a specific area of work within the analytic relationship, in which the relationship with corporeity and with the sensory and emotional events that stem from it is explored. Seen in this light, the psychoanalytic experience becomes an opportunity for working through conflicts inherent in the mind–body relationship, whereby both the physical and mental manifestations of the individual are joined in a single context – "attempting to overcome any dualism by proposing a unitary picture of the human being in which all functions are complementary" (Mancia, 1994: 1284).

This has important implications in the so-called psychosomatic disorders (as well as in psychic manifestations in which the bodily dimension is directly present), in eating disorders, or in panic attacks. Unlike the authors who developed the concept of alexithymia (Nemiah and Sifneos, 1970), Ferrari takes the view that there is no such thing as the "psychosomatic patient," because he sees the question of the mind–body relationship and its disharmonies as a general problem of the person's internal functioning. Through the correlation between body–mind and the analytic relationship, it is possible, by way of certain transference levels, to explore phenomena and relations typical of the body–mind relationship, thus opening the way to perception and change. Of course, not all somatically activated processes are reversible, because, after all, the body has rules and organizations of its own, which must be not only learned but also respected owing to the limit they constitute for the mind.

Solano (2000) describes the case of an analysand suffering from diabetes mellitus as embodying a disorder of the relationship with an internal and/or external regulating object. The patient had systematically disavowed the physical signs of attacks of hypoglycaemia, acting against his own needs so as to triumph over relational and biological necessity, including that of survival; in his analytic development, the capacity for control of glucose arose in parallel with the ability to make use of his four analytic sessions and to retain connections in his thought. In a significant vignette, while in the street the patient experiences an intense need for sugar, but instead of going into a nearby bar for some food he buys a pencil at the stationer's next door. Apart from the enactment of infantile mismatching experiences as described by Stern and others, it seems to me that this case is also a good example of a disharmonic disposition to reject corporeity, as well as of the correlation between the vertical body–mind relationship and the horizontal relationship with external objects.

The COO concept implies that the body furnishes the constitutive elements from which are derived both the precursors of the emotions and the perceptual structures out of which the ego functions develop. It is thus assumed that it is the very nature of sensation that presses towards psychic expression, which is somehow innate in it by virtue of a natural tendency to make connections with the perceptual resources when marasmic tension is reduced through the mother's *rêverie*. With the eclipse of the body, the area occupied by the sensory world is progressively reduced, eventually giving rise to the constitution of a "mental space" in which sensations and emotions can be received and recognized. In this space, the apparatus of perception and consciousness is extended towards sensations, producing "nodes" that give rise to visual representations, which can in turn progress towards better defined and more conscious configurations; in this way, "significant correspondences" are achieved between sensory and representational data (Ferrari and Stella, 1998). This is the area of transition from the concreteness of sensation to the first forms of abstraction and representability. Ferrari uses the term "contact network" for the multi-dimensional function activated at all times by the intersection of sensations and thought; this hypothesis describes the dawn of thought not only in its primary constitution but also in its constant structuring by the continuous flow of sensations from the body. Hence the process of thought is considered in terms of its potential for expressing current emotions, such as "I am afraid; I don't feel well; I feel lost" or "you are beautiful; I love you; I hate you," and so on – which expresses the construction of identity as something "ever changing and alive with internal contradictions, so that it is never static or absent" (Ferrari and Stella, 1998: 102). If the distance from the emotions is excessive, the significant correspondences will be lacking and a barrier disposition will replace the network.

The entropic area is therefore constantly involved in the genesis of thinking phenomena, and its exclusion gives rise only to imitative manifestations, which lack the containing characteristics of genuine mental phenomena; hence thinking is deemed to be at all times dynamically connected with feeling. Arguing along these lines, Ferrari makes interesting suggestions about the various manifestations that precede more structured forms of thought, describing the different ways in which the primitive sensory world reveals itself, from dream-type representations to delusional, phobic, obsessional, and other expressions. In the absence of more developed mentalization instruments, the subject resorts to emergency languages, seen by Ferrari as language registers, or primitive linguistic aspects that function pending the onset of conditions more favorable to mentalization – such as an encounter with an analytic *rêverie* – which afford an opportunity for their development towards language proper and hence thought. There are surely many points of resemblance between this view and the approaches of other authors such as Resnik or McDougall, especially with regard to the role of analysis in facilitating the construction of a language to enable corporeity to speak.

Of the various hypotheses derived from the eclipse of the body, I shall mention only one concerning adolescence (Ferrari, 1994), which sees this period and its various clinical manifestations as an expression of autonomy as opposed to childhood – as a period more dramatically involving the body–mind conflict and its possible harmonization, providing a foundation for future adult identity. For the bodily transformations of puberty lead to a new configuration of the COO, which, for the second time since birth, assumes a decisive relationship with the mind; however, it is not the mind that is born of the body, but the body in adolescence that presents itself for the attention of the mind, which consciously witnesses the radical transformations in hand. In this sense, adolescence is always a critical and highly conflictual period, in which developments and changes may be extremely rapid. For example, the claustro-agoraphobic conflict central to anorexia and bulimia proves to be a typical adolescent oscillation that, if contained within certain limits, contributes decisively to growth. Even acting out, which seemingly has pathological or perverse connotations, may perform an important growth function in adolescence, giving rise to an alternation of "doing in order to gain knowledge and gaining knowledge in order to do," thus making for emancipation from childhood and opening the way to adulthood.

Corporeity and transference

Psychoanalysis is primarily a source of experience in the present (Bion, 1990 [1973/1974]; Ferrari, 1982; Sandler and Sandler, 1984), in which the analysand is called upon to activate self-observation and self-consciousness. Whereas Bion, on the basis of the ideas of Klein (1975e, 1975f), had taken the absence of the breast as his starting-point to account for the activation of thinking phenomena (Bion, 1967d), Ferrari shifts the focus onto the role of the sensory component internal to the subject. A child is stimulated to become aware of her body and of the sensory phenomena taking place inside her, and consequently constructs a "verticality" of her own, which is the area of the dramatic impact of her own disorganizing sensations that press for containment and organization. One is reminded of Winnicott's statement that everything that happens to one is creative, with explicit reference to bodily activity (1971). Reflecting on this passage, Marion Milner emphasizes the importance of awareness of the body and of its constant changes if the subject is to have a creative perception of the world: in her view, the body presentation leads not to "the narcissistic impoverishment of one's relation to the external world that one might have expected, but [to] an actual enrichment of it" (1987 [1977]: 282).

Ferrari thus distinguishes two main elaborative axes, both of which are present in the analytic relationship. The first, the vertical axis, refers to the mind–body relationship and, more generally, to the subject's relationship with himself; while the second, the horizontal axis, has to do with interpersonal relationships, the first and most important interlocutor here being the analyst. In his interventions in the session, the analyst will stress one of the two axes depending on the analytic context. The horizontal axis relates to what is customarily understood as the transference, seen both as a displacement of archaic relationships onto the analysis (Freud, 1912) and in the wider sense of the analytic relationship as a "real relationship" (Greenson, 1971) or an "alliance projected into the future" (Ferrari, 1982).

Ferrari's distinction between the two transference levels in certain respects parallels the distinction between self-object transference and object transference in the Kohutian tradition, and the two transference patterns described by Killingmo (1989) as deficit transference and conflict transference, the first of which is characterized by a pre-structural relationship to the object, i.e., a relationship that thus precedes internalization phenomena. Whereas one common feature is the specific attention paid to the quality of being and to growth needs, rather than to repetition of the past, it is nevertheless surely the case that the conceptualizations of the self-psychologists always have to do with object needs, such as the correction of distorted object representations or of object relationships awaiting internalization, rather than the organization of a primarily bodily area in which the structural aspect can never be separated from the sensory pressure awaiting thinkability. An interesting approach that resolves the conflict between the need to evaluate the material in extra-transferential terms and the importance of the analytic relationship is James Fosshage's distinction between content and process in the transference:

> All the communications within the analytic setting have transferential meaning: the meaning, however, may not be related to the content but to the process of communicating. For example, a patient may be recounting an abusive experience with another person, not because she is "latently" experiencing the analyst as abusive (that is, interpreting the content as applicable to the transference), but because she is experiencing the analyst at that moment as sufficiently safe and protective as to enable her to communicate the painful experience (that is, interpreting the communicative process as having transferential meaning).
>
> (Fosshage, 1994: 276)

According to whether vertical- or horizontal-axis phenomena predominate, the analytic relationship will unfold on one of two levels. An initial phase of the relationship with the analyst is deemed important to the function of the transference in facilitating the unfolding of the internal world: in this case the analyst identifies with his function of facilitating representability and dimensionality in the primitive sensory world.

On the one hand, the infant can construct a verticality of his own through the relationship with the mother, while on the other, on the mental level, horizontality confers representability on the vertical dimension, which it could not otherwise have (Ferrari and Stella, 1998: 150).

Only later is the relationship with the analyst as such confronted, with its specific connotation of otherness; it will then be the "task of the analyst to bring up the horizontal dimension, with the consequent intense perception of the limit set by the impact of external reality" (Ferrari and Stella, 1998: 151).[2]

The postulate of the two axes is, in fact, not altogether new, because it gathers together and formalizes a number of hypotheses already present to some extent in psychoanalytic tradition from Freud's primitive model, in which the object is "at one and the same time internal to the drive and external to the body. The object is therefore two-fold, internal and external" (Green, 1984a: 390). Although the correlation between the intrapsychic and relational levels of the transference is considered essential by some authors (Fornari, 1979; Loewald, 1960; Green, 1984b), it tends to be underestimated. The term "transference" was first defined by Freud in *The Interpretation of Dreams* (1900 [1899]) as an intrapsychic mechanism whereby dreams use the day's residues to gain expression through the transfer of an unconscious trace onto a preconscious idea; only later was this primal definition developed in external relational terms into the more classical, generally accepted concept of the transference, as the displacement of feelings, wishes, and attitudes connected with the infantile objects onto later objects – in particular, the analyst (Freud, 1912). Bion, for his part, took care to distinguish the analysand's various relational levels in analysis – specifically, within one and the same psychic manifestation, the relationship with himself, and that with the analyst:

> We are trying to introduce him to a character which we think it would be worth his while to respect, namely, himself ... These two people dislike each other and do not want to be introduced. Not only do they hate each other, but they hate this psychoanalyst who is trying to introduce them.
>
> (Bion, 1990: 90)

The importance of the vertical axis follows directly from the theoretical assumption that the body is the mind's first and most fundamental interlocutor:

At the beginning of the process the analysand is predominantly a "participant," because the lack of a contact network entails almost complete saturation of the mental space; in this situation the capacity for self-observation, the essential condition for the formulation of thought, is suffocated if not totally inhibited. By paying attention to the vertical dimension, we are allowing the patient to have a genuine confrontation with himself, which involves the specific identification of anxiety, the recognition of the inefficacy of the defences adopted, and a realistic evaluation of his own responsibility in the search for new equilibria.

(Ferrari and Stella, 1998: 155)

On the basis of this primitive aspect of the transference, the analysand's psychic responsibility can be rated initially as the direct expression of his somatic processes (Isaacs, 1991 [1948]), which find expression in the external world in the phenomena of projective identification (Klein, 1975e); these are not then misinterpreted as conflicting with an intersubjective and interactive conception of the transference (Ogden, 1994). In the transference, the analysand's "unconscious delusions" (Money-Kyrle, 1968) become so real that they are experienced as concrete realities. In this way the patient transforms his vision of the analyst by incorporating him into a system of categories that directly express his internal functioning, so that the analyst "establishes himself as 'the mental space' within the analysand's potential mental space ... and thus in effect acts as a mediator between his conflictual aspects" (Ferrari and Stella, 1998: 156).

Sensoriality, thought, and bi-logic

An interesting convergence is observed between Ferrari's standpoint and an approach that is at first sight remote from it – for Matte Blanco's research (1975, 1988) aims at an abstract and epistemological reformulation of the logical implications of Freud's science. Some authors (Ginzburg, 1993; Bria, 1996, 2000; Lombardi, 2000a [1998], 2000b) have suggested a rapprochement of Ferrari's and Matte Blanco's formulations on mental functioning, in view of their shared lineage in Freudian clinical research and certain Kleinian developments (see Bon de Matte, 1988, 1994). Ferrari and Matte Blanco both start out from an interest in the most extreme manifestations of the mind, attaching only secondary importance to the individual pathological manifestations of narcissism and the destructive instinct. Again, both authors concentrate on the structural difficulty of achieving discrimination and thinkability in the face of the disturbing bio-psychological thrust of the emotions, and ultimately condense the forces acting within the psychical apparatus into two fundamental principles (entropic/negentropic; symmetrical/asymmetrical), which can be traced back to the structural opposition between order and disorder and between harmony and disharmony respectively; the subject-matter of psychoanalysis is thus seen to parallel a fundamental issue in contemporary science.

Matte Blanco's interest in the tendency of certain manifestations of thought towards the infinite finds its counterpart in Ferrari's attention to the indefinite fluctuation of physical sensations, or to the multidimensionality and intense symmetrization involved in the emergence of the first traces of thought from the sensory level: in both cases, "infinite" and "indefinite" are regarded as the central and most extreme challenge within the complex problem of thinkability, so that they become essential aspects of a psychoanalytic observational standpoint. The two vertices in my view possess a latent complementarity, so that in-depth research in both fields could fruitfully be stimulated by their combination: one would contribute the epistemological precision of logic and mathematics, and the other the application of the concrete element of corporeal attachment.

For both authors, psychoanalytic technique is seen as a medium, subject to no prior conditions, for the differentiating force of thought whereby a primal matrix that is structurally alien to it can "unfold" (Matte Blanco, 1975) – in the words of Freud as recalled by Matte Blanco, it is a way of making a camel pass through the eye of a needle. For example, the clinical application of Matte Blanco's thought proposed by Fink (1993), concerning the importance of mental work on time in an otherwise unanalyzable patient, could be regarded as akin to Ferrari's "vertical" axis, the perception of time being one of the first organizing principles behind the onset of the eclipse of the body and the constitution of a mental space.

Owing to its focus on the most primitive aspects of mental functioning, the clinical application of the hypothesis of the eclipse of the body is proving particularly valuable in the psychoanalytic treatment of the psychoses, including the serious forms susceptible to violent acting out (Piperno, 1992; Lombardi, 1992, 2000a), child analysis (Milana, 1992; Lombardi and Carignani, 1998), and clinical work with adolescents (Bon de Matte, 1994, 1998, 1999; Del Greco, 1996), as well as in various clinical psychoanalytic contexts (Ciocca, 1998; Turno, 1998).

I shall now present a brief case history taken from an analysis with four sessions a week. My account will be limited to essentials for reasons of confidentiality.

Case history

Arturo is an atypical male anorexic, being 40 years of age. He is as thin as a rake and since adolescence has expelled the little he eats by vomiting daily and systematically. In his analysis, he speaks like a TV newsreader and agrees to everything, as if lacking any views of his own. He is always in a hurry and always busy "thinking" something. In particular, he has no time to eat and to digest; this he says, would take time and lay him open to the risk of slowing down and losing efficiency, which he sees as unacceptable. In a moment of insight, Arturo describes himself as surrounded by a shell that cuts him off from the outside world; in his analysis, it is indeed very difficult to communicate with him, particularly as sensory and affective experiences appear remote from him at all times.

The absence of emotion in Arturo is associated with a pronounced difficulty in distinguishing between abstract and concrete, since, for him, everything is abstraction, as the following clinical fragment shows. Arturo tells of a friend he has not seen for some time, who has put on weight. At dinner, his friend's chair collapses; half an hour later, a second chair also gives way under him and his friend once again falls to the floor. At this point Arturo exclaims "The conversation tonight must be particularly heavy." Although this might have seemed a witticism, those present feel the lack of irony and look at him aghast, as if he has gone mad; for Arturo, however, everything seems normal, apart from his embarrassment at the others' reaction. The communication of these events in the session took on a dreamlike connotation, which I therefore saw as indicative of his internal state. For when concreteness appears, Arturo is deploying drastic defenses of negation, extending to the point of negative hallucination: in this sequence the concrete is so confused with the abstract that what causes the chair to collapse is not a real body with its concrete weight, but the abstract subject-matter of the conversation. At the same time, particularly in light of later developments, which I shall mention below, the fat, heavy friend was well suited to representing Arturo's body, relegated to the role of an externalized imaginary twin detached from the representation of himself – and this body-as-other was bound to collapse because it was inaccessible to a mind that ought to have held it up. Indeed, any form of sensory perception indicative of a connection between corporeity and self-representation was lacking at all times in the sessions.

In the sessions with this patient I had to take care not to collude with his requests for "analysis" of relational and historico-reconstructive contexts, which would in my view have constituted a pseudo-analysis rather than leading to a genuine process of growth. Instead, I repeatedly drew Arturo's attention to his disregard for his personal experiences, the anonymity of his judgments, and the most obvious common-sense contradictions of his communication. In other words, I felt it essential to get the patient to be responsible (Bion, 1965: 155) for his internal attitude, which led him not only passively but also actively to set up obstacles to genuinely listening to himself on the level of sensations and emotions.

This work in the first year resulted in his becoming conscious of his artificiality and extreme intellectualization; in this way, little by little, the system of certainties that had acted as a rigid barrier against involvement in his internal world became less monolithic. The appearance of doubt and uncertainty heralded some signs of change, with the emergence of new and unforeseen phenomena. In one session Arturo suddenly and for no obvious reason interrupted his mechanical, repetitive discourse; he looked stunned. He said that he had noticed a concrete presence in the room: a solid, spherical mass hovering underneath the ceiling. A few minutes later, he saw the same mass closer to him, almost within arm's reach. In a later session, the solid, spherical apparition gravitated to a point just above his abdomen, so that he even seemed to perceive it in contact with the palms of his hands. Arturo came out of these experiences exhausted, as if he had performed a tiring physical task and needed time to recover.

These bizarre events signaled the onset of an experience of corporeity in Arturo, in the form of hallucinatory extracorporeal phenomena that expressed his extreme defense against sensory inputs. His body, although subject to dissociation, nevertheless tended to betray traces of its existence, especially in the presence of an analytic *rêverie* capable of recognizing and receiving the communications stemming from the authentic nucleus of his personality.

In a subsequent session I witnessed an important change. Once again Arturo's verbalizing stopped abruptly in midstream; after a while he began to tell me that he had felt the presence of an enormous mass within him, as if his arms and chest were swollen up. A little later, his entire body was experienced as a swollen entity. In my effort to imagine what was happening to him, I internally associated the image of his swollen body with that of the "Michelin Man," representing the famous restaurant guide. This spontaneous association of mine proved to be somehow anticipatory, because not long afterwards Arturo told me that some days earlier he had stopped vomiting. He had resolved to allow himself time and begun to make small meals; small as they were, they nevertheless seemed enormous to him. He said he could still feel the effort of digesting what he had eaten several hours before, as if he had only just eaten it. He added that he felt most pain not in his stomach but in his temples, which were throbbing intensely. This shift from the stomach to the temples struck me as an original mode of expression, as if Arturo were seeking to communicate something; I wondered if he might be articulating a shift – linking belly and head, body and mind. Oddly enough, this movement immediately had a concrete reflection in the analytic relationship: while Arturo was telling me of his experiences, my stomach began to rumble noisily, and was immediately answered by borborygmic manifestations from his. The session had become a conversation for four voices, those from our heads taking turns with those from our bellies. Before leaving, Arturo commented that he would never have thought himself capable of enduring a process of digestion. Meanwhile, I for my part was astonished to consider how Arturo had set his digestive apparatus in operation just at the point when our intestines seemed to have coordinated their workings as if they were one.

A few weeks later, as Arturo was speaking to me, I suddenly started up: a shadow had appeared at the edge of my field of vision. I had the impression that a big scorpion had entered the room and I took fright. Turning my eyes towards the apparition, all I could see was the shadow of the bookshelf ladder. My hallucinatory experience was echoed on the couch by Arturo, who interrupted his associations and told me that he had noticed sensations in his stomach: "Oddly enough, they seemed more familiar to me and less frightening." As I struggled to breathe normally again after my moment of fear, I thought with surprise of the sensory and emotional trends in the analytic relationship that were making it possible for Arturo to move closer to his corporeity. I too had found myself experiencing bodily sensations as hallucinations, just as Arturo was, as if there were no distinction between us. Far from being a sterile evacuation, this exchange of parts, mediated by projective identification (Bion, 1962) and by an intense symmetrization in the relationship (Matte Blanco, 1988), marked the beginning of a process of development whereby Arturo was gradually enabled to draw closer to his sensory experiences and to tolerate them.

Let us now turn to a later session, which included a dream. In it, Arturo was a little turtle in a kind of well, which someone covered over with a lid. In the water there were other little turtles of other colors – not only green but also yellow, and so on. While dreaming, Arturo wondered whether he could stand living the rest of his life in the body of a little turtle. Associating with the dream, he said that many years before he had preferred to give his turtles away when they grew up, to avoid the bother of setting up an aquarium. Without a break, he began to talk about a meeting at work and about the fact that things always had many meanings for him; from then on, his words became more and more chaotic and ultimately incomprehensible. Then he fell silent. After a while I asked him what was the matter. He answered that there were abstract figures moving in his mind and that he could not understand them. At this point I asked him what he felt in his body. He stirred on the couch and seemed revitalized: "Hungry [a pause]. I think I shall eat something without waiting for midnight as I usually do. I have had this feeling for a few days now and have begun to eat a little piece of pizza in the afternoons. I never used to feel anything before." He went on to say that he never managed to connect with what he was doing: he felt detached, as if he were somewhere else; everything seemed useless and meaningless to him. I told him that he hated his body – hated it so much that he never recognized himself in the place where he was: he could not stand living in a body, which he felt to be constricting and slow. Arturo replied that in the dream the feeling of being a little turtle had aroused great anxiety in him; he continued: "Now it occurs to me that I felt like Kafka's beetle: I wanted to run away, but could not."

By the representation of a closed space and the turtle in the dream, Arturo was approaching the perception of his bodily space as an experience shared by the presence of other little turtles. This was a visual translation of the fact that the emerging experience of corporeity had been, and was continuing to be, shared with me in the analytic relationship; the color differences here betrayed an incipient differentiation, based on the color of emotion rather than on abstract thought. The bother of setting up an aquarium for the turtles when they grew up was very reminiscent of Arturo's stoppage of development in his adolescence, intended to avoid the pain resulting from a period of change.

During the session Arturo was unable to associate and elaborate the dream with symbolic instruments because he was preoccupied with meaningless abstract figures – no doubt because the sensory level that he was beginning to experience still presented him with great difficulty with regard to the construction of symbols. Elaboration was possible only on a basic level such as that of physical sensation: when Arturo said "hungry," he was actually having a sensory perception, expressing a communication between body and mind, which allowed him to remain contained within the oscillation between concreteness and abstraction. His language gave the impression of an infant trying to find words to express his sensory experiences. In such phases, dreams assume particular importance because they can convey connotations of representation and thinkability still remote from the more abstract levels of the personality. The metaphor of the beetle in the associations made it possible to develop the visual image of the little turtles in the dream: the image of the insect represented the intense claustrophobia and the "uncanny" experience of his approach to the body – a shift demonstrating a greater permeability to emotional experiences, to the extent of transparently revealing his contempt for his own corporeity (after all, a beetle arouses reactions very different from one's tender response to a little turtle). The literary reference to Kafka's metamorphosis also seemed very relevant to the theme of bodily transformation, which was connected with Arturo's adolescent problems as crystallized in the anorexic symptom of the rejection of corporeity.

The above clinical fragments illustrate the movement that can potentially be achieved in analysis in a context in which the mind has artificially emancipated itself from the bodily substrate that generates sensations and emotions. When the words spoken in the sessions tend to reveal a world of meaningless "abstract figures intended to make one forget sensations" (as Arturo acutely observed in one session), the function of analysis is to lead the analysand back to a real lived dimension so as to generate fragments of authentic experience – as when Arturo gradually drew closer to the sensory perception of his body, or merely noticed internal stimuli that he could verbalize, for example by saying "hungry." Repeated experiences of sensory registration and "significant correspondences" (Ferrari and Stella, 1998) weave a mental fabric, which, with time and growth, will develop containing functions (Bion, 1962). By virtue of these acquisitions, Arturo was able, at later stages of the analysis, to confront the emotions unleashed by the relational world, including the transference, without recourse to imitative defenses (Gaddini, 1992).

Even if this material admittedly does not reflect all aspects of the hypotheses I have outlined, representing as it does only one moment in the progress of this analysis, I nevertheless hope that it might convey some idea of an approach centered on the body and on primitive mental states, and of how that approach might be applicable to a case seriously at risk of impasse.

Notes

1 Ferrari (1992: 37) considers marasmus to be a transitory condition in newborn babies as a result of sensory pressures from their bodies. Marasmus is the starting-point of the entropic phase that, mediated by maternal *rêverie*, stimulates the activation of the negentropic area.
2 This second level seems to me very close to the "use of an object" described by Winnicott as "the subject's placing of the object outside the area of the subject's omnipotent control; that is, the subject's perception of the object as an external phenomenon, not as a projective entity ... this is a departure from theory which tends to a conception of external reality only in terms of the individual's projective mechanisms" (1971a [1969]: 89, 90).

Chapter 5

The body in the analytic session
Focusing on the body–mind link

> The poet Donne has written "the blood spoke in her cheek ... as if her body thought." This expresses exactly that intervening stage which in the Grid is portrayed on paper as a line separating beta elements from alpha elements. Note that I am not saying that it is either beta or alpha but the line separating the two which is represented by the poet's words. The practising analyst has to be sensitive while the conversation is taking place to what is taking place ... a situation of change from something which is not thought at all to something which is thought.
>
> (Bion, 1990:41)

Maria, a young woman in her thirties, suffered from severe panic attacks and various skin problems. During the first months of her four-session-a-week analysis she looked very rigid, bent almost at a right angle when she was lying on the couch. One day, after a comment of mine, I felt that a space for communication had opened between us. She was silent, however, and her anxiety seemed almost palpable. I asked her what was on her mind. She replied in a serious tone "The trouble is that it is not only on my mind." When I asked for some clarification, Maria said "When you stopped speaking I felt oddly relaxed and I was comfortable lying on the couch ..." Then, sounding frightened all at once, " ... but I come here to think!" I actually felt Maria's

---

A previous version of this chapter was presented at the Fourth British–Italian Conference in London; at a Meeting on the Body in Rome sponsored by the Centro di Psicoanalisi Romano; and as a lecture at the Centre for Psychotherapy, Knockbracken Healthcare Park, Belfast, in February 2007. A wider version has been published in Lombardi (2008a).

fear of coming into contact with her sensations, which arose in relation to what I sensed was a possible transformation of her internal disposition from her former intellectualizing impermeability. I imagined that this was her way of telling me how unsuitable she considered her relaxation to be, and that she was frightened of overstepping professional boundaries. Thus I sought to comment in a way that would foster the new experience of herself that Maria was having, as regards contact with her physical sensations. So I replied "You seem to be frightened now because your body is participating. Instead, you might view it as part of your experience and make a distinction between 'sensual' and 'sexual.'" Maria immediately seemed calmer.

What Maria expressed about thought revealed a misconception (Money-Kyrle, 1968): she conceived of thought as an abstract entity, something quite removed from physical and affective reality, rather than as a function that acts in conjunction with "an awareness of emotional experience" (Bion, 1967: 8). I realized that I had the impression that, had I attempted to spur her on to a more developed level by focusing on the transference and object relations, she would have been deflected from an intimate experience of her bodily sensations that she was, for the first time, allowing herself in a session. Hence my intervention underlined the entry of the body into analysis and was intended to show the possibility of thinking and discriminating within the experience of the body (body–mind relationship) as the patient began to approach her own sensations.

This experience of sensory contact and her associated burgeoning mental perception seemed to heal her body–mind dissociation within the context of this session. During the first few months of her analysis she had manifested this dissociation through physical rigidity and obsessive speech. The only dream she had hitherto brought in seemed an attempted pictorial representation of her condition at the time. There was a woman all alone in a castle at the top of a hill, while lower down, at the foot of the castle, another woman was wandering, as if lost, along a narrow path. In fact she could not at that point rid herself of the mental armor that kept her from getting in touch with her real sensations and emotions. But in the session under consideration, by feeling relaxed on the couch and talking about it, Maria was able to allow her body some space and to relate to it mentally. Since her body, when it made its appearance, had generally been connected with an immediate tendency to panic, with a resultant risk of mental paralysis, my intervention was aimed at stimulating a conscious distinction between "sensual" and "sexual." Thus the activation of her mind could help turn down the emotional heat that exposed her to bodily turmoil.

This first clinical vignette, which I have chosen to introduce a discussion of the body in the analytic session, was one of many that showed me how a focus on the body makes it possible to approach the wide range of patients who suffer from a "defect of thinking" (Bion, 1962). This material illustrates how helpful such an approach can be in those cases in which this defect is not fully evident until concrete and bodily aspects begin to emerge in sessions.

Fluctuations between the vertical and the horizontal axes: the case of Antonia

In this second clinical case I hope to show how helpful a technical approach based on the vertical relationship was in fostering the working-through in an analysand with evident dissociative traits in her bodily experience. We shall be able to follow the oscillation between the vertical axis (body–mind) and the horizontal axis (analysand–analyst) in the context of the material from one week's work. The working-through allowed the analysand to strengthen both her body–mind relationship and the analytic relationship.

Antonia, a 35-year-old woman, was in the midst of three-session-a-week psychoanalysis. Her relationships were shallow and precarious, and she had almost no sex life, somewhat surprisingly for someone with her feminine appearance and outgoing manner. At the beginning of the analysis I observed that Antonia seemed unaware of her physical sensations and that she found her own reflection in the mirror alien. The subject of her body came up in analysis because of minor plastic surgery followed by lymph drainage and regular activities such as massage, exercise, and workouts at the gym. It was during her time at the gym that she began to confront her own mirror image as something unfamiliar and disturbing. Later she reported a revealing dream: "A woman came up close to me and sat in the very chair I was sitting in. At that point I turned into a piece of paper and disappeared." Thus she communicated her trouble in conceiving of herself as a real person with a body that had its own three-dimensionality, and her tendency to relate to others by submitting to external demands and disappearing as a separate person. Clinical work with her was problematic because of the analysand's non-perception of her body, as well as because of the sense of emptiness and internal death she conveyed, which produced a sensation of paralysis and boredom in me. My attempts to approach the problem through its transferential and countertransferential implications, by proposing interpretations of her tendency to deny the emotions provoked by a greater closeness between us, met, however, with no success.

During the working-through it was possible to analyze her tendency to "keep her body in jail" by not going out, thus avoiding meeting new people and excluding the possibility of a sexual life. At this point the sessions began to include constant references to bodily sensations: she felt hot, she felt cold, she had backache or a headache, she suffered from indigestion or a stomach ache. It was as if her body were being concretely released from jail, and were testifying to its sensory presence by means of these complaints.

Now we can look briefly at some material from three consecutive sessions from one week during her fourth year of analysis. During the first session Antonia said:

P[atient]: This week-end I went to a crowded party where I met a few young men. It was quite some time since this had happened to me. The party took place in a grand old Roman palace that housed the War Ministry during Mussolini's time. The music was loud and I felt deafened by it. At a certain point I didn't feel at all well and I thought I might faint. It's odd that something like that should have happened to me.

A[nalyst]: [I note her new ability to venture out into a social situation but also her inclination to disappear.] When you permit yourself to make room for your body and your internal music by going out to a party, war breaks out inside yourself. In this war you become the Mussolini who needs to control everything, even if it means that you have to faint so as to get away when you are not in total control.

P: I'm not used to staying at a party, but this time, perhaps for the first time, I felt that I myself and "the feminine Antonia" could stay there together. I've come to understand that I'm used to blotting out the fact that I'm a woman sexually.

A: [Here I am annoyed by the intellectualized and imitative way she expresses herself.] You treat your mind and your body separately, so that you almost become two separate people: you and "the feminine Antonia." [In a somewhat sarcastic tone of voice] Excuse me, aren't you always the same person?

P: [She seems embarrassed.] As I was leaving the palace I noticed that the banister was unsteady and I couldn't lean on it. [Silence.] I feel some pain in my back.

A: [I am struck by the way her body enters the analytic session. It makes its appearance just as she is referring to an external support – the banister – which was unsteady.]

P: These sensations in my back seem reassuring to me. They make me feel that I am staying in myself. The back is ... I don't know what to call it ... a "ring finger – a ring road." [The Italian word *anulare* has both meanings.] I feel connected to myself. It's sort of like the ring road, the road encircling Rome that connects various areas of the city and allows drivers to go off it in a variety of directions. I feel I have boundaries, but at the same time I can go off in different directions. The shaky banister made me think how I've got used to leaning too much on things outside me. I'm always placing too much importance on things outside me – that's what happened at the party too.

A: If you place "too much importance on things outside you," you will expose yourself to the risk of losing your connection to yourself, losing the ring road that binds you to your sensations. And it's not surprising that your body should then disappear that way. [As I make this comment I see that Antonia is making some small movements on the couch and I feel she is more in touch and more present emotionally.]

P: I still have some backache, but it's not as disturbing as before. I feel my entire body quite clearly, as though the sensations in my back were delineating the boundaries of my body.

One might wonder at my tendency not immediately to interpret either her hatred for the weekend separation manifested in the patient's first statements of the session, or the transference as it appears in the unsteady banister (Flanders, 2007). In this case a by no means negligible element was my emotional perception in the real time of the session: indeed, it is not by chance that the analyst generally "feels" whether or not the patient is ready to accept a transference interpretation. My impression in this context was that it was too early for an intervention of that sort, so I made the choice described above.

As I reconsider the material, my impression seems to be confirmed by Antonia's reference to the deafeningly loud music and to her almost fainting, as well as by her first response, which indicated a profound dissociation in relation to herself. When, with some annoyance, I noted her dissociation, I made active use of my countertransference to construct an intervention in a sarcastic tone about her still being one and the same person, by which means I intended to involve a less intellectualizing and more basic level of her personality (see Lombardi, 2004). This sequence seems to me to be pervaded with emotional fluctuations that set in motion transformations and changes (Bion, 1970) leading towards authentic interaction in the analytic couple (horizontal relationship), and associated with the analysand's first approach to her vertical relationship.

With the emergence of the body in the session, her back started to function like a "ring road," connecting her upper and lower parts. Here her tendency to place too much importance on things outside herself comes to the fore. So in this sequence we can see a body–mind "contact network" that enables her to express her bodily sensations and also her working through defensive theories (Bion, 1962), such as considering herself two separate people and giving too much importance to things outside herself. At the end of the session Antonia perceptively delineated the boundaries of her body, starting from her bodily sensations. The working-through that favors the vertical relationship in the session catalyzes a drawing nearer to the body.

In the following session, Antonia, who is a social worker, told me that she had had a session with a very difficult child that went better than usual. The boy said he was a steel robot, but then he asked if he might go and have a pee. As they left the loo she asked him how it was that steel boys could have a pee. Maybe if they can, she suggested, it is because they don't have steel bodies, but real ones. Things got complicated towards the end, when the child moved a cupboard and slipped behind it. She had the feeling that he wanted to disappear. At this point in her account, Antonia's tone of voice changed as she said she had a terrible headache; she then retreated into silence, which I perceived as full of hostility. I asked her with what she connected this sudden headache. She answered that she had the impression she had already left the room. I wondered, out loud, whether it could be connected with the imminent end of the session. Antonia replied that she couldn't bear the end of any experience, and then restated it, "I've never been able to bear it," adding "it's strange that I don't feel my body anymore." I told her that she was behaving like the boy hiding behind the cupboard: she was making her body disappear. It was her way of not going through our experience of today, in which our time was ending. "I don't know what's going on," she replied, "I just know that I feel a strong hatred for you. It starts in my back. I feel I just can't stand you." I felt that her hatred was authentic. It was real hatred, because it was linked to her perception of me as a person with real limits, in contrast to her omnipotent fantasy, according to which I would be a kind of "banister" she could lean on however and whenever she wished. I said that if she accepted hating me as a real person, she would accept feeling her own body as well, instead of making herself disappear, as she had done on other occasions. Now she could see the correspondence between her back and her hatred, and think about it all with her own head, rather than cutting everything off.

During the final session of the week, Antonia told me how sorry she felt about her hatred for me of the preceding day. She didn't start to feel regret until quite a while after she had left my office. In the course of this session her back pain surfaced once more. She said she again experienced it as a "ring finger/ring road," and from it she was able to outline her body in her mind. As the session developed she carried on a dialogue with me and, at the same time, a continuous dialogue with her own bodily sensations, rhythmically alternating the two. Thus it was as if Antonia could relate to me without losing the connection to her bodily sensations. Towards the end of the session she said she felt some sadness: she was sorry to be finishing the session, but she was also glad because she was about to go on a weekend trip to northern Europe with some friends for the first time. She had checked the weather, and the temperatures were much lower than in Rome. She would have to be sure to pack some warm clothing. As she prepared to leave the office her movements seemed slower than usual, and as she crossed the threshold she most unusually turned and looked at me for few seconds.

If we track the evolution of these sessions we can see that in the second one the patient is confronted with her trouble in keeping herself integrated before a relational separation (headache, the impression of having left the room, the inability to feel her body). In this sequence the "horizontal relationship" affects the "vertical relationship." In other words, working through separation from the analyst (horizontal) tends to trigger the defense of body–mind dissociation (vertical). Here the body–mind dissociation provoked by confrontation with a limit (Matte Blanco, 1975, 1988; Green, 1990 [1976]) takes the form of disappearance of the body into some sort of hiding place. In this context recognizing hatred and respecting perceived limits play an important integrative role, making it possible for her to have an authentic relationship with the analyst as well as a relationship with her own bodily sensations.

The last session of the week starts with working through the patient's experience of hatred as separation looms. In the course of this session Antonia proves able to maintain contact with her bodily sensations and, at the same time, with the analyst. That is to say Antonia no longer disappears when confronted with the other, as she had in the dream from the beginning of her analysis (in which she turns into a piece of paper and disappears). And this continuity of her own presence is not derived from abstract understanding, but rather from a continuous input originating in her bodily sensations.

Previously my attempts at processing separation and absence had drawn a blank. To one of these attempts Antonia responded by telling me about one of her rare dreams: in it she viewed herself as she was sleeping and she saw that she was unable to wake up, despite various attempts she made to rouse herself by touching her body. I then realized that Antonia was trying to communicate her internal state of paralysis – of what Bion (1992) would have called the waking dream alpha – with the consequent non-differentiation between sleep and wakefulness and a blocked ability to learn from experience. At the time of this sequence of sessions she had long since got past this condition, with the result that the material that appears here is much more differentiated than it had been previously, but I felt I must nevertheless keep on carefully monitoring the continuity of her sensory presence. The dissociation is countered by revealing her "disappearance behind the cupboard" (namely her body–mind dissociation) in the course of the middle session and by recognizing the emotion of hatred. At the end of the last session Antonia feels both sadness and happiness as a result of separation. Not by chance, the separation is represented in terms of a bodily experience, such as a change in temperature, and the need for warm clothing.

These sessions seem to show the importance of the "vertical relationship" in a context in which the analytic working-through cannot altogether count on the analysand's inner integration to anchor the symbolic processes of the analytic relationship in the body.

Hindrances and integration in the body–mind relationship: the case of Roberta

Here I should like to present some material in which the analyst's interventions place the "vertical" body–mind relationship at the core of the working-through. Thus the "horizontal" analyst–analysand relationship (thanks in part to the analyst's *rêverie*) simply fosters the process by catalyzing the focus of the analysand's intrapersonal disposition.

Roberta, a nearly 30-year-old woman, was undergoing her second analysis, now three sessions weekly, because of persistent depressive symptoms. In the past she had had a lesbian relationship but had recently established a stable relationship with a man. Her past homosexual orientation had contributed to her growth, particularly in helping her approach her body, which she had formerly experienced as beyond reach. Recently, however, this kind of attraction seemed to be regressive, disguising a conflict in the body–mind relationship. One session should serve to demonstrate this kind of conflict and my clinical approach to the material.

Roberta began the session by telling me that she had been feeling strongly attracted to a lesbian colleague who was strongly attracted to her, and that she had been thinking of arranging to go out with her. She immediately added "Anyway, how am I to handle physical attraction? The best way is just not to think about it." I pointed out how she responded to sensory stimuli: when she felt the anxiety provoked by the power of her physical sensations, she was guided by the folk wisdom "What the eye doesn't see the heart doesn't grieve over." If she neither saw nor thought, she interrupted the relationship between her mind and her body, erecting a barrier rather than permit a body–mind network and fall prey to the physical urges she feared.

After my intervention Roberta associated a dream.

> The tenant who lives one floor below rings me up to congratulate me and make a pass at me. I invite him to come upstairs to our party, where I'm with my boyfriend. The tenant comes with his girlfriend. After a while this guy becomes too pushy and I decide to throw him out by pushing him out the door. While I'm trying to get him out of my place I realize that he has a marked physical trait: a very big nose. We push him out of our flat and his nose is the last part we manage to push out. It's like throwing something out of the window.

The hypotheses I worked on with Roberta emphasized her capacity to keep in touch with her own body and emotions (communication with the floor below), which was closely connected with the capacity to allow inner space for a relationship with a pair of internal parents (the tenants from downstairs): thus, integration in her vertical relationship with her body proceeded in correspondence with an integration of her internal objects. But she tended to perceive this emotional contact as anxiety-ridden – the anxiety of contact with overly violent emotions – so she was inclined to expel her body (throw it out of the window), and she represented the body – using the form of synecdoche involving naming a part but meaning the whole – as a nose (Freud, 1900; Matte Blanco, 1975).

In theoretical terms this dream is an expression, within the dream-work, of the contact network: i.e., the patient was representing to herself the acceptance of her own body (the marked physical trait of the tenant from the floor below) and, simultaneously, the expulsion conflict in her relationship to her body. The party is imbued with an atmosphere of arousal associated with the appropriation of her physical sensations, and their intensity probably contributed to her non-containment anxiety.

Roberta responded to this working-through by reporting a second dream she had had some time earlier. "There are two dogs fighting. Then the bad dog bites X's parents first – that is, my former girlfriend's parents – and then it bites me. But I accept the bite and so the dog bites less hard. It bites just to leave a mark." By way of association Roberta commented "X's parents may represent my past, how I used to be in the past." I then pointed out the image Roberta had created of an inner conflict (two dogs fighting). She was grappling with her own body because she was frightened by the violence of her emotions, both erotic and aggressive, as she had experienced them in her relationship with her parents in the past (the dog biting two parents first). But in fact she was now able to bring new resources into play and accept her emotional violence instead of rejecting it (the dog then biting her). This new acceptance of her emotions meant that they bit her only to the point of leaving a mark, allowing her to access consciousness of her feeling. The dream displayed the difference between her old line of conduct and her newly acquired learning. The conflict involved me as well, since she had kept the dog dream from me, although she had had it some time previously. But this also seems like an expression of her old modus operandi, which implied not fully recognizing what she felt and perceived.

Roberta seemed intrigued by my comments. She said:

> I thought that my attraction to my colleague might have more to do with me than with her. I'm the one who feels more positive, more interested, more open to the world lately. But I'm also frightened about feeling more vital and more physically present. Perhaps I dared to attribute this state of mind to her because it's reassuring to keep it outside myself. But this way I lose it and can't enjoy it as a thing that involves me as a person in a more general sense.

I replied:

> This nose would seem, to some extent, to be mediating your relationship to the world, as is the case with dogs, whose olfactory sense is a primary way of knowing about their surroundings. If you push this "curious body" of yours away from you, you will be in danger of losing your vital relationship to the world.

The above material clearly reveals my preference for emphasizing the body–mind relationship as an interpretative approach to this session. The working-through was focused primarily on the "vertical" relationship, with the "horizontal" relationship with the analyst remaining in the background, from which it briefly emerged in my comments, when I pointed out the parallel between the analysand's distancing herself from a recognition of her bodily sensations on the one hand and, on the other, her delay in bringing in a dream that would have helped her understand her current internal state.

"I … feel more positive, more interested, more open to the world lately," Roberta said. Thus she highlighted the analytic evolution that made her feel integrated with her body, so that it became the basis for her relating to the world with curiosity. At this point Roberta was having to deal with anxiety associated with the aggressive component of the epistemophilic instinct (Klein, 1975c [1928]), an expression connected with the instinctual and bodily nature of the cognitive processes linked to curiosity. As a result, our working-through had a moderating effect on Roberta's inclination towards projective identification, fragmentation, and action divorced from thought, and it also reintegrated her in terms of her relationship with herself and her sense organs. An indirect effect was the strengthening of her interpersonal relationships. Her new openness to the world was in fact a sign of a notable openness to object relations beyond the direct transference relationship with the analyst, thanks to her reappropriation of aspects of herself that she had hitherto projected onto him.

It is easy to imagine what a very different direction the working-through would have taken had I focused on transference issues. For example, I might have identified the big-nosed figure as a representation of the analyst, and seen the nose as a phallic symbol reminiscent of seductive and persecutory factors in the analytic relationship. Or perhaps I could have taken her acceptance of being bitten by the dog as a masochistic submission to her own sadistic destructiveness. Instead, I feel that giving due weight to elements connected with the body–mind relationship enabled me to get at Roberta's archaic anxiety about sensations and emotions, which then fostered her ability to deal with them by strengthening a trusting internal relationship with herself and her own body.

This case seems to me to provide a chance to observe how making room for the body as an object of the mind can help to distinguish between the body–mind relationship and a relationship with an external object. Failure to differentiate between these two levels can lead to impeding or delaying analytic progress and to establishing a pathological dependence on the external object.

Discovering the concrete body and the beginning of a body–mind relationship: the case of Carlo

The case I am about to present illustrates some implications of the idea of the COO, seen here as a source of confrontation, experience, and stimulus to mental growth in a patient suffering from phobic-obsessional symptoms and a general state of inertia. I shall discuss a dream and some aspects of a session in which various elements of the progress begun in analysis emerge through a strikingly original language register.

Carlo, a man in his mid-fifties, in his fourth year of four-session-a-week analysis, recounted a dream:

> I dreamed I was masturbating Bertinotti [the president of the Chamber of Deputies and a communist]. He told me that later he would bugger his brother-in-law, who, in the dream, was his daughter's husband. (Doctor, please don't ask why, in the dream, this was not my son-in-law, but my brother-in-law. That's just how it was.) The relative's wife was in the next room, perfectly aware of what was going on, but she didn't mind. She knew that was how her husband was.

Then he associated:

> I really don't know what the dream means. But I do know that this dream, this absurd dream, is one I've never had before and, until now, would never have even thought of having. As I look back, I see that many things happened last year and if anyone had told me they were going to happen I would have thought he was crazy. Like buying a horse and riding it regularly. Or going to prostitutes. This week for the first time I had intercourse with two women at

once. Would I ever have imagined I could do something like that? I'd have panicked at the very thought. They were as efficient as two nurses in changing my condom when I switched from one to the other ... Of course, they are nurses: they nurse the wounds that have made living impossible for me up to now. They had small breasts. I'd have liked to touch them, to feel their contours, but I held back. Next time. The main thing is that now, unlike before, I feel alive. The concentration camp is still there, just a step away, but now I have a concrete reality I can turn to. The real pitfall is abstraction. With abstraction anything can happen and you never know how to hold subversive anxiety at bay. It's different with concrete reality: things exist and have definite boundaries. So I have room to live, while the other way it's just terror and nothing else.

As the session proceeded, Carlo associated his dream with the film *The Crying Game* (dir. Neil Jordan, 1992), in which an Irish terrorist searches for the girlfriend of the man he killed and discovers she is transgender, going on to have a conflicted and erotic relationship with her. Then Carlo started to speak about two paintings by Caravaggio that were rejected by the ecclesiastical authorities of his time. He mentioned the violence of the Counter-Reformation Church, expressing outrage at the rejection of a painting by Caravaggio, who was already "Caravaggio" even back then. At this point I felt I might comment that he was trying, by means of eroticism, to revivify the body that his ideological terroristic violence spurred him to blot out in his own world. If a painting by Caravaggio is valuable, his body, his unique body, should be all the more so, but he had nevertheless effaced the very body that made it possible for him to live.

With his dream and the subsequent associations, Carlo recapitulated the experience that enabled him to use analysis as a way of approaching his COO, i.e., the concrete reality of his body and of his relationship to his animal and sexual dimensions. This encounter with his biological self made it possible for him to begin to make some progress with his severe obsessive syndrome, the tip of the iceberg of a more general condition of internal death. His first analysis, which took place in his youth, some thirty years earlier, had not achieved anything of the sort.

This sequence shows the role of the body, not only as regards events in the analytic relationship, but also in the broader context of the analysand's life experience. The parasitic relationship between his obsessive system and abstraction had led Carlo to lose contact with life and had resulted in a chronic persecutory state he referred to as "Auschwitz," the ubiquitous fantasy of his own concentration camp. As the unconscious is linked to a relationship with concreteness (Freud, 1915a) and the illogical (Freud, 1932: 73; Matte Blanco, 1975), Carlo's developing a relationship to his own body enabled him to integrate a concrete level of functioning as well as a tolerance for the illogical, and thus to be more prepared for experiencing the unconscious. At the same time the relationship with concreteness as connected to the body introduces the presence of edges, boundaries, and differences in a relationship, as Carlo pointed out. Thus there is room for a burgeoning discriminating and thinking capacity (Matte Blanco, 1975), as well as a capacity to shift between the concrete and the abstract (Freud, 1915a; Bion, 1965).

Not by chance did Carlo mention, in this session, the two women's breasts, whose outlines he would have liked to sketch with his hands. The breast apparently evokes the lack of sensory and bodily *rêverie* Carlo experienced with his obsessive mother and an absent father. As the family moved about constantly during his childhood, he could not even develop a bond with a definite geographical place. His adolescence was dominated by his ideological infatuations, based on an inclination towards imitation and compliance that deprived him of the integrative potential inherent in adolescent corporeality. Through his analysis Carlo was able to open the door to the adolescence he had never experienced and, despite a delay of more than thirty years, he activated a realm of experience that is indispensable for the development of the personality.

These facts would be too fragmentary were they not related to Carlo's conflicted internal system in such a way that, dominated by a primitive persecutory super-ego, he had become a terrorist threatening himself, committed to the systematic murder of his own physicality and to a personal 'Counter-Reformation' *auto-da-fé*, which was meant to do away with his own body. A devastating and pernicious mixture of this sort cannot, in my experience, be transformed in analysis by working exclusively on the mental level, which could provoke a defensive pseudo-mentalization. What it needs is a systematic catalyzing of the body–mind relationship, from which the analysand can get a direct experience of his own real body.

This material seems interesting also because it forms a convenient bridge between certain theoretical and technical elements I should like to mention, although I cannot now enter into much detail. If taken literally, the manifest content of Carlo's dream gives prominence to what could easily be considered perverse elements, such as auto-eroticism, arousal with a manic coloration, and homosexual elements. Particularly if we place it in a transference framework, the dream could easily be used to evoke regressive fantasies and a transference perversion. Conversely, if we start by focusing on the relationship to the body – as I have tried to demonstrate – the consequences can be very different indeed.

We tend too easily to assume that working-through, in which the body is prominent, has to do with attacks on the analysis in the form of destructive acting out (see, e.g., Rabih, 1991). An understanding of bodily representations and functions in terms of perversion can be achieved even when the patient responds negatively to such an interpretative approach (see, e.g., Baker, 1994; Good, 2006).[1] Similarly, the tendency to understand the so-called erotic transference in purely defensive or manic terms (see, e.g., Smith, 2006) involves neglecting to explore certain levels: indeed, "the erotic component that some analysands bring to analysis could be seen as an attempt to draw nearer – by means of the analytic relationship – to the corporeal levels that were never completely integrated into the personality" (Lombardi, 2006a). This is true as well of many situations in which shame plays a major role: where shame is linked to relational hostility and triumph manifestations in the transference (see Steiner, 2006b). I would instead hypothesize a more archaic level of denial of one's own bodily reality (Lombardi, 2006b, 2007).

Thus the question seems to be whether the absence of a clear theoretical status for the body in contemporary psychoanalysis should now claim our attention, so that we can correct the misunderstanding by which the body is mistaken for its potential symbolic meanings, while its basic quality as a concrete object is quite neglected – whereas it is not a symbol but something real. Stressing the fact that the body is a concrete object from which the mind evolves and with which it is continually confronted would mean recognizing the corporeal foundation for psychic reality (Freud 1911a) and paving the way to a functioning body–mind relationship. From this perspective, situations that might have been viewed as examples of perversion, destructive acting out, erotic transference, etc., could instead reveal the emergence of the analysand's primitive needs connected to her existence and her ability to live. This would legitimate a clinical approach more focused on helping the analysand relate to her own physical sensations and would emphasize the need for a perceptual recognition of the body, leaving the recognition of the relational other to a later stage of the analytic process.

If we consider Carlo's material as the expression of his attempt to link body and mind, we can find a sort of proto-representation of the body–mind relationship, in which his dream "recognizes" the mind's specific function in fulfilling the life-promoting urges of the body. The analysand unconsciously chooses Bertinotti as the protagonist, i.e., a communist recently promoted to one of the highest offices in the country. He functions here as a representative of the "revolutionary" changes Carlo has brought about during his analysis. Because of these changes there must now be a new "constitution" regulating his internal balance, with full recognition of the cardinal position of his body: something that could never have been imagined before. For Carlo this connection to the body serves to counter the action effected by his internal "architect of terror," embodied in his obsessional and terroristic thoughts. Carlo's acting out should therefore be understood as an experience that contributes to the working-through (Rosenfeld, 1964), even becoming "in some ways our chief clinical ally" (Khan, 1974 [1964]: 67). Thus the analysand's mental approach to his body seems to fulfill the conditions of "a new psychic action" (Freud, 1914b) that can meet the vital needs of the person as they come up. The body is, however, still a concrete object, the reintegration of which into the analytic process enables the patient to open up to experience, change, and life, even before opening up to thought.

Before concluding I should like to consider, however briefly, the subsequent evolution of this patient. In a later dream, where he had expected to find just one building, he found two buildings instead, and he was somehow particularly aware of the spatial dimension. In the dream he felt an intense hatred for that change, a hatred that, he said, he felt again at the very moment of describing it to me. Thus I was able to interpret it to him as his hatred for a change that explicitly made me an actual partner in his analytic experience.

The analytic relationship came to hold the stage, and the analysand explicitly recognized the quality of the work we had accomplished together. This working-through of otherness made it possible to make room for a clear differentiation between the sexes and also to endorse his process of identification in the transference, which contributed to his sexual identity. In addition to working through analytic otherness, Carlo was distinctly more capable of tolerating his hatred of surprises, which he now viewed as symbolic otherness for which he was ready to allow space in the context of experience. Thus he modified his need to seek reassuring habits and repetitions. This kind of reassurance had led him to a form of psychic death. Even his experiences with prostitutes seemed, in the end, repetitive and predictable compared with the surprises that took place within the analytic dialogue.

For my part, I was particularly impressed when his reflections enabled him to talk to me about death as the "last surprise" that life can have in store and, as he said, "the last possibility of continuing to be alive." Carlo's meditation about death amazed me, also because it reminded me of the very moving words of Donald Winnicott when confronted with his own death (see C. Winnicott, 1978: 19). It is a secular prayer that seems, in its essential simplicity, to condense the experience of the last challenge to the connection of body and mind in the face of the irremediable loss of life. It means being able to be mentally alive even when our body is about to leave us forever:

> O God, may I be alive when I die!

Note

1 In Baker and Good's clinical cases the patients respond to the analyst's failure to register their physical presence by reasserting it through means of flatulence during the session, i.e., by manifestations of a concrete body that is not eclipsed by the mind's shadow.

Chapter 6

Body and mind in adolescence

In this chapter, I will consider primarily the topic of the body in adolescence. The body–mind conflict assumes particular characteristics during this period of life because of the imposition of changes in the body, which takes on the defining attributes of the adult body. The mind, adapted until recently to living in the body of a child, finds itself confronted by an otherness that has powerful new aspects. Hatred of one's own body and others' – characterized at times by extreme violence – thus moves to the foreground.

> One thing I could never stand was to see a filthy, dirty old drunkie, howling away at the filthy songs of his fathers and going blurp blurp in between, as if it might be a filthy old orchestra in his stinking, rotten guts. I could never stand to see anyone like that, whatever his age might be, but more especially when he was real old like this one was.

This voiceover in one of the violent opening scenes of *A Clockwork Orange* (dir. Stanley Kubrick, 1971), conveying the sentiments of the main character, Alex, evokes the adolescent's hatred of the body. The violence perpetrated by Alex and his group against the old "drunkie," the tramp with the "rotten guts," is dramatically retaliated in the violence that Alex will use against himself, throwing himself out of a window in order to be rid of intolerable physical sensations.

A first draft of this chapter was read at the Foundation for Adolescent Psychotherapy, Helsinki in October 2014; at the San Francisco Psychoanalytic Center in March 2015; and at the Psychoanalytic Institute of New England, East (PINE), Needham, MA in May 2015. Translated by Gina Atkinson.

Of interest is the correlation suggested by Kubrick between Alex's hatred for the "filthy old orchestra" of burps and intestines on the one hand, and his loving idealization of "Ludwig van's" music on the other: a split between *hatred of* and *idealization of* bodily sensations, here sublimated in musical data, which in the film is destined to fail following the "Ludovico technique" that allows Alex to get out of prison. And this method of treatment – through a coincidence that does not seem to be entirely by chance – has the same name as the revered composer. The retrospective sequence that portrays the "Ludovico technique," with Alex wide-eyed at the scene of violence, symbolically indicates the reconnection within the protagonist *of the conscious gaze* with *the violent bodily action*, which by contrast had earlier been dissociated. And from this point onward, a *conflict that sets body and mind in opposition* is restored to the protagonist – a conflict that impedes muscular discharge and awareness, a conflict that will also expose Alex to the risk of suicide.

The hatred for the body to be found in many adolescent clinical manifestations is similar to what can be observed in psychotic situations, which typically have their onset in adolescence. This was noted in the early 1900s by the Swiss psychiatrist Emil Kraepelin, who assigned the name *dementia praecox* to what we now call schizophrenia, because he had seen that its symptoms of degenerating mental functioning tended to make their first appearance during late adolescence. In the detailed account of her treatment of her psychotic patient Susan, Marion Milner pointed out the importance of *hatred of one's body* or of a conception of the *body as an enemy*, which applies to adolescent situations as well as to psychotic conditions.

> Certainly, at times it seemed clear that her way of interpreting the sensations from the inside of her own body was in terms of *her body being her enemy*. Certainly, also, her body had been a frustrator, as for all of us, by comparison with what one can dream of doing. And certainly *this idea of the body as an enemy because of its setting limits to the omnipotence of her thoughts* was confirmed, I thought, by various statements of hers, for instance when she one day said that she could not get into her body because that would mean the acceptance of the fact that one day she would die.
> (Milner, 1969: 46; my italics)

The body is hated because it acts as a limit to the omnipotence of the mind: a limit that emerges principally with the patient's perception that her body is not infinite, but subject to the limitation of death. While the mind tends towards atemporality, in accordance with the atemporal characteristics that Freud (1900) found in the functioning of the unconscious, the body tends to force it to be aware of linear time, particularly through the confrontation with certain incontrovertible real events such as birth and death (cf. Lombardi, 2013a). This emerging awareness of our human limits, which is connected to our bodily reality and to the objective reality of time, is in the foreground during adolescence and contributes decisively to the formation of the profound body–mind conflict we encounter there, as well as to the relative tendency towards body–mind dissociation. Thus adolescent manifestations often present various discordant patterns in which body and mind each seek control of the personality, the consequence not infrequently being that one of the internal contenders dominates the other.

Before approaching some clinical experiences on our main subject I will briefly consider some ideas of A. B. Ferrari about adolescence: this author's tendency to place the body at the center of his reflections offers an original perspective, which is useful as an introduction to my clinical study.

The second challenge

Ferrari (1994) characterizes the child's primary development as a body awaiting evolution of the mental capacity to contain overwhelming bodily pressures. The child's mind arises from its body. In adolescence, the situation is very different because a mind capable of curiosity by now already exists; this mind assists in the discovery of a new body that is unlike that of the child. *The adolescent's mind does not know the body in which it lives, but must discover it.* If the birth of the mind from the unformed chaos of a body inhabited by an ethological turbulence corresponds to an initial challenge during the first months of life, the confrontation between an already-formed mind and a new body that assumes its definitive adult configuration represents the *second challenge* of adolescence to the internal organization of a body–mind relationship. From this it follows that some discordances may be rooted exclusively in the adolescent experience, putting into perspective the more common idea that all disturbances must have a root in infantile development.

The body comes to the forefront of the adolescent's mind at around the age of 11 to 13, and the mind will have to take on the body, caring for it over the course of a lifetime. Adolescence involves confrontation with a *choice* that becomes decisive for all subsequent development; this choice consists of either facing up to adolescent turbulence or mobilizing all possible strategies to avoid it. Facing the adolescent challenge becomes an important element of stability for subsequent mental development, in that the rejection of adolescence leads to an enormous waste of resources and to developmental paralysis. If the child, even when involved in social relations, is always attracted to his vertical dimension and to the chaotic jumble of his fantasizing imagination, the adolescent will have a vital need to confront external reality and the horizontal dimension in order to learn from experience and to know himself.

Acting out becomes essential for the adolescent, because *only through action can the adolescent gain experience and knowledge*, even if the price of this action is very high, because the adolescent must continually cope with an intense anxiety about the unknown in order to discover step by step what reality can teach him.

The role of choice in adolescence is an important tool with which to orient oneself in the various phenomenologies of adolescent discomfort. From this point of view, a "calm" adolescent can be paradoxically more worrisome than a troubled one; for Ferrari, turbulent and intensely discordant behaviors must not be confused with pathological elements, as they are the organizing part of the living torment of adolescent experience. Adolescent torment not infrequently takes delusional or phenomenologically psychotic forms, but even in these cases, it is only a lack of working through of the experience connected to the area of psychotic language that can lead to the crystallization of an actual, stable psychotic disturbance. This fact is pointed out as strongly encouraging for the analyst who is faced with so-called "intractable" situations – as demonstrated by all those cases of adolescents considered to be without hope, who then, in actuality, respond well to the psychoanalytic approach (see, for example, some clinical cases described by Steinman, [2009]).

Working with adolescents requires mobilization of *great empathic resources*, given that the adolescent continually tests the analyst's participation and affective resonance, not least through absences that put the analyst's tolerance and human interest to the test. The analyst *must not fear his own adolescent experience* and must keep the way open for a continual working-through of her own adolescent layers, *in primis* with the hatred and destructiveness that are so much in the foreground in adolescence (A. H. Williams, 1961), in order to be able to accompany the development of her analysands. The adolescent lives out his experiences with a *forceful intensity* of which he has not had any experience beforehand, waiting to acquire the tools with which to modulate it; he therefore requires an intensely empathic analyst.

When the adolescent experience entails significant involvement of the psychotic area of the personality (Bion, 1967c), the analyst must not fear this area's turbulence. Ferrari (1994) emphasizes that we are all *carriers of an entropic dimension* tied to the area that is organized in close proximity to somatic processes, with related unstable points of equilibrium; these unstable points can be clustered together in a fairly stable way or may assert themselves in a state of explosive magma. It is necessary for the analyst of adolescents not to fear the downpour of explosive, emotional magma if she is to accompany the processes of fluid and unstable transformation, without which adolescence would not be adolescence, nor would the construction of a mind capable of thinking in the presence of emotions ever be possible (Bion, 1962).

Adolescence has strongly subversive characteristics linked to the inexorability of the pressure that *time* exerts on the adolescent situation: without time, in fact, adolescence would not even be launched, and childhood would be an immutable, golden condition as in the myth of *Peter Pan*. Time is thus a primary object of working-through in the context of analytic work with the adolescent (cf. Lombardi, 2003b).

The attempt to hold back the progress of time can lead to the generation of those claustro-agoraphobic conditions that are so evident in disturbances of eating behavior: the adolescent feels himself a prisoner without noticing how much he himself tends to put his own body in prison in trying to control what he feels is subversive and explosive in his own bodily experience. In reality, conversely, *nothing can halt the eruption of change that leads from childhood to adolescence*. This is an undeniable fact, even if in certain analyses of adult patients we may sometimes discover, with surprise, that an intense opposition to the adolescent experience may have involved mysterious physical consequences that remain stable in the configuration of the adult body. Through such processes, an adolescent who rejects the loss of childhood can become strangely "capable" of arresting her own growth in stature or of causing a regression of the development of sexual characteristics secondary to adolescence itself, such as the shape of the breasts or of the hips.

The working-through of adolescence needs time, and this all too easily clashes with certain demands of the productive cycle of the society into which the young person is pressed to enter as early as possible, blocking an indispensable process of working-through. Ferrari writes:

> Our culture does not seem to take account of the fundamental importance of this phase of a man's life for his future and for his insertion into the group ... How much time do we need in order to learn to become adolescents? Will they let us become adults, or will they immediately throw us into the fire, stripping us of the time necessary to do so?
>
> (1994: 53)

Violence, body, and mind

At this point I will move to a brief consideration of some clinical situations encountered in my practice that can lend themselves to the illustration of the body–mind conflict in adolescence. My agenda in this chapter precludes an in-depth discussion of a single clinical case, so my illustrations will be brief and suggestive.

Dario, a young man of 20 in analysis with me, told me about having been taken ill and experiencing a transitory loss of consciousness at the cinema on seeing the scene of aggression against the tramp in *A Clockwork Orange*. In subsequent sessions, his anxieties relating to hatred and violence emerged, which he tried to hold back with denial and a claustrophilic disposition that kept him at home. An intensely symbiotic relationship with his mother, furthermore, led him to feel stuck in the condition of being a small and powerless child, negating every aspect of growth and the emotional urges arising from his adult body. Violence mingled with omnipotent negation primarily took the form of worrisome suicidal fantasies in which his body became the privileged object of his hatred. Later, subsequent analytic working-through brought to light an intense conflict with his father, which took the form of strong homicidal fantasies towards him and the extreme idealization of a person described in the news who had killed both his parents.

After a series of dreams in which he faced violent situations and managed to react, Dario's hatred took concrete form on the occasion of a classmate's repeated provocations. In a sudden outburst of rage, Dario grabbed the other boy violently by the collar and flung him to the ground, causing him, now terrified, to struggle to his feet and run away. In Dario, dreams functioned as a network of connections between body and mind, which began to sensitize him to his hatred, encouraging an appropriation on the part of the ego. It was, however, especially the confrontation with concrete experience and in the interpersonal dimension with his classmate that permitted Dario to have a direct experience of his destructiveness and his hatred, as a way to begin to recognize the intensity of his emotions and the tools with which he could manage them. Beginning with this episode, Dario was able to develop a basic trust in his ability to manage his hatred, instead of giving way to it as a hidden, crushing force, as had happened in the episode of his loss of consciousness while watching *A Clockwork Orange*.

The attack on the body in Giorgio, age 19, took the form of repeated unconscious attempts at suicide. For example, one day he told me about driving his motorcycle very fast down a one-way street that he frequented regularly; that day, however, he took it the wrong way, convinced that the cars, which almost killed him, were driven by criminals. It took a few minutes before Giorgio got a hold of himself and discovered the absurdity of what he was doing; he guided the motorcycle to the edge of the street, terrified and astonished at his own behavior. At that point, working-through began and his suicidal fantasies emerged, such as when he planned to throw himself off a fourth-floor balcony to confirm his ridiculous conviction that his legs could elastically withstand the impact of his jump.

In all these circumstances, the attack on the body was mingled with the negative hallucination of the *existence of the body as a concrete entity*, subject to the laws of physics and space-time. In Giorgio's delusional conviction, *a body that had no weight* emerged, a body that could absorb the shock of impossible jumps as in an animated cartoon, or a body that was not subject to the incompatibility of penetration by other bodies, as in his crazy spin in the wrong direction on his motorcycle.

A psychoanalysis of eating behavior disturbances

> J'ai craché sur l'amour et j'ai tué la chair!
> Fou d'orgueil, je me suis roidi contre la vie!
>
> [I have spat on love and I have killed the flesh!
> Crazy with pride against my life, I dig in my heels.]
> (Jules Laforgue, "Pour le livre d'amour")[1]

The treatment of eating behavior disturbances is an important challenge for present-day psychoanalysis, and a new frontier that requires attentive management integrated into the treatment, with close collaboration between the psychoanalyst and the medical team together with consultative work with the family. I will not now discuss the practical aspects of this type of management, but will focus on what emerged during the course of the psychoanalytic treatment of an anorexic analysand whose life was at risk through body–mind dissociation and conflict.

Let us look at the case of Laura, a young girl whom I followed in supervision.[2] She had begun psychoanalysis at the age of 17 for a serious form of anorexia associated with marked agoraphobic symptoms. She was brought to me by her analyst at around the third year of analysis, when Laura climbed up onto the parapet of a five-story building, ready to challenge the force of gravity, convinced that she could hover in the air. The paradoxical aspect of Laura's clinical picture was that the trend towards her attempting suicide appeared simultaneously with the first perception of her body as a real and autonomous entity. With the acute risk of suicide that Laura was bringing into the analysis, there was a coexistence of both a homicidal attack on the body and a search for the body's true nature that had to be recognized and distinct from the world of her fantasies: until then reality and fantasy had been separated only by a blurry boundary.

It was therefore necessary to follow the analysand's verbalizations very carefully and to help her disentangle the various levels of perception of reality and of anxieties, on the one hand, and of omnipotent fantasies that led to a concrete attack on her body, on the other. The risk of her killing the body, even though it had been overcome at the moment of greatest peril, remained present in analysis for a long time, in fact, on account of Laura's low body weight and precarious metabolic conditions, which necessitated attentive medical monitoring. We will see in greater detail, however, some aspects of her psychoanalytic working-through.

"To go out means to get dressed, to comb your hair," Laura said, immediately bringing in a correlation between this area of disturbances and the acceptance and care of her body. In fact, she preferred to avoid every occasion of encountering her own body, including looking at herself in the mirror. "Being thin is a way of disappearing, of not being there," she tellingly remarked of a relative's thinness, and unintentionally offering a key to understanding her internal situation.

In a session on the eve of summer vacation, Laura spoke of having dreamed of an acquaintance, Carmen, whom she saw every year while camping. Carmen was quite curvaceous and had a baby-doll manner, meant to attract boys – even though, Laura noted, she herself would never be attracted by a big bottom. In the dream, Laura meets Carmen, who is wearing a bathing suit. She sees that Carmen doesn't look worn out. They both say they'll see each other at the beach.

Laura thought that Carmen might *spoil* her vacation; if Laura was interested in a boy, Carmen would *interfere* and Laura would feel forced to *withdraw*. Actually, when Carmen puts on her baby-doll act, Laura chooses to play the censorious male and disapprove of her pose.

Dreaming of Carmen, the analysand approaches the perception of her body and the associated conflict. In fact, Laura disparages the form of her body, considering it an obstacle to her life and her experience. With anorexia and vomiting, she prevents her development of a feminine form, preferring to nourish the illusion of being able to exist apart from her body. Her body confronts her with the deterioration and decay that she fears will be instantaneous and not the result of years that would allow the unfolding of her experiences over time; she is surprised, in fact, that Carmen does not look worn out, as she would expect of anyone who accepted having a body.

When, after some medical tests, Laura learned that she had osteoporosis, which in her case was the result of poor nutrition, but which is analogous to what may be experienced by women in menopause, she observed: "But I was only thinking of going backwards!" – which offered the analyst an opportunity to call attention to the paradoxical position in which she was placing herself by attempting to control time; it led not to a prevention of the much feared decay, but to precocious physical deterioration.

In another dream, after the vacation, Laura is organizing a train journey with an old school friend. She is happy at the prospect, but when it's time to leave she decides to back out of the trip because she's anxious about the unforgiving schedules of traveling, and about the fact that she won't be able to weigh everything that she is about to eat. At home everything is a mess because her flatmates are packing for their own trips. Laura is relieved to be totally uninvolved. Having decided not to go, she feels calm; she sees that the kitchen is clean and orderly, just as she likes it.

In this dream, too, we find evidence of the control that led her to reject the sensorial world of the body, and with it the world of vacations, experiences, life. Limitations of time, such as schedules and deadlines, are rejected, even if the price of this rejection is the paralysis of life. The scheduled journey between her body and her mind is cancelled, impeding every form of constructive continuity between inside and outside, and between self and other.

On another occasion, Laura dreams of an outing to the zoo in which she sees two dogs who are coupling. The female dog doesn't want to do it, but the people present say that if she lets herself go and follows her instinct, she'll like it. The analysand's comment is that to her the scene seems "horrible and disgusting" – a replay in the sexual dimension of her attitude of scorn and rejection, which we have seen with regard to bodily issues in general, even though in this way she reaches the point of preventing herself from having pleasurable experiences.

In the next session, Laura returned to the dream and commented that "my body does not agree with my head," connecting it to a similar problem that she experienced in relation to food. And she asked herself how it was possible to eat or to make love "without its becoming an illness." And then: "I understand that I cancel everything out because *I can't achieve a balance.*"

In cancelling everything out, Laura was again escaping from the body–mind conflict and thus denying herself the development and growth that could lead her to a certain form of balance, though an unstable and dynamic one, between body and mind. In particular, she feared the violence of her drives, their monopolization of her, likened by her to an illness – which led her defensively to take refuge in a withdrawal that assumed the exterior forms of "suspended animation" (Winnicott, 1958a [1935]: 132). It is thus precisely the rejection of the mind–body conflict that led her to regress to a state of body–mind dissociation, treating her body as though it were non-existent, but having to suffer for this decision.

In the case of Laura, it becomes evident how the rejection of the body may lie at the root of a discord in the mind–body relationship that has oppressive consequences in the balance of life. This is a discord in which the mind excludes the body for fear that the body could exclude the mind: an amalgamation organized according to a theory that the body could only be an extraneous obstacle to mental participation.

In the case of adolescents such as Dario, Giorgio, and Laura, it seems evident that rejection of the body and violent attacks, to the point of murdering the self, are expressive of an otherness that is not easily acceptable or integratable into one's own internal parameters, but are largely constructed in accordance with fantasized omnipotence – an omnipotence that is quite characteristic of a child's mental world. Conversely, the mind's confrontation with the otherness imposed by the reality of the body, subject to the biological laws of growth, is an indispensable, catalyzing aspect of mental growth. The working-through of this conflict not only permits the integration of body and mind, but also confronts the ego with the intensity of the force of emotions, thereby stimulating important resources of containment.

Learning to tune into the body in adolescence

Claudio, a 20-year-old man of slight build, asked for analysis because of an undefined malaise associated with a fear of fainting.[3] His anxiety was distinctly phobic, despite his never having actually lost consciousness; thus his lack of confidence could be said to be altogether based on a preconception.

Claudio's problems began in pre-adolescence; in fact, he had a conscious memory of violent and hitherto unknown feelings when he was 12 during his first encounters with a girl of the same age. These feelings seemed so threatening as to make him *promise himself that he would no longer pay attention to his bodily sensations*. It's interesting to note Claudio's drastic way of rejecting his body at the beginning of adolescence because it demonstrates how important the traumatic impact of a new adolescent experience can be to the body–mind relationship – an impact that has its own particular role, quite distinct from the experiences that characterize childhood.

Claudio's body, now that he was 20, had become the chosen object of his suspicions, regarded as unreliable and potentially dangerous because it could provoke new feelings that he couldn't know about in advance. Already, at the beginning of analysis, his fainting phobia seemed a desperate attempt to control what his actual adolescent body, unlike his childish body, might put before him. Together with the intense anxieties related to his sexuality, it was his general perception of a body that seemed completely foreign to him, to the point that he didn't *perceive hunger*, and forgot to eat – reaching anorexic levels – and he *didn't perceive tiredness*, because of his interminable and obsessive athletic activity.

With the start of his analysis, new attempts at exploration were put in motion. In a session during the first year, Claudio spoke of his interest in a female classmate, with whom he had experienced something new and formerly impeded by his tendency to avoid every kind of physical contact. They met at the park, and she sat down very close to him, with her leg touching his leg. He began to sweat, fearing that he could faint at any moment. At this point, his account dramatically came to a halt, as though he were quite without resources for symbolizing what he had experienced. Nor were the analyst's efforts to encourage him to describe the malaise he had alluded to of any use. After a long silence, Claudio started to speak again, but he could only recount that he'd become aware of an erection, without being able to say whether it was pleasurable for him or not. He had wanted both to stay and to run away.

In his behavior, as well as in the way he told his story, Claudio revealed a tendency to observe his body from the outside, as though he were a spectator. In fact, both in the episode in the park and in the course of his account to the analyst, one would have expected a level of participation that was oddly absent. His sense of paralysis during physical contact with his classmate, his tendency to clam up, and his incapacity to associate freely in the course of the session showed the effects of his profound dissociation between body and mind, which tended to become all the more estranged from each other in precisely those moments of intense physical emotion, in which there was an urgent need for the mind to take on its role of registering and containing the strong sensorial surge associated with such experiences.

Subsequent analytic work gradually allowed Claudio to get into contact with his body and with his emotions, so that he might be able to learn to recognize and distinguish among them. For example, he began to understand that a certain feeling of malaise can arise from the exhaustion caused by excessive physical activity, and he started to tolerate the eruption of intense sexual excitement – to the point of being able to have an actual sexual experience with a girl, which was then discussed in a session.

In this entire period, covering three or four years of work, the analyst, although it was clear that much of the content of Claudio's discourse might be connected to the analytic relationship, felt that focusing his interventions on the patient's relationship with his body took priority, and she privileged the construction of a mental space from which to approach sensations and emotions that Claudio had previously feared would be unbearable.

Let's move on to another case that demonstrates the role of sensorial perception as a springboard for the development of mental knowledge of the body and a sense of bodily identity.

Magda was a young woman who presented with a compulsive tendency to touch her own intimate anatomical parts in order to smell them, and who was assailed by obsessive thoughts with continual self-accusations that impeded her constructive integration with reality.[4] After an early period of analytic work lasting about two years, she brought in a dream: "There are some kittens that my mother allows me to keep in a little room – not in our house, but near it. Then she lets me keep them inside the house. My father, on the other hand, agrees to let me have a dog."

The patient associated this dream with the fact that her parents had never allowed her to have an animal, but only, at a certain point, some fish, because they don't get things dirty, they're no trouble, and they stay inside a tank. She added: "But I would have liked animals with more presence." The dream was worked through in analysis as the expression of an important development in coming closer to an early animal-like dimension of the patient herself, like what her own body represented.

From this moment on, an important process of working-through began, in the course of which her compulsive tendency to touch her intimate parts, so as to smell them, was discovered to be an attempt to approach her own body, which she had feared was inaccessible, and then to try to know herself, as is the case with a newborn when its first sensations are activated. This procedure was indispensable to Magda for not losing herself and as a protection against falling into psychotic confusion. The urge to touch and smell herself, then, did not arise from a "bad mind," as she had previously thought, but from a personal, vital stimulus, even though it was very rudimentary in form.

Through utilization of a working-through focused on the importance of keeping communication open with the animal world of her own body, her compulsive tendency to smell herself – which she had always considered intensely negative and shameful – began to be used in the analytic work as a cornerstone from which to initiate the construction of her body–mind relationship. The analysis could thus make use of this compulsive symptom as an unconscious proposal waiting to be worked through – using the sensorial level of smell as a helpful tool for progressing towards a bodily identity of her own.

In the analytic situation, a development took place, so that the patient – initially rather dirty and smelly – was able after some working-through focused on the recognition of her body, to buy soap for her personal hygiene and use it regularly. This simple and basic activation of personal hygiene was accompanied by the general psychological dawning of a mental perception of the self – that is, the possibility of perceiving herself not only through a smell, but also through the construction of a mental space. From this space arose the awareness of a bodily self connected with the concrete action that allowed Magda to take effective care of her body. Something of this sort happens in the course of the infant's development when the baby, soiled by excrement, connects with a mother who cleans him. In Magda's case, it is the patient herself who discovers the ability to become her own mother, to the degree that she accepts recognition of her body and her sexuality and, thereafter, of taking care of her own personal hygiene, and at last reaching a more acceptable and concordant experience of her own corporeity.

The kitten dream appeared at a moment in which it was beginning to be possible to pass from a primal area of "pure sensation" to the perception of an animal dimension through the visual image of the dream. The step after the recognition and care of her own corporeity coincided with important changes in her daily life, when she could look after her room and the rhythms of her life, in a more practical and realistic way. The dream about kittens and a dog represented the possibility of opening a new horizon where the mind could begin to function, fostering a representation of the self and the care of her own body.

The intellectual's missing identification with the body

The body's conflict with otherness, which is particularly evident in the course of adolescence, can be significant in other situations as well: for example, in the relationship with illness and impending death. The philosopher Jean-Luc Nancy has given a lucid account of his personal experience of a heart transplant, describing "my own immersion in a self that had never identified with this body" (2000: 15). In recognizing his lack of identification with his own body – or rather, a sort of dissociative implant from the body that can characterize the philosopher or the intellectual, as we have seen in adolescents – Nancy embarks on an actual self-analysis that reveals the omnipotent component of an internal orientation, in which the mental plays a hypertrophic role, to the point of denying its own bodily reality.

Not by chance, the western philosophical tradition from Plato onwards – though with some exceptions, such as Spinoza – is decidedly mentalistic. So the philosopher's failure to identify with his own physicality is not surprising, to the point where the body becomes "other," rather than being itself the subject – an other that can then become an "intruder," like the transplanted heart, as Nancy experienced it. Bearing witness to the extreme scorn regarding the body, felt by an intellectual and philosopher who wishes to be identified only with his own mind, Nancy cites the writer and playwright Antonin Artaud, who meaningfully wrote "There is nothing in fact more ignobly useless and superfluous than the organ called the heart, which is the vilest means that one could have invented for pumping life into me" (quoted in Nancy, 2000: 1).

To this body–mind conflict, well described by Nancy, according to which the body becomes the *other* and an *intruder*, one must add an entire series of complications tied to the medical management of transplants. For example, medical intervention can pharmacologically lower the organism's natural immune response in order to make the transplanted heart tolerable. This fact, which on the surface could be considered merely a biological factor, in reality plays an important psychodynamic role, by further complicating the already very problematic context of an organ transplant. "The possibility of the rejection leads to a *double alienation*," Nancy states:

> [o]n the one hand, that of the transplanted heart, which the organism identifies and attacks as alien, and on the other, that of the condition in which the protective medication places the person who has undergone the transplant. It lowers his immunity so that he can withstand something alien. So it makes him an *alien* to himself and to the immune identity which is in some sense his physiological signature.
>
> (2000: 25; my italics)

Lowering the immune response thus creates a condition in which the features of one's biological identity are lowered, which is registered mentally as a heightening of the sense of the body's alienation – an alienation that extends to the objective alienation of the transplanted organ.

The body as a resource of change

We can utilize the situation of the transplant as a springboard to another clinical context, which merits its own particular exploration, but will here appear only peripherally. In fact, just as the transplant of a vital organ can save a life, so the physical body can function as a reservoir of new resources to be activated in the personality as a whole. This is interesting here in that it shows us how adolescence can be a new and particular source of experiences, conflicts, and possibilities. In the case I shall now briefly describe, the existing resources in the actual body are revealed to operate in relation to the mind as a sort of transplant of a new object, or rather, as the activation of new experiences connected to corporeity, which can lead to admitting the assumption of a new sexual choice or a new sexual identity. In other words, the body permits the emergence of new possibilities and occasions that made it possible to escape from a paralyzing and bottomless mental void, as we can see in certain films by Pedro Almodóvar.

The case in point is Filippo, a young adult who had been a perfect child, adored by his parents and teachers. But behind this apparently delightful harmony there lay hidden a sham adaptation to external demands. Hence, well trained to be what others wanted him to be, Filippo had condemned himself to play the thoughtful husband, the compliant partner in a marriage devoid of all affective life, in addition to being a model civil servant with a dull, bureaucratic job.

Having initially sought help from me to "cure" what he considered a "perversion" and "aberrant behavior" – namely, the compulsion to go out at night in drag – Filippo could instead make use of the analysis to sketch the first true outline of his own identity, recognizing in his transvestism an emergency device for combating his severe agoraphobia, which threatened to bury him in his own home. Thereafter we could establish a working-through focused on the recognition of his body, a process that was able to modify the sense of non-life that had long tormented him. Thus, his primitive super-ego could be put into perspective – a super-ego that had isolated him from the awareness of his authentic bodily sensations; this emancipation mobilized a radical change in his life, as he discovered an interior freedom he had never known.

The uninhibited experience of his body that Filippo began to discover through a new and original way of experiencing his sexuality was a decisive contributor to this freedom. As he followed this developmental trajectory, he also discovered within himself some important creative – indeed artistic – resources, that had previously been hidden, but that during the analysis were gradually revealed publicly to considerable acclaim. This creativity had remained hidden and private, not unlike his sensorial and affective life, which had been kept rigorously apart from his relationship with the outside world. But the discovery of his bodily resources set in motion an identity based on reclaiming the adolescence that he had never really faced; instead, he had taken refuge in a pseudo-identity and a strategy for managing interpersonal relations through compliance. Now, however, constructing a body–mind relationship allowed Filippo to make a place for the *creation of a vital, original, and creative self*.

I have used various illustrations to examine what we encounter in the psychoanalysis of adolescents in relation to the body–mind conflict. This discussion has no claim to be exhaustive, as the subject deserves a whole book of its own. Elsewhere (Lombardi and Pola, 2010), you can find a detailed discussion of the onset of psychosis in adolescence and the modalities of intervention in the context of an adolescent's acute psychotic crisis. Analytic work with adolescents who are at risk of chronic psychosis may offer the occasion for a decisive developmental turning-point for those whose existence might otherwise be compromised forever. At the same time, psychoanalytic work on acute crisis can offer an important contribution to the development of psychoanalytic research.

Notes

1 Laforgue (1986: 425). English translation by Gina Atkinson.
2 I thank Dr. Enrica Fondi for her clinical material.
3 I thank Dr. Luisa Colantoni for this case.
4 For this case I thank Dr. Paola Natali.

Chapter 7

Working with the body–mind dissociation in three psychoanalytic sessions

In this chapter I present an example of psychoanalytic work with a patient who showed signs of body–mind dissociation. I shall limit myself to the bare essentials of the case, both for reasons of confidentiality and because I am not interested here in a reconstruction of the patient's history, but instead in her mental arrangements, particularly her way of organizing a body–mind relationship.

Marta is just under 30 years old. She suffers from an eating disorder and agoraphobia. The latter takes the form of her not being able to go out without a bottle of water; when she takes a sip and feels the water in her throat, she then feels able to go on. She also presents with various phobias, incipient alcoholism (7–8 liters of beer every evening), and tobacco addiction (about forty cigarettes per day). She was in analysis once before, with another analyst, but was dissatisfied and broke it off in the third year.

We are now in the fifth month of Marta's analysis. For most of that time, she has seemed constantly out of touch and unable spontaneously to express or formulate any kind of emotion. Early on, she asked if we could reduce the number of sessions to half, which I thought would make her analysis impracticable.

First session

In this, the second of Marta's four weekly sessions, my first impression is that she is a little more present than usual.

This chapter was previously published as Lombardi (2004b). Translated by Karen Christenfeld.

M[arta]: I saw a pair of socks on my way here and was reminded of a dream I had last night, which I'd forgotten. [At this point, I start to feel rather bewildered and have difficulty focusing; this persists for the whole of the first part of the session. The patient continues.] In the dream, I had on a pair of red socks with holes in them, so that my toes were sticking out. Someone was with me – maybe Pietro, my boyfriend, and a girlfriend who said "Why don't you get a new pair of socks from the sock shop?" I answered "I don't wear them." In the dream, I realized the absurdity of what I'd said, since I had on a pair of socks.

I then ask some questions to try to understand what Marta is saying; I am finding it difficult to "see" the dream. I think of the strange connection between my not seeing the dream and the patient's not seeing the socks that she's wearing in the dream. I keep quiet and listen to Marta's answers.

M: This sock thing came back to me on the bus while coming here, when I saw a girl wearing red socks. There was also a blind man on the bus, accompanied by a woman. The blind man was talking about some place near the stop he'd asked to get off at; he must have remembered the area from when he could still see. Then he started to give directions to some people who'd asked something. It must be awful not to see! It bothered me that the woman with him didn't even touch him, as she could've done, if only to let him know where she was. Not having this contact, he got the wrong person – he turned and talked to me, thinking I was the woman accompanying him.

Here I begin to think about the blindness that has come upon me in the session, and the theme of blindness in the dream. I imagine that this emerging theme of blindness in the analytic office reflects an attack on my mind by means of projective identification. But it is also indicative of *internal* problems regarding the patient's relationship with herself. Is she communicating to me that *she* cannot see? And in particular, that she cannot see *her body*? This could underlie her denial of the socks she is wearing. Can the fact that the blind man talked to Marta be read as the patient's implicit allusion to her *own* blindness?

A[nalyst]: [Trying to collect my thoughts, I make the following comment.] You tend to be blind to your body, treating it as if it weren't yours to the point of neglect. For instance, in the dream, you say you don't wear socks, while you are in fact wearing socks with holes in them. In this way, you make it impossible to get new ones for yourself. But the point is really that if you aren't aware of your body, you can't do what's needed to take care of it.

M: [She responds immediately.] Just think – this sweatshirt I'm wearing isn't even mine; it's my boyfriend's. I don't feel comfortable in it because I know it's not mine and it doesn't feel right; and I think it might smell of cat pee, which makes me worried that other people might notice that I smell.

A: [I note here Marta's absence of emotional participation.] So why don't you wear something of your own?

M: [She speaks in an expressionless voice.] I never bother. I don't bother about my underwear, either – not like my friends, who really give it a lot of attention. I had a loose jacket that I'd left on the back of a chair when I went to bed. When I was in bed, I noticed it had fallen off, so I asked Pietro to pick it up. He didn't, so the cats peed on it.

A: Peed on it doubly, I'd say, seeing that you, as well as the cats, pee on your clothes by not looking after them and leaving them on the floor like garbage to be peed on.

M: [She seems disturbed and moves around on the couch. She then speaks in a different tone of voice.] But I had asked Pietro! He was the one who should have taken care of it.

A: [I emphasize my surprise.] Wasn't it your jacket? Wasn't it your body? You don't seem to take that into consideration at all; on the contrary, your attitude seems to be that "it's none of my business."

M: [She is a little ill at ease, but speaks in an arrogant tone of voice.] You're right, but the fact is, I detest having responsibilities that I can't delegate . . .

A: [I sense a feeling of hatred. I think of the rigidity of Marta's splitting and her use of rejection of her responsibility as a means of reinforcing it. I modulate my emotions and speak in a calm, detached manner.] But a responsibility is a responsibility precisely because it can't be delegated. You seem to delegate everything, even your body, so that you can't even see the red socks you're wearing on your feet.

M: [She seems less dissociated when she replies.] But I saw someone else's colored socks on the bus and then remembered my dream.

A: [Here it feels to me as though Marta has her head "screwed onto her shoulders" again.] In general, though, you don't seem used to using your eyes for seeing.

M: Exactly. Even now, it sometimes happens that I see everything through a fog. I can't bear to see the light fade. I never go out in the evening.

A: [I'm struck by how pregnant Marta's association is. I think to myself that she attacks her perception of sunset so as to eliminate her awareness of the limitations of time.] You can't stand seeing limits – not the limits of your body, or even signs of the end of the day. But what happens is that, in rejecting boundaries, you cut away pieces of life.

M: [I sense something at work inside her when she starts to speak.] That's strange! I just suddenly thought how I could administer my money better. Before coming here, I thought that, since I only have €50, I could buy a carton of cigarettes and pay off part of a debt with the rest. But now it occurs to me that I could just buy four packs instead of a whole carton and have some money left to buy fruit and yogurt; that way I won't get back home and stuff myself with whatever I can find. I can take care of my body, which I usually forget about. I treat myself like I treat my plants: I always let them die, even succulents that you only need to water once a year. With me, they dry up.

A: [I think to myself that the patient does not like being "succulent" or fat, since even "succulents" die – mentally – in her hands.] Plants are like royalty, needing constant attention. It might be something really simple like watering, but it's still constant attention. It's as though these physical matters, even the simplest, don't exist for you.

Marta seems abashed and is silent. I sense that she is emotionally present and receptive to what has emerged. After she has remained silent for a while, I signal the end of the session.

Second session

Five months later, Marta managed to get herself a rented room, giving up the precarious lodging she had at her boyfriend's house. This external change coincided with my impression that the patient was starting to develop some personal boundaries.

Then, just prior to our last session before the summer holidays, Marta dreamed that she had written in bold letters on her stomach "He's not coming back." She seemed quite guarded in relating the dream, and I discovered that she had not been able to make any connection between it and the upcoming summer break. This missing link was only partially related to her separation anxiety; given her usual level of mental functioning, she lacked a realistic knowledge of time, and therefore of the change and continuity that time implies. When I was able to bring her closer to her fear that analysis would end with the holiday break, she started to cry. It seemed like an important breakthrough.

In the first session after the summer holidays, Marta seemed fairly integrated, but was running a temperature and so missed the rest of the week. She missed further sessions the following week. The material I am about to present comes from the third week after the break, which was the first week she felt able to attend all her sessions. What follows consists of the first and last sessions of that week.

M: I woke up late. The weather was glorious and I thought I'd like to sit at the table in the sun forever. Obviously, I didn't want to come to analysis. Even when the weather's bad, I don't feel like coming. I understand that's only my way of fantasizing, and in reality I don't sit in the sun forever. I should also learn to enjoy limited experiences. [She pauses.] I want immobility . . .

A: At the end of one of our sessions last week, you regretted that there wasn't more time. [In my mind, I connected this fact with Marta's sense of greed, her "all-or-nothing" attitude: if she could not have infinite access to something, she tended to throw away what she did have.]

M: Talking of which, I've dreamed a number of times about a beautiful place in the mountains. I dreamed about it last night, too. In the dream, we stopped climbing at a point lower down than where I wanted to go; I didn't get to the town higher up. [I wonder whether she is talking about her analysis or the fact that the dream experience does not correspond – fortunately – to her total ideal.] In one scene, I saw a boy and girl chatting while they were on the toilet; I felt ashamed to be there. [Again, I think of the analysis in relation to her representation, which calls to mind both the body and a sense of loss.] The earth begins to shake and there's an earthquake in the dream.

I was in a real earthquake in Friuli when I was 1½, so I'm told; and when I was 4, I was in another earthquake in Basilicata. I remember my mother taking us down the stairs and the stairs were shaking. Then, when they were collecting aid for the earthquake victims, my mother sent a dress of mine that I liked a lot. Something happened and all the donations ended up in the mud. My mother felt guilty about taking the dress from me for nothing. [I think of the dress as the disappearance of Marta's body image. Had her mother thrown away a mental image of her daughter's body? And had Marta's body, deprived of maternal *rêverie*, become unthinkable?] I remember other earthquakes, in Rome, but they weren't as bad.

Going back to the dream, the two on the toilet thanked me for warning them and said I was sensitive. At a certain point in the dream, I saw I was going into a bedroom that wasn't my own. [I think of the symbiotic confusion hiding behind last week's missed sessions.] This place is in the Dolomites. It's called Vipiteno and the town higher up is called Colle d'Isarco.

A: [I think that Marta's fear of earthquakes, as of a life in motion, is causing her to resist coming to analysis, where she senses that things are moving – her feelings, changes in her sense of time, and so on.] What does this dream make you think of?

M: I've always been afraid of change, of things moving. I'm used to behaving as if nothing was happening. I pretend not to notice that my body is getting fatter.

A: And the toilet?

M: It's always like that when I'm in a group. I feel ashamed, whereas the others are more free and easy about it.

A: [At this point, I decide to tell the patient about a scene from a Luis Buñuel film on this subject, but she says she has never heard of it. I think to myself that Marta, like other patients with defective thinking, unconsciously uses pieces of film to help her alpha function organize internal representations.] "Vipiteno" sounds a lot like the need to go to the toilet: *vipi–pipì*. And how do you see yourself in the dream? [I am thinking that the concrete and the abstract are converging here and signaling something important.]

M: I had colitis a lot this summer. Then, at Vipiteno, I didn't go to the toilet for four days. [I think of how the four missed sessions during summer have become a concrete missing toilet.] Now everything's back to normal and I'm always amazed that I'm just like a normal person. After I talked to you about my fear of taking trams with sealed windows, I've taken them a few times. I've also tried to go out without water a bit, even though I still use it like Linus's blanket. While I was waiting for my father to come back, for instance, I didn't have a bottle with me, but I had some later from the bottle he had in the car.

A: [I am curious about what happens to Marta when she is not in the throes of the bottle/omnipotent breast confusion.] What do you notice when you go without water?

M: I have sensations that are almost unbearable. My lips feel dry, I have no saliva in my mouth, I have difficulty swallowing and breathing. Without water, I can feel my body, and then I start to panic and feel like I'm dying. Now I'm able to be without water for a short while; then I go into a café. [I think of the interaction between Marta's increasing ability to tolerate being in touch with her body and the analytic café, where we tolerate her feelings together.] I feel naked without my bottle of water, as though I don't have my purse with me.

A: [I feel the patient's suffering. When she uses the word *naked*, it is as though she were talking about not having a skin.] With these experiments, you're allowing yourself to have sensations, and you're finding out that internal earthquakes don't kill you.

M: It's true that I try to hang in there, and then I see that, in fact, everything *doesn't* break up. I'm afraid of exploding; I'm afraid of the air staying in my lungs.

A: [The patient seems to be talking of violent, psychotic anxiety, and I want to help her discriminate between the feelings she experiences and the objective reality that her body does not actually explode, in order to create a "film" in which, for the first time, she can contain these fears.] But then you don't explode. On the other hand, your habit of controlling things by keeping everything stationary only confirms your anxiety. Besides, by keeping things stationary, you harm yourself, like when you skip sessions, for instance.

M: This is the first time since I've been coming here that I've noticed these tendencies of mine.

A: [I sense a clear feeling of participation, and I believe that Marta's perception is accurate.] When you're here, you discover that things are moving. It may seem like we're only talking, but really there are lots of feelings and emotions moving around. They are like the bowel and bladder movements of those two on the toilet. There's something alive that's in motion.

After a few seconds, I get up to signal the end of the session. Marta starts to leave without the book she brought with her. I think to myself that, faced with the earthquake of the end of the session, she tends to lose the "dress" (the representation) of the event in the mud.

Third session

At this last session of the same week, Marta starts off by saying that she will have to miss one of the next week's sessions for work reasons. Investigation reveals that this work commitment coincides with a new experience and is an important opportunity for growth. The patient talks about how she lets herself be absorbed by situations, to the extent that, if she takes on a commitment, she can think of nothing else until she has fulfilled it.

I think of the sessions that Marta missed after the summer holidays and of her symbiotic control of me and all events. I decide not to raise the subject of the transference directly, but to allow it to remain implicit for the time being.

A: You let yourself be swallowed by work commitments rather than facing up to the hatred that makes you recognize real limitations.

M: [She seems a little embarrassed.] I always get stuck in life. For instance, I went to Pietro's house to do some work on his computer, but ended up watching TV instead. [She goes on to talk about all the ways that she wastes time. I point out that she fritters her time away and uses work commitments more as a pretext than as something she really cares about. Marta replies that she tends to put herself in situations in which she ends up at a standstill. Then she goes on to talk about her not sleeping well.]

Yesterday I slept over ten hours, but it wasn't the right kind of sleep. Maybe I was tired.

A: Perhaps one reason you don't sleep well is that you spend your waking life trying to stay in a state of suspension that is similar to sleep.

M: Every so often, I feel my vitality being sapped.

A: What do you mean?

M: It's as if I have to fight against an idea I start off with: the idea of not being alive. [She then tells me about "experiments" she has been doing recently. I think to myself that these experiments are the first real *experiences* that she has tried to open herself to.] I've always thought of the day as something external, where I can go or not go. Now I think of it more as something that flows from me. Before, I used to go out without paying any attention to my clothes. Now I feel more *myself* because I get myself ready, and I pay attention to my body. Starting the day that way is very different: it feels like an achievement. The morning becomes beautiful.

I find what Marta is saying here to be authentic and coherent. This new, more personal involvement in life and her newfound attention to her body and clothes are concrete but important elements in an authentic relationship with herself. They seem to be the direct results of the work we have done in analysis so far. I find the reference to the beauty of the morning, coming from a patient who earlier on could not bear to see the sunset, very moving. I think that this initial entrance into temporality is a striking achievement. I respond to Marta by emphasizing her ability to accept and tolerate change, and she continues as follows:

M: A while ago, I stopped wearing a watch because of an allergy. [I am struck by her bringing up a watch – that is, the reality of real time – immediately after I suggested to her, in a general way, how she might see these changes.] Before, I never knew what time it was. Now when I look at the time on my new watch [she raises her arm to show me], I feel so satisfied. [I sense that she is being spontaneous, not artificial.] I feel the need to have my hair looking nice. These are small things, but important to me.

A: [At this point, I feel I can directly introduce the subject of the patient's relationship to time as a key area where the conflicts between psychotic and non-psychotic areas are played out.] This allergy of yours makes me think of your hatred of time ... [Marta remains silent; I feel that the atmosphere is relaxed. I hear the ticking of her new watch.] Your ability to allow yourself moments of silence during a session is new.

M: I was thinking that I'm really hungry. I've been drinking less beer recently. [As noted earlier, the patient formerly drank several liters of beer a day.] But I've been eating pizza. Drinking less and eating make me feel more normal.

A: [I notice that she has passed from the subject of time to an awareness of her body, indicating her ability to apply her discovery of spatio-temporal limits to the area of physical instincts. The improvement that Marta describes seems real to me, since it coincides with how I perceive her.] Now you seem less obsessed with filling yourself up.

M: Maybe I use bottles of beer like a baby's bottle. I don't know if it's a coincidence, but when I'm with my parents, I never drink. Anyway, I thought I'd like to buy myself an appointment calendar with the days printed out. I've never had a proper calendar, but I'm fed up with writing things in a notebook and then getting them all mixed up. But maybe I'm becoming obsessive ...

A: [I conclude that Marta's analogy of the baby bottle is accurate in terms of the concrete level at which she appears to be stuck. I sense that the idea of the calendar – which makes me think of babies' feeding times – is about to crumble in her hands. In this context, I feel that analytic neutrality would be a mistake, and I decide to intervene in a way that aims to protect her nascent perception.] Everybody has an appointment calendar. It looks like you're discovering that calendars are as helpful to you as they are to other people.

Before leaving, the patient picks up her handbag and book with care, in contrast to her behavior in the last session, when she seemed to want to leave her newfound self-representation in the mud, and I have the feeling that she is more together. It seems that the session has likely provided a direction in which Marta will be able to develop further.

Commentary

I shall focus a few brief comments on some basic points, so as to assist the reader by elucidating my clinical orientation. I hope that the approach I have presented up to this point in the book, together with the following concise commentary, will succeed in making my choices during sessions understandable.

The body–mind dissociation

I would distinguish splitting, in the classical sense – i.e., the mechanism that breaks up the contents of the mind – from dissociation, a more primitive event relating to the separation of body and mind, which should be approached with a full awareness of its peculiar qualities (see Lombardi, 2002, 2003a).

"I treat myself like I treat my plants: I always let them die," "I want immobility," "I pretend not to notice that my body is getting fatter": these communications convey an idea of Marta's state of internal dissociation and of the possible consequences. What happens to Marta, on the other hand, when she begins to approach herself as an actual person? "I have sensations that are almost unbearable. My lips feel dry, I have no saliva in my mouth, I have difficulty swallowing and breathing," "I'm afraid of exploding; I'm afraid of the air staying in my lungs."

It does not seem a far-fetched supposition that in a state in which thought has lost its roots in bodily experience and functions on impersonal levels, a psychoanalytic working-through by means of symbolic interpretation could run a serious risk of not reaching the analysand, or even of increasing the already present dissociation. For all the variety of psychoanalytic perspectives that have been put to work to describe this kind of analysand in the literature, one common observation seems to be the difficulty of getting through to them.

The analytic dialogue in which the analysand seems to rally and to become emotionally available and responsive is hence not only a confrontation, but also a fundamental component of a way of understanding the analytic microprocess of the session, such that the analyst does not intervene with traditional interpretations, but rather by developing the emerging aspects of the analysand's perceptions and working on less intellectualized and more basic levels of her personality (Lombardi, 2003c). In the course of the dialogue, the analyst shifts the vantage-point so that Marta's communications can take on a new dimension: thus, the criteria that Marta had used without being aware of them become recognizable. This reformulation is often expressed in a condensed and unsaturated manner in order to stimulate the analysand's thinking, as, for example, when I reply, using Marta's own words, "Peed on it doubly, I'd say." This concise intervention conceals, in actual fact, a faithful utilization – even if shaped by the analyst's subjective style – of the model the analysand herself has unconsciously proposed in her statement, in which not looking after her clothes is associated with the behavior of an animal who pees on an object that is not its own. The force, even the apparent anger, of my early interventions is thus directly derived from the emotions that inform the way in which Marta relates to her reality.

The analysand's wavelength

This kind of dialogue, in any case, produces a twofold propelling effect, on both cognitive and emotional planes, which are two sides of the same coin. On the cognitive plane, Marta approaches some important perceptions: her dissociation from her body ("this sweatshirt I'm wearing isn't even mine," "I don't bother about my underwear"); her hatred for responsibility ("I detest having responsibilities that I can't delegate"); her inability to use her sense organs, particularly sight ("I see everything through a fog"); and her intolerance of limits ("I can't bear to see the light fade"). On the emotional plane, on the other hand, we witness Marta's progression from an absence to a height of emotional participation, which manages to involve me and to provoke surprise ("I'm struck ... by Marta's association").

When, during this session, I touched upon the clinical phenomena, I deliberately did so in the analysand's own language, for the most part. The use I made of *rêverie* presupposes a willingness to take up Marta's transference, placing myself on what I perceive to be her wavelength (based on a series of observations, both objective and subjective) as a springboard for beginning to think. As I proceeded, I found myself experiencing in my own person the analysand's frame of mind, which I enriched with the perspective resulting from my own mental experience. Thus, I made use of the relational dimension to place myself mentally inside the analysand and to try to observe – and then to encourage – her internal functioning, particularly with regard to the interaction between sensation-feeling and thought (the body–mind dialogue).

On the basis of this internal dialectic, I, as an analyst, interacted with Marta to set in motion experience and thought. This orientation tends to safeguard spontaneity and to leave room for a certain transparency of emotional reactions on the part of the analyst. The construction of statements that have not been formulated according to a preconceived code of communication reproposes, in part, the emotions the analyst has experienced in the countertransference, and in some cases it makes use of emotional impact as a means of communicating with the analysand, so as to create the requisite conditions for internal change.

The oscillation between the hazy realm of emotion and the well-defined world of thought is a real challenge for the analyst's inner resources, putting to the test her "irreducible subjectivity" (Renik, 1993), without there being, however, any neglect of what is generally considered objective reality.

The impact of experience and change

What I have written above explains my decision not to interpret the analysand's anxiety and projective identification, and why I chose to conduct the first session by means of a series of events that generate experience and change, which are essential components of mental functioning and a principal goal of clinical analysis. This approach towards change in analysis seems important also because of my belief, in agreement with Jacobs (2001: 153), that "despite learning much about themselves, patients were able to change little ... [and] as the number of such patients grew, the reputation of analysis declined."

I tend to read Marta's anxiety as connected to her difficulty in achieving a relation with herself. This view leads me not to stress her dependence on me in the transference, and also not to interpret her absence for work reasons as an attack. The respect for reality and the responsibility the analysand has assumed by giving up a session, as

I understand them in this particular context, are elements deserving of respect as an expression of autonomy that can reinforce both her ego and her belief in the possibility of a non-claustrophobic relationship.

When there is something awkward to be seen (a hole in a sock), Marta banishes confrontation with any problem connected to her relationship with her body (the sock on her foot) by claiming to be absolutely unconnected with it ("I don't wear them").[1] This tendency to dissociate herself from both her body and her emotions was in keeping with her constant intellectualization during sessions.

Thus, the red socks with holes appear to me to be a very intuitive visualization: i.e., of a dissociation that left out basic aspects of her personality – just as a part of the foot is left out of a sock with holes – and that this explains Marta's symptoms. Such dissociation was also very probably one of the main factors, if not *the* main one, that undermined the analysis she had been in for three years before coming to me.

It should be interesting for the reader to consider these two interpretations of the associative material about the blind man being "left alone." I treat this material as a manifestation representing an intrasubjective condition that does not by any means exclude a relational significance.[2]

An alternative relational interpretation of the story of the blind man and the woman who "didn't even touch him" could, for example, refer to the lack of *rêverie* introjected by Marta from her primary relationship and from the parental couple. In contrast to the effects created by this internalized couple, the question in the dream, "Why don't you get a new pair of socks from the sock shop?," might promote consideration of a further meaning. It would stand for the possibility of change offered by the new analytic couple. Marta's reply, "I don't wear/use them," indicates her holding fast to the old internalized relational model. But the interactive working-through during this session changes Marta's initial orientation and allows her to have a new experience in the here-and-now – an experience along the lines of a new pair of socks without holes.

The birth of consciousness

My approach takes as its starting-point a greater attention to the analysand's intrasubjective processes, as well as the interaction created in the relationship with the analyst. Sometimes confusion "floods the dyad": transitory states of confusion in the analytic relationship should be considered an actual tool, one that I here employed to facilitate in-depth communication with Marta and to utilize my *rêverie*.

My way of getting more inside the patient's neglect of herself involves an awareness that there is a more urgent level than the historical and reconstructive one: this more urgent level involves the endangerment of mental functioning that I found in Marta.

"Describing the institution of the reality principle, Freud said, 'The increased significance of external reality heightened the significance also of the sense organs directed towards the outer world, and of the consciousness attached to them'" (Bion, 1962: 45). To go back to Marta's associations to the blind man and the woman "who didn't even touch him," I would suggest that what are represented here as the sense organs of sight and touch are not regarded as functioning by Marta. In other words, despite her intelligence and sensitivity, she, as she recognizes, is not in the habit of using thought or of feeling emotions in relation to herself. And the hazy emergence of this perception makes her discover, perhaps for the first time, how terrible it is not to see. The danger inherent in Marta's self-hatred thus seems to me to stem essentially from the non-activation of consciousness, which causes the hatred to remain unthought, dissociated, and at the level of concrete attacks against herself.

In replying to my intervention about her being "blind to" her body, Marta says at one point "I think it [the sweatshirt] might smell of cat pee." I interpret this comment as indicative of her hesitant approach to a sense of smell as an expression of an attempt to set in motion a consciousness attached to sense organs and an inchoate body–mind relationship. If I were to try to characterize my interventions, I would say that they had in common a tendency to stimulate the activation of Marta's consciousness, and to protect the fragile threads that were starting to connect her mind to the reality of her body, to her feelings, and to space and time (see Lombardi, 2003c) – in effect, to mend the holes in the sock, to use the language of her first dream.

I must conclude my remarks here, in the hope that this clinical material has been a useful occasion for considering some of the varieties of choices the analyst is called upon to make in a clinical situation, and that these various approaches will be productively stimulating to the reader.

Notes

1 In Italian, one can say, as Marta literally phrased her remark on this occasion, "I don't use them," meaning "I never wear them."
2 I use the word "intrasubjective" here to convey a broader meaning than "intrapsychic," in that I wish to refer to the body, the mind, and the relation between the two.

Chapter 8

The body, feelings, and the unheard music of the senses

In the 2009 film *Surrogates* (dir. Jonathan Mostow) – a commercial flop in the United States – human beings, at some time in the near future, never leave their houses. The mechanical bodies that interact with the outside world are replicas, images, surrogates, and not real people. The few actual human beings are considered deviants, and are contemptuously referred to as "meat bags": they are embarrassingly saddled with the weight and fragility of their bodies, with all their attendant physical and aesthetic limitations.

In modern painting, the body, as it is represented, often seems to express the torments of the body–mind conflict adumbrated in Oscar Wilde's 1890 novel *The Picture of Dorian Gray*. For example, in the paintings of British artist Francis Bacon, the outlines of the human figure seem unsettlingly indefinite. Entire body parts vanish while jaws gape in space. Legs cramp, contract, get muddled together, and ooze beyond the outlines of the painted figure, creating the effect of a hemorrhagic dissolution into nothingness. But even as we witness corporeity being engulfed in a dimensionless abyss, we see an opposite movement, in which the body laboriously gains access to a spatiality of its own and to representation, acquiring original and unpredictable dimensions that offer visual substance to a complex conflictual world.

I mention these things as examples of the suggestiveness of the cinema (see Tylim [2012], on David Cronenberg; Lombardi [2004], on Stanley Kubrick), literature and painting (Lieberman, 2000), and

A first version of this chapter was read at the Thirteenth Symposium of the Massachusetts Institute for Psychoanalysis: "Minding the Body: Clinical Conversations about the Somatic Unconscious," Boston, MA, May 1, 2010. Translated by Karen Christenfeld.

other art forms that confront us with the state of conflict that assails the corporeal nature of contemporary humankind. Humanity's relationship with our own corporeality is more problematic today than it has ever been, in part because of recent developments – most notably in the increasingly important field of information science and the new frontiers of artificial intelligence. Indeed, as a result, this relationship needs to be brought up to date and reformulated in contemporary psychoanalysis. In other words, it is important for us to realize that intelligence and thought are no longer the exclusive prerogative of human beings.

If the analytic office is visited by "surrogates," the subject comes in, stretches out on the couch, and recites her free associations. It may all seem like a real situation, but actually the real subject is absent because her real sensations are absent. And this situation can become even more problematic if the analyst is particularly concerned about providing an analysis that is scientifically correct in terms of analytic neutrality as well as providing an orientation towards a historical reconstruction of the patient's childhood relationships: then you can wind up with two surrogates in the office.

"I guess this is how it's supposed to go," a patient of mine murmured to herself – she was my official training case – when faced by my tendency to interpret the transference, and it was only my previous experience with psychotic patients that allowed me to let myself be guided by the patient herself (Lombardi, 1987) in mapping out the route we would follow.

Our most difficult patients can teach us a lot, partly because they are not willing to relinquish a certain authenticity, even if they are not capable of following it completely and making sense of it mentally. In general, the analytic relationship requires particular conditions of authenticity if it is to develop. In this context I prefer the word "authenticity" to "truth" (which Bion used): an authenticity that is as essential to the development of the personality as breathing, drinking, and eating is necessary to physical development (Bion, 1962: 42). It is not easy to maintain this authenticity, because it is countered by the human propensity to tell lies – described by Bion (1962) as the conflict between K (knowable) and –K.

With psychoanalysis widening its scope to include the treatment of serious cases, we now find ourselves approaching more primitive levels of functioning than those described by Freud and Klein. Our patients are constantly threatened by mental paralysis and the fear of annihilation. The danger comes not so much from limited areas of intrusion of the unconscious or specific schizoid mechanisms, as from the maelstrom of non-thinking and non-existence.

Being unable to achieve a relationship with her body traps the patient in an unthinkable anxiety that can drive her to madness and death. Maria, a 20-year-old anorexic patient, began, at a certain point in her analysis, to sit from time to time on the cornice of a building, wondering whether to jump off. "I wish I were a balloon," she declared, epitomizing her desire for lightness. Maria said she could not understand why she should not be able to fly like her beloved balloons. Only by focusing the psychoanalytic working-through on a recognition of the body and on the irreversibility of death did it become possible for Maria to come in off the cornice. Giorgio was a 19-year-old survivor of a five-floor jump who still had dramatic trouble mentally integrating his body. "Surely I'm not just an abstraction, am I?," Giorgio wondered. And his answer was "No, I have bodily functions, so it must be true that I exist." Rosa was a psychotic patient who, thanks to our psychoanalytic work, succeeded in liberating herself from a world populated by "grey men" who existed without the weight of bodies or emotions. One day she said to me "What is all this about grey men? [Pause.] Now there are no more grey men; I eat, I smoke, I pee [yelling]: I'm alive!" For Rosa, as for Maria and Giorgio, bodily functions such as eating, peeing, and smoking offered perceptual evidence of being alive, instead of being imprisoned in a delusional world of phantoms and abstractions.

The inability to integrate the body mentally applies not only to obviously psychotic cases but also to the deepest levels of patients, who sometimes seem perfectly integrated with external reality. The personal life of these patients is often reduced to a mere façade, behind which lurks the same "sense of nothingness" characteristic of certain psychotic conditions. "I've always had the impression that I had a body on loan. It seemed that I was present, but I wasn't there" was the significant comment of Anna, a very bright patient of mine who, however, could not even have a bath in a tub for fear of being sucked down the drain.

Hence, on the basis of my clinical experience, I would be inclined to shift Freud's focus (1915c) on the relationship between the body and the repressed unconscious to a consideration of the relationship between the body and the dimensionless abyss that the unrepressed unconscious becomes for difficult patients (Bion, 1965; Matte Blanco, 1988; Lombardi, 2009a, 2009b). The unrepressed unconscious implies the absence or disintegration of spatio-temporal coordinates, so that any possible experience or thought seems "won from the dark and formless infinite" (Bion, 1967b: 165).

Thus, the challenge that many patients now pose for the analyst does not consist primarily in interpreting the repressed unconscious – an unconscious that is already structured with a view to acceptance and evolution towards consciousness – nor is it the analysis of the ego's defense mechanisms. The challenge is encouraging the patient's emergence from the dimensionless abyss of non-existence, because his principal conflict concerns, in the most radical way, the polarity between being and not being. Hence I consider that a central element of the therapeutic action of psychoanalysis is the discovery and working-through of sensory and bodily experiences in order to reach a first authentic form of subjective existence. From this perspective, a variety of manifestations that are considered worrying and pathological – such as acting out, uncontrolled explosions, "perversions," or "negative transference" – can become conditions that are favorable to the patient's drawing nearer to being and thinking.

The fact that our patients' problems are ontological does not, of course, imply that we are straying into a philosophical realm, because the problem is posed in pragmatic and clinical terms. In addition, functioning at these primitive levels is characterized by the same tendency towards conflict that Freud found to be a distinctive trait of the human mind. And functioning at these levels coexists – with variable results – with other more evolved levels that are better understood in psychoanalysis. Thus it is important that we make room in the course of clinical evolution – putting aside any preconceived ideological criteria – for the level that most urgently requires working-through in a given session.

I believe that there is too much emphasis in contemporary psychoanalysis on object relations and the role of the other, and that this has contributed to a loss of contact with the deepest areas of the personality: those that have to do with life itself. In other words, we have underestimated the analysand's capacity to show a good adaptation to external reality and interpersonal relations to the detriment of an actual connection with his own most intimate sensations. Not that I consider intersubjectivity inessential, but rather that this intersubjectivity should be placed at the service of the analysand and we should first focus on his being able to develop a relationship with himself. Mario, who arrived in my office after two long psychoanalyses and whose sexual life had completely vanished years before, told me one day that he had been struck that morning by how he could be in a good mood, despite the whole complex series of difficult situations and health problems he was facing, and that now he felt alive inside, with a sensation of living that he had never been aware of before.

Together with the loss of a more intimate connection with the body and life, psychoanalysis is in danger of losing its connection with the originality that belongs to it, together with the implications of creativity that originality can have. "I'm beginning to realize that I'm a woman out of the ordinary," Grazia said to me, not long before the end of her analysis. "It's that now I see myself: I see what I am."

In order to approach the subject of the body as something real that allows the subject to emerge from a dark and formless unconscious, I shall present two clinical cases: each of the two came to me after a long psychoanalysis of many sessions a week for a number of years.

Vittoria

Vittoria, an attractive young woman, asked to be analyzed because she and her husband wanted to have a baby, but, despite undergoing medical procedures, she was unable to get pregnant. She was thin and in uncertain health, with an oral complaint that threatened to cause the loss of her teeth. Her situation was such that she could not see me frequently, so we agreed to start with two sessions a week. Over the course of time we moved up to three and then four weekly sessions, at her request, because she felt that the experience was fruitful.

She did not speak easily and the flow of her associations would repeatedly be cut off, so I had to be careful from the outset to introduce "interaction" into our sessions in order to provide active support for dialogue, whatever the importance of the subject under discussion. At the same time, I had to watch out for her tendency towards apparent compliance and her habit of delegating the role of thought leader to me.

In the first dream she reported, the patient saw herself stretched out, completely motionless and unable to move any part of her body, as if a watchful consciousness had reawakened in a body without life or resources. The dream was accompanied by a dramatic feeling of death. The patient, having described her dream, was silent at first, but then, with obvious difficulty, she connected the dream to her general sense of paralysis, as a result of which she experienced every important initiative of hers as a danger and source of error. I replied that the danger came rather from keeping herself paralyzed, in part because any error could be remedied more easily than paralysis.

It became increasingly obvious that no conventional working-through based on free associations could possibly take place. Hence I was particularly careful during the sessions to seize upon any manifestation of her subjective presence, starting with sensory manifestations, and to support any potential willingness to face reality, to catalyze the growth of her resources and awareness.

Bit by bit, Vittoria began to take note of a crisis in her marriage that she had denied up to then, and her hope of having children turned into a conscious choice – indeed into an active position of refusal – to have them, because she was discovering that pregnancy did not correspond to her real desires. This was followed later by the establishment of an actual separation from her husband. I shall present some material that will give an idea of the role played, in this phase, by the presence of the body in the session and by the activation of a body–mind relationship as the analysand's first occasion of getting to know herself.

She said to me one day:

> It's only here that this stomach makes these noises. I really just don't understand what it wants ... whatever it needs, it would certainly not need food ... [and then, without interruption, referring to some situation at work] Today I'm really mad: this girl who thinks she's Madame President has really driven me up the wall ... they were right to report her.

In parallel with the analysand's verbalization I noticed considerable peristaltic movement in my gastrointestinal tract, so that I had the impression of an interaction between the two bodies involved in the session: in fact, thanks to my sensory re-echoing, the patient's body began to make its entrance. I was struck by her reference to Madame President, so I said:

> Undoubtedly when you give up playing Madame President even with yourself, you can grant your body the right to move around, to express itself ... while you tolerate not understanding what it's all about ... Little by little, as you allow your body and your sensations to express themselves, perhaps you will be able to understand something about your own needs ...

This brief sequence gives some idea of how Vittoria's body began to make its appearance in analysis. And the rumbling of her stomach and her tolerance of not understanding paved the way to the first perception of what the analysand considered to be her needs – needs that, in fact, arose from her body. This progression towards the mind effected by her body coincided with a reappraisal of an arrangement based on omnipotent control ("Madame President") and a denial of emotions. This sort of evolution is ideally accompanied by the presence of an analyst who is careful not to saturate the potential mental space and not to rush to the interpretation.

In a subsequent session Vittoria started by saying "I've understood that I do not for any reason want to get pregnant. I've realized that all these problems arose just when we began to think of getting pregnant."

At this point I became aware of enormously disruptive internal movements in my belly, as if I were a pregnant woman with a baby shifting about and kicking inside her. I had the novel sensation that Vittoria, at that moment in the session, was particularly authentic and in touch with herself, having decided at last to "give birth to herself," just as she was willing to pay attention to herself and assume the responsibility for this attention.

I replied "It would seem that up to now you have regarded getting pregnant as a duty rather than your own free choice."

Vittoria nodded and went on to tell me about her decision to take a room in a hotel, although she could have stayed with her parents.

"It was so sweet, this room, so sweet: it had a lovely bathroom with a tub as well as a shower," she said, associating immediately thereafter about the control her father exercised over her during her childhood and adolescence.

In this fragment of a session the analysand's symbolic statement was strikingly echoed by the analyst's bodily reaction. The analysand's getting closer to herself – to her own body – was mirrored by the confrontation the analyst finds himself having with his bodily sensations. Vittoria's father was given to an obsessive control of his daughter and a denial of her independence, whereas her analyst functioned in a new kind of partnership, by experiencing, in his *rêverie* (Bion, 1962), how his own physical sensations were independent of mental control, and by witnessing the spontaneous activation of his peristalsis. At the same time, the analyst accepted the patient's development in an area other than her dependence in the transference, so that she approaches a room and a bathroom of her own – or rather she is primarily engaged in listening to and developing an intrasubjective dialogue – rather than accepting suggestions that come from the other.

In one of the following sessions Vittoria was relaxed when she appeared, and the first thing she did was go to the bathroom. Then, when she was stretched out on the couch, she said she felt contractions in an ovary, so she thought that she was ovulating at that moment. During her last cycle she had not ovulated, and on the twentieth day she discharged some blood, but it was not her period. Usually when she ovulated she felt it in her belly and had some leucorrhea. Her gynecologist had said she should have an ultrasound to see if there was a fibroma, which could block ovulation. Then she spoke about her marital problems: she was still having sex with her husband, but she noticed that it was not the same as before. Then she described a dream. "I was in my childhood house, together with my brothers, and the drains were blocked up, so a lot of expensive work had to be done outside and inside the house." And she added at once, in some agitation, "But why does it always have to be like this? Why, tell me why? [And, in a loud voice, almost panicking]: Why all this shit? I've got to be steeped in shit if the drains aren't working. [With increasing agitation.] Please, say something: tell me what you think!"

At this point I could distinctly hear Vittoria's stomach rumbling. I thought of her anxiety at being dirty and "steeped" in guilt, although her intestines indicated that peristalsis was proceeding; that is, her own "drains" were not blocked, but were allowing movement. Even her agitated tone, as she sought to involve me directly, seemed to be saying that she was interested in how her life was moving and in activating her own ability to think. I noted that her urgent "tell me what you think!" was addressed to herself, as well as to me. In other words, it seemed that Vittoria's body, through the resumption of ovulation and through intestinal peristalsis, was indicating that she was reacting to the existential blockage we saw in the first dream: and that all this physiosensory pressure was pushing her towards an awareness of need and desire to change. I replied:

> Clearly you now realize that there's something not working inside you and outside in your relationships, and this means you have to pay the costs of the task of restructuring yourself: something that obviously has an inevitable "cost" for you on the personal level. But this is an essential way of opening yourself to change. And if you agree to pay the cost, you can also begin to unblock the drains.

Vittoria seemed to calm down immediately, which appeared to confirm my impression that she feared she was guilty of the crime or fault that crammed her full of shit, because of some "pathological hatred" of hers that led her to destroy her marriage.

> My husband says that my uterus bleeds because I mortify my femininity by not having a baby. I told him, "It's really clever, this thought of yours; what a pity that it doesn't correspond in the least with reality! If you really want to know, I don't have the least intention of having a baby. Despite what you think, it's possible to be a woman even if you don't have babies."

From that point on to the end of the session, Vittoria spoke about her new projects, about starting to study a foreign language, and other possibilities that seemed now within her reach.

In one of her next sessions Vittoria told me about a dream in which she saw that one of her eyes had drooped. The muscle was relaxed, revealing the red of the blood vessels below. She felt unsettled by the whole scene. And, by way of association, she immediately remarked, "It's as if I were displaying my internal organs. In fact the blood vessels you can see in an eye are like internal organs that appear to a bystander."

I felt, meanwhile, that her comment was shrewd and to the point, so I replied:

A[nalyst]: You're discovering that you can think without losing track of your internal organs, without losing track of what you feel.

V[ittoria]: Maybe it's because now I'm thinking in my own way. My husband would like me to think like him. I've always done that sort of thing all my life, but now I've had enough. If I go out with just €5, I don't care in the least. It's my own business, but he says that I can't possibly go out with so little money. I asked him "Who are you, my father? Or maybe I'm crazy?" [Disconsolately, nearly demoralized.] All right, let's say I am crazy.

A: Out of fear of being taken for crazy you have, up to now, relied on thinking in the way that you believe others expect you to think, blotting out your body and your feelings.

V: That's what I've always done. With my parents there was no other way except thinking as they expected you to. But now I've had enough. I can't take it any more.

In this session as well, Vittoria's working-through arose from something corporeal: her eye. This time it was something corporeal represented in a dream, rather than the actual thing: an eye-mind nourished by its explicit relationship to the internal organs of the body – a representation grounded in the continuity that Vittoria now succeeded in establishing among her body, her affects, and her thinking (Lombardi, 2009b). On the basis of the attention she was paying to her sensory and bodily urgings, Vittoria could now "think in her own way" – tolerating the uncertainty of thought and her fear of madness ("Or maybe I'm crazy?") as her way of succeeding in thinking authentically, in contrast to the imitative orientation that caused her to be dominated by someone else's thought.

Sandra

Sandra was a good-looking analysand in her late thirties who had a job with considerable responsibility in the intellectual sphere. She had trouble feeling emotionally alive, and her relations with her partner, and her sexual life, were problematic. She had recently had health problems, had undergone surgery, and still suffered from inflammations that were going to require further operations. Our analytic work proceeded gradually, and passed from twice- to thrice-weekly sessions, in keeping with her request.

In a dream from the beginning of her analysis Sandra saw herself shut inside a mortuary chapel, enclosed in a tomb, as if she were dead. From within the chapel she could see someone approaching the tomb – she soon discovered that this was herself. The analysand appeared to be declaring her condition of internal death, together with her dissociated external presence.

After an initial period of analytic participation, with a certain tendency to intellectualize, Sandra began to manifest intense erotic feelings towards me in the sessions, and to suggest openly that we go somewhere to spend the weekend together. The proposal became explicit: "So do you want to fuck?" At that point I could perceive the sexual excitation that lay behind the proposal, which was not without a certain managerial component. I felt it would be clearly counterproductive to interpret this as an attack against thinking and/or her analysis, so, containing my embarrassment, I attempted to give her proposition a symbolic value by saying "You are asking me to form part of a couple with you, but this can take place right here, in keeping with our analytic context." The patient's reply was concrete. "I want to know if it's yes or no. Give me a straight answer." So I became more explicit as well:

> If it's a question of having sex together, my answer is no: you came here for analysis, not for anything else. If, instead, it's a question of creating greater emotional closeness between us, which can let you feel that you are understood and help you get closer to yourself, then the answer is yes, within the context of our shared analytic experience.

This exchange took place in an agitated atmosphere, in which the analysand's evident palpitation was accompanied by my own rapid heartbeat. Our bodies were paving the way in this analysis, so that, although no concrete sexual encounter was taking place, our symbolic dialogue proceeded in conjunction with a clear involvement of the presence of our bodies. In contrast to the internal death of the patient's dream and her initial intellectualization, a definite sign of life in the form of an emotional and erotic dimension had made its appearance.

In addition, if one manages not to be thrown off by the concreteness of her formulation, one is struck by the considerable force and immediate incisiveness ("So do you want to fuck?") with which the analysand was capable of placing the subject of the body, sexuality, and desire at the center of the analytic gaze, as a core of an undeferrable confrontation that requires from both participants – although in different ways – the activation of resources of "containment" and "responsibility" for coping with the impact of corporeal reality in the analytic relationship. The body had been completely buried throughout her previous analysis but was destined to emerge in a variety of forms in the course of our experience together. It should not be overlooked that body, sex, and desire went in the direction of language and representation, which led from the body to the epistemophilic development (Klein, 1975c) of the analysis.

A short time later the analysand brought in a dream in which she entered an underground passage and, after walking for a while, saw a great hanging river of fire crossing the bowels of the earth. She held out her walking stick and a small amount of this flaming liquid began to issue from the river; the flow ceased as soon as she drew back her walking stick. The patient produced no association whatever, saying that she was simply astonished by the strangeness of her dream. I asked whether she was not discovering incandescent emotions within herself, like the incandescent emotions she brought to her session when she asked me to fuck, but also discovering that she could approach them without being drowned or scalded. And she was discovering that she could draw near her incandescent emotions, in small doses, as had been the case when she held out and drew back her walking stick in her dream, or when she was willing to speak with me about her more or less burning emotions: in this way she found that she could call a halt to emotions that she felt were so extreme that, if they once appeared, they would have to be acted out in some way. Sandra seemed content and noted that she felt emotionally warmer and more positive than she usually did.

In a subsequent dream Sandra found herself in an exciting situation with someone, so that it seemed there could be some sex involved, and then the scene changed and she saw herself walking in the center of town, going into shops to look at clothes and then into perfumeries where she stopped to sample various perfumes. Her associations were that, because she was always too taken up with her work, she had never thought she could allow herself a restful and relaxing day going around the shops, not to mention sampling perfumes. Now it seemed like a good project for the winter break. I observed that she could now allow herself forms of gratification connected with her body – such as relaxing strolls, or looking for clothes and perfumes – rather than confining herself to intellectual pursuits or attempting to satisfy other people's needs.

This development coincided with an improvement in sexual relations with her partner, and also with the first occasion on which she was able to talk about some of her sexual problems in a session. Specifically, her idea of sex seemed based on the expectation of having to respond to her partner's desires, whereas she perceived any form of more directly personal arousal as somehow threatening. And in fact she said "You don't think I get worked up on my own, do you? I'm hardly some sort of pervert, you know!" I replied that there is a certain amount of arousal that is centered on oneself and is always present in any kind of sexual relationship with another person, otherwise one would be in danger of becoming a puppet. This working-through led not long afterwards to some material in which the patient spoke about discovering the pleasure of a sensual contact with herself, for example by granting herself time to have a bath, or discovering her image in the mirror, because she could look at herself naked with some satisfaction, taking pleasure in her physical shape, and this did not make her feel guilty of any perversion.

This discovery that she had an erotic body of her own occurred in conjunction with a new series of erotic fantasies connected to the analytic relationship, which allowed us to make further progress with our working-through. During this phase Sandra no longer seemed cheeky: instead she was more sensitive, and had moments of acute anxiety and feelings of impotence in the presence of the intensity of the attraction she felt. "Why do I have to have these feelings when I come here? There must be some way of blocking them, mustn't there?" I pointed out that if she had these feelings it was a sign that we should be dealing with them, and denying this was like denying her body and her real emotions.

In a later session the analysand began by saying:

> This morning I woke up to a leaden sky. Everything seemed oppressive. But little by little, as the time for coming here approached, I felt that my inner state was changing. And I could feel my heart pounding, as I still do. I don't know why it's pounding, but I feel it's pounding and I'm glad it is.

I was quite moved by her discovery that she had a heart that was pounding in her chest and that it marginalized her sense of internal leaden oppression. I was struck by the fact that the experience of the pounding heart began in my absence, and not directly in an aroused and agitated interaction with me. So I answered:

> Coming here allows you to find a space of your own and a relationship with your body and an emotion of your own, which you find here in relation to your getting closer to me; but it is nevertheless your own personal experience: the discovery of your pleasure in finding that you are emotionally alive.

To which she replied "It's lovely to feel emotions in myself: it makes me feel contented. My whole day becomes different."

Thus I welcomed the sensation of heightened heartbeat and emotion she experienced in relation to analysis, and I related it to the sensory awareness she was acquiring; and by so doing I shifted the accent from the relational component involving me to her internal experience.

Sandra accepted and developed this emphasis on herself, discovering that she was pleased to have feelings of joy and contentment that had hitherto been almost beyond her reach. In a matter of moments, before my eyes, a concrete physical emotion (a pounding heart connected with approaching her analyst's office) had turned into a feeling ("I'm contented"), or a general mood ("the whole day becomes different").

A significant development took place later in relation to the discovery of an aggressive component in her erotic feelings, and it seemed to contribute to a further differentiation in the context of her initial jumble of emotions. And our relationship acquired a broader mental dimension thanks to her recognition of her aggressive feelings, without entirely losing its erotic components.

During a session, in a shaky voice, her face distorted by panic – which seemed tangible evidence of the touching effort it cost her to approach and find words for the emotions she could feel rising in her body – Sandra said "When I come here I feel an urge to devour you. I feel like a panther." Then, after a long pause that seemed proportional to the effort she had made to express herself, she added, in a calmer tone of voice, "I've only just remembered an old film in which a woman turned into a panther. It scared me to death when I saw it. Now I know I have to decide whether to be a woman or a panther."

I too remembered the black-and-white film *Cat People* (dir. Jacques Tourneur, 1942) – known as *Il bacio della pantera* (*The Kiss of the Panther*) in Italian – with Simone Simon as the terrifying main character who was herself terrified by the discovery of her animal nature: a feeling of terror that I felt was consistent with what Sandra was experiencing in analysis. In the last part of her communication ("Now I know I have to decide whether to be a woman or a panther"), however, I noted the danger of a disconnection between the human and the animal: having only "the woman" in my office might imply her dwindling to a bloodless surrogate without animal emotions, whereas having only "the panther" meant my being exposed to an instinctual acting out that could easily get out of hand. I sought within myself some turn of phrase that might help keep her connected to the emotions of the panther inside herself, without losing her human resources of good sense along the way, so I said "You are both woman and panther when you recognize your sexual attraction and your desire to tear me to pieces and possess me as a way of satisfying your love as well as your hatred and your thirst for total control." Thus I attempted to make explicit the two elements, love and hatred, that were at last recognizable and distinguishable. This made it possible to explain the violent component of possession that contributed to transforming her urge to appropriate me into something concretely sexual.

And in fact, after my comment, the analysand seemed immediately calmer: it was as if the idea of having recognized the aggressive component of her nature had brought her closer to being able to exist within herself while tolerating the intensity of her physical emotions and the interpersonal distance that separated us.

The conflict about death that had appeared in the first dream, in which Sandra was imprisoned in a tomb, gave signs of having evolved: she dreamed she saw her mother – who had in fact died a few months previously – emerge alive from her coffin. In her dream, Sandra, amazed, could not understand how her mother had managed to breathe during all the time she was enclosed in her coffin. I wondered to myself whether this was a delusional denial of death, the same denial that had led her, in the past, to be unsure whether she was alive or dead, as she was in that first dream. Sandra added that she had also had another dream, in which she saw herself snorting cocaine.

It emerged that she had taken this substance in the past, during a relationship with a cocaine addict. Her association was that the cocaine had the effect of completely anaesthetizing one's nose and mouth: "it leads to not feeling anything." Thus it was possible to work on her cocaine-addicted aspects, which seemed to be connected with her denial of death and her tendency to attack her relationship with her body and sense organs (Freud, 1911a), and hence to do away with her vital relationship with feeling ("not feeling anything").

In the light of this material it became possible to have a better understanding of the role of eroticization, in the sense that her eroticized emotional participation was a way of laying claim to the ability to feel emotionally alive, in contrast to the psychotic part (Bion, 1967b), which canceled the difference between life and death. In terms of her tendency towards substance abuse, the eroticization of the analytic relationship kept her connection with sensations and emotions going, allowing her an experience that could be further defined in representative terms by my interventions.

Sandra's reference to blotting out the differentiating function of her sense organs through drug use revealed an important component she used in her attack on her body–mind relationship. At this point it also became possible to understand some episodes that had emerged in the course of our analytic relationship, in which she had in various ways introduced the subject of her sense organs through occasional concrete references. These episodes now revealed their significance as approaches to the utilization of her sense organs. For example, she had once brought a bottle of wine to an early-morning session, and she asked me to taste the wine so that she could have my opinion of it. At the time I felt that a refusal on my part would be interpreted as proof that she was a dangerously seductive person who had to be driven away, so I tasted the wine, spitting it out – as professional tasters do – and gave her my actual impression. This opened a channel of communication between us, so that, after this concrete smelling and tasting experience in the session, the patient was able to tell me about her gastronomic and tasting experiments. On other occasions, hearing and music became the subjects under discussion, so we were able to consider her experiences connected with her musical feelings, which she cultivated by attending concerts and also by comparing musical interpretations (for the role of music in the analytic exchange, see Lombardi, 2008b).

Before concluding I should like to consider two final clinical examples of how the subject of body–mind integration or dissociation can emerge in the session.

One day Sandra, referring to the previous session, observed:

> I was really amazed when you said that in any case our bodies are always there in the session. Although it may be obvious from one point of view, it's not that way at all for me, because, without realizing it, I lose my body all the time.

This assertion increased my awareness of the value of integrating the body into the analytic process, but at the same time it indicated how necessary it was to continue working on the body–mind relationship, because it was an area urgently in need of working-through.

In the next session she began to complain, as she had in the past, about her runny nose, a condition that afflicted her repeatedly.

S[andra]: Who knows why this nose of mine is always so runny?

A: [I make a mental connection between her comment and the appearance on the horizon of the body she complained about constantly losing.] If you have a runny nose, you obviously have a body. This too is a way of not losing your body when you're here for your session.

S: [At once more responsive and present.] That's really a good observation. It just hadn't occurred to me at all!

In this case the runny nose is a sign of the presence of the body, but it is the analytic working-through that must introduce that body to the conscious contemplation of the mind.

In another session Sandra, speaking of a book in which a journalist writes about his experiences in the Far East, recounted the episode of a visit to an Indian guru. This man, when he received the journalist, had beside him his female companion, who was completely naked, with her eyes closed and her legs open, in a state of total yoga concentration. I noted the analysand's tendency towards emotional absence, as she described an episode that did not seem directly meaningful to her, so that I wondered if she was sensorially elsewhere, splitting in two like the characters in her description. I therefore suggested that she might be organizing herself as if she were split in two – either only body like the naked woman, or only mind like the Indian guru – and in this way she disappeared as a person, together with the real limits that are part of a real person. As I finished speaking I saw that Sandra's eyes were filling up with tears.

S: [Annoyed.] Look at what happens to me! I don't understand why I should be starting to cry now.
A: It would seem that by crying you can discover yourself and what's happening inside you! By giving room to your emotions you allow yourself to feel and to become aware of yourself, instead of losing yourself.

The runny nose from the earlier session seemed to evolve towards an experience with some emotional resonance, epitomized by the crying in the later session. In both contexts the emergence of sensations and emotions allowed the analysand to enter into contact with herself and to discover that she was alive and present there and then.

From all these clinical fragments of Sandra's analysis we can see how the working-through can make various uses of intersubjective dynamics, the exploration of the patient's conceptions and misconceptions (Money Kyrle, 1968), and the experience of the body and the emotions during the session, so as to catalyze the basic forms of experience of the body and of thinking in the presence of emotions (Bion, 1962) that make it possible for the patient to emerge from the abyss of indifferentiation and body–mind dissociation.

Bodily feelings in the analytic encounter

The integration with the body realized in these two analyses allowed the analysands to free themselves from an existential paralysis that might have been attributed to particular forms of perversion or to a death instinct (Freud, 1920). The analytic experience made it possible to initiate a complex mental relationship with the world of physical sensations and emotions. Vittoria stressed the decisive contribution that sensations made to her learning to "think in her own way," just as Sandra – farther along in her analysis – recognized that she had at last come to terms with her passion, the very passion she had always been afraid she would not be able to manage.

My focus on the body–mind dialogue does not imply repudiating the essential role of the relational dimension: intersubjective impact is, indeed, the only source of experiences capable of generating internal changes. The analytic relationship is where sensations, anxiety about losing one's mind, and the anarchic fire of passion all meet: the analyst becomes the interlocutor who can exercise emotional containment, thus facilitating the analysand's access to the catastrophic turbulence of the body–mind relationship. Faced with relational experiences, the analysand and the analyst remain separate subjects, each one alone in confronting himself and the task of performing the notation and containment of sensory-emotional pressure (Freud, 1911a; Bion, 1970).

The body not only reminds us of the importance of instincts and sexuality: it is also the concrete core of the personality, playing a role whose significance is equal to that of the mind, although the latter has generally monopolized attention in psychoanalysis. So we should not mistake the centrality of the body for a reversion to a Freudian unipersonal view, the inadequacies of which have been pointed out in various ways by relational analysts (e.g., Aron and Anderson, 2003; Fast,

1992, 2006; Seligman, 1999). The failure to integrate the mind with primitive physical experiences comes about, in fact, in a relational context of absent or distorted maternal *rêverie* (Bion, 1962), which gives rise to invasive and paralyzing introjections (Williams, 2010). It is also because of the toxic and invasive nature that object relations have had in individual development that analytic working through centered on transference interpretations runs the risk of simply reinforcing a dissociation from the body.

In neurological terms, Antonio Damasio (1994, 1999) has stressed the cardinal importance for the organization of the self and the generation of self consciousness of representing the body, stating that "emotion, feeling, and consciousness depend for their execution on representations of the organism. Their shared essence is the body" (1999: 284). Up to now, psychoanalysis has failed to assign a specific psychoanalytic status to the body as a level absolutely differentiated from that of the mind: as far as I know, A. B. Ferrari's concept of the COO is the only move that has been made in this direction (Ferrari, 2004; Lombardi, 2002, 2005b, 2009b; Meissner, 2005). A standpoint that starts with the body could contribute towards modifying the somewhat moralistic tendency to discount the "primitive" manifestations with which the body makes itself felt in the session. Freud (1915b: 166–167) used the disparaging expression "the logic of soup, with dumplings for arguments" to describe the behavior of those women who, in their so-called "transference love," "refuse to accept the psychical in place of the material" and threaten to destroy the doctor's authority. Subsequent literature about the erotic transference has confirmed this focus on object relations and the Oedipal level, while neglecting the specific needs of the internal body–mind axis: thus those forms of transference in which we can find an explicit affectionate and nostalgic reference to the object are classified as "benign," whereas those manifestations that directly involve sexuality and the body are considered "malignant" or delusional (Blum, 1973; Bolognini, 1994; De Masi, 2012). Freud and the Freudian tradition's desire to assign a charismatic and absolute value to the authority of the analyst – even to the point of inducing an identification of the analyst with her own super-ego (Reeder, 2004) – seems reflected in the psychoanalytic tendency to underrate bodily manifestations.

Concerned first of all to preserve his authority, the analyst is in danger of not working through the elements of sexual attraction that surface in the analytic relationship, and of being exposed to drastic repression and dissociation, even to the point of violating professional boundaries.

There is a not infrequent tendency in psychoanalysis to be apprehensive of patients' disorganized and primitive manifestations, which are attributed most often to destructiveness and insanity. The patient who brings his crude bodily feelings to a session is consequently labeled narcissistic, sociopathic, perverse, intolerant of otherness, etc. Actually, these patients are in many cases incapable of being physiologically "narcissistic" enough to have access to themselves and their own needs. In this context, a tendency towards action seems more like an attempt at being receptive to new experiences that can contribute to the development of subjectivity, rather than regressive and destructive acting out.

Focusing on the continuity among body, action, feelings, and thought helps us to bear in mind the extremely important concreteness of the bodily feelings connected with living, or rather the raw feelings that precede the more organized form of defined emotions. In a context where the actual human body comes to the foreground, confronting feeling is a constant challenge to the subject's containment resources.

The Greek poet Sappho wrote, at the dawn of western civilization:

> Love shook my soul, just as a sudden wind, down from the mountain, falls upon an oak.[1]

The force of sensations and passions agitates the subject, just as the wind, with its unruly strength, bears down upon the oak.

The psychoanalyst must be aware of the genuine danger that accompanies the impact of emotions on the mind, and of the real risk of destabilization that can ensue from a healthy interaction between the psychotic and the non-psychotic areas: it is not possible to think without confronting this risk, if it is indeed the case that thinking can take place only in the presence of emotions (Bion, 1962). The practice of psychoanalysis consequently requires a mind that is not systematically oriented towards theories, or taken up by the "irritable reaching after fact and reason" – to use Keats' words (as quoted by Bion, 1970: 125) – so that it can instead make room for the confrontation with the intrinsically catastrophic nature of bodily feelings. By the way, I find that some contemporary authors run the risk of becoming so beguiled by Bion's enchanting abstract thought that they end up with an intellectualized and self-referential sort of psychoanalysis, while losing sight of the somatic mainspring that inspired him.

Conclusion

Despite the desire for intellectual control and omniscience that seems to characterize our profession, we ought to recognize the increasingly important role that the body has recently been playing in our analyses: an area that is not thought, but is capable of anticipating and generating mental functioning (Bion, 1988 [1979]; Lombardi, 2008b).

> Wait without thought, for you are not ready for thought:
> So the darkness shall be the light, and the stillness the dancing.
> (T. S. Eliot, *Four Quartets*: *East Coker*)

Contemporary practice increasingly challenges us to move closer to areas dominated by "oceanic feelings," in which organizing the experience of sensations and bodily feelings counts more than abstract comprehension. The body–mind relationship that is formed in the forge of the analytic relationship leads to a new manner of experiencing, which begins at the bodily roots of subjectivity, and proceeds towards containment and thought. As the analytic experience develops, the working-through increasingly highlights the otherness of the analyst, together with the limits this implies. The subject takes with her, beyond her analysis, a practiced capacity to effect exchanges along with the body–mind axis, constructing her relationship with others in continuity with the bodily sensitivity that characterizes her being herself.

Note

1 Sappho, fragment 42. Translated from Greek into Italian by Riccardo Lombardi; translated from Italian to English by Karen Christenfeld.

Chapter 9

The hat on top of the volcano

Bion's O and Ferrari's body–mind relationship

In this chapter I shall be attempting to indicate parallels between Bion's O and the body–mind relationship – which I have explored on various occasions in the light of my clinical experience – setting out my own variations on several theories of A. B. Ferrari's which assign a central position to the body as the COO (Ferrari, 2004; Lombardi, 2002). The theoretical and conceptual spheres represented by Bion and Ferrari do, of course, differ, since they are grounded in diverse perspectives, but the two men's thinking can reveal some interesting points of interaction and, given the fact that Ferrari was a student of Bion's in Brazil, they can give us an indication of how some of Bion's theories might be developed.

In his theory of the eclipse of the body, Ferrari maintains that mental functioning is set going by the cooling down of primitive raw sensoriality which was originally incandescent and overwhelming. Maternal – or analytic – *rêverie* contributes to lowering the sensory tension, but the actual operation of putting the sense data into perspective takes place inside the infant or patient. Ferrari discriminates between a *horizontal relationship* between the analyst and the analysand and a *vertical body–mind relationship*: they are both constantly present, but distinguishing one from the other points the way to a specific working-through on the vertical axis in all those cases in which this represents the patient's most urgent needs and can further analytic development.

The phenomena of intersection between mental notation and sense data are a constant point of reference for mental activity. As regards Bion's emphasis on symbol formation, Ferrari stresses that the body

This chapter was translated by Karen Christenfeld.

continues to be present even during the most abstract mental processes: it is only temporarily eclipsed by the mind's activity, but is ready to re-emerge in the foreground with its overwhelming structural ethological baggage on any occasion on which emotions are intensified. Thus what is sacrificed by Ferrari is the distinction between thought-friendly alpha elements and thought-hostile beta elements: it is especially the viability of the body–mind relation, which, when functioning, creates the conditions for access to thought or, on the contrary, blocks access when it has shut down.

While for Bion (1962) thinking always takes place in the presence of feelings, Ferrari favors the microphenomena of sensory perception to the more developed interaction between feeling and thought. Thus, the eclipse of the body has the advantage of being a hypothesis oriented specifically towards the way the body and the mind interact, focusing on the areas in which most primitive phenomena responsible for mental functioning are organized. In this sense Ferrari's hypotheses seem particularly up-to-date, since they foreshadowed the most recent findings in neuroscience that reveal a close connection between awareness of the body and the ability to feel – emphasizing that "feelings are likely to arise from maps of body states" (Damasio and Carvalho, 2013: 146) – and consider our bodily self-experiences determinant for the understanding of intersubjectivity (Gallese and Ebisch, 2014).

Bion's psychoanalytic contribution unsurpassably develops the thought-centered analytic perspective introduced by Freud. At the same time it marks a blockage point, such that psychoanalytic research can acquire new impetus and explore new horizons *only* by starting from the pre-mental generative levels: the body, in short, can become the new starting-point of psychoanalytic explorations (Ferrari and Lombardi, 1998).

So we shall now consider some areas of intersection between Bion's ideas – his O hypothesis in particular – and the body–mind relationship.

The mystery of a constant conjunction

Bion reminds us of the need for a "constant conjunction" within the analytic setting, although it might take us years to understand what it is in our experience of analysis that is doing the conjoining and what exactly this conjunction means. This puts us in mind of how the analyst must constantly bear the anxiety of the unknown, together with a "becoming" that contains certain terrifying characteristics: "of all the hateful possibilities, growth and maturation are feared and detested most frequently" (Bion, 1970: 53). It is from this central presence of the unknown that there ensues the disproportion between the massive engagement required by analysis and the scarcity of means at our disposal for explaining to ourselves and communicating what is happening.

The anxieties that are called forth in the analyst can be so strong that they activate a tireless quest for external approval: a "popular repute" that reassures the analyst that his analytic ability is not in question. Bion is trenchant on the subject, as he considers "popular repute" to be "notoriously fickle and unreliable, and unsuited for use as a foundation for any judgement" (1970: 62): a point of view that is decidedly polemical for the analytic current that cleaves ever more closely to the notion of the identity of analytic capacity with institutional power (Lombardi, 2006b).

One cannot deny that there is something defensive about a certain verbal "Bionism," in which it seems that "the container extracts so much from the contained that the contained is left without substance ... An illustration would be the word used as a metaphor until the background is lost and the word loses its meaning" (Bion, 1970: 106–107). Reference to Bion is thus in danger of serving to *deactivate* the explosive nature of the psychoanalytic experience, rather than to *develop* it, so that – to paraphrase Bion himself (1970: 78) – we can fear that Bion "risks being loaded with honors and sinking without a trace."

The endurance of darkness and mystery is most particularly necessary when dealing with so-called severe cases that confront us with our limitations in the matter of translating and communicating our analytic experience, given that the "available verbalizations do not provide the psychoanalyst with appropriate formulations": a problem that is made all the more complex by the fact that, when we seek to transmit our clinical experience, "no vertex at present recognized is adequate" (1970: 63). So psychoanalysis cannot survive except in a context that is open to the quest for new vertices that are in line with the experience of our most extreme analysands. In his attention to the toleration of mystery and uncertainty, Bion seems to be a direct heir of the Freud who loved the midnight gloom described by Goethe:

Nun ist die Luft von solchem Spuk so voll,
Dass niemand weiss wie er ihn meiden soll.

(*Faust*, II.v.5)

[Now is the air with horror's brood so dense
That no hope flickers of deliv'rance hence.]

Bion's O

In an attempt to open psychoanalysis towards new horizons, Bion summons up the Kantian concept of the thing-in-itself and suggests that psychoanalytic events cannot be known directly. O denotes the "ultimate reality, absolute truth, the godhead, the infinite" (Bion, 1970: 26) of the psychoanalytic experience, which cannot be known "in itself" since it is "darkness and formlessness." O has, however, the potential of "becoming" and of being knowable (K) at a certain point of its evolution.

If the analyst becomes O, he is capable of becoming acquainted with the events that are a development of O; and this particular "becoming O" has to do with Being, rather than with knowledge. The analyst cannot *know* the patient's O, but can *be* the O that corresponds to that O (Bion, 1970: 27). Since Being is involved, the interference of lying takes on ontological even more than cognitive characteristics, so that "there can be no genuine outcome that is based on falsity" (28).

Memory and desire are an obstacle to becoming O, to the extent that they introduce an element of saturation that stands in the way of at-one-ment with O. In the case of memory, the element of saturation introduced is an obstacle to the free unfolding of mental functioning: "an analyst with such a mind is one who is incapable of learning because he is satisfied" (Bion, 1970: 29). Similarly, sense conditioning – derived from the desire that the patient be well – is damaging. By avoiding memory and desire "the psycho-analyst and the analysand achieve a state in which both contemplate the irreducible minimum that is the patient" (59) and develop a faith in a "psychoanalytic experience which remains ineffable" (35). Failing to follow the "difficult discipline" (56) connected to the suspension of memory, desire and knowledge "will lead to a steady deterioration in the powers of observation whose maintenance is essential" (51).

In its tendency to counter the force of sensual desire coming from the pleasure principle (Freud, 1911a), the experience of O introduces a series of important features:

- an observational framework for the analyst and a discipline that is not subject to personal will;
- an approach to unknown internal experiences in a context of intersubjective syntonization;
- a temporal syntonization that opens to a continuous updating in the context of the session and of the analysis;
- an obstacle to intellectual control;
- a specific focus on unknown phenomena that should be explored.

From his psychotic patients, Bion had learned to recognize the danger lurking in symbol saturation, which leads to transforming all acts into symbolic acts, with a possible delusional outcome. The tendency towards constant symbolization represents a serious danger for the functioning of a so-called normal mind as well: when the analyst keeps himself constantly anchored to his knowledge and his symbol-forming ability, he or she falls into a "premature saturation," which impedes the experience of an unsaturated mind and the development of the normal process of symbol-formation (1970: 68).

Bion's misgivings about the operation of memory and desire seem to extend to all cognitive activity when he cautions his readers not to assume they can reach O through knowledge: "At-one-ment with O would seem to be possible through the transformation K→O, but it is not so" (1970: 30). This reveals important implications about the role one should attribute to feeling and to the body–mind dialogue, which I am exploring in this book.

The marginalization of K in a universe dominated by O should have important implications for psychoanalytic training as it is provided in seminars. This training is only too often reduced to mere cognitive activity with strict monitoring: indeed, in some psychoanalytic societies attendance is now required at an established schedule of seminars, and candidates are subject to annual evaluations. This emphasis on the mandatory nature of knowledge and on well-policed inspection – which was conceived essentially to rear new generations of a "ruling caste" that is "not by nature fitted to have direct experience of *being* psychoanalytic" (1970: 73) – can have nothing but harmful effects on successive generations, given the current state of psychoanalysis, already afflicted with conformism and a lack of creativity.

Borrowing a concept from Keats, Bion focuses on "negative capability"; "that is, when a man is capable of being in uncertainties, mysteries, doubts, without any irritable reaching after fact and reason" (quoted by Bion, 1970: 125). He also underlines the role of "patience," by means of which the analyst can "relate to what is unknown," even for long periods. Exercising "patience" leads to "security," in which the analyst becomes able to put together her scattered observations, think symbolically, and produce interpretations (1970: 124).

Bion's O and the body–mind relationship

I believe that the emphasis – introduced by Bion – on the unsaturated condition can be traced to the experience of one's relationship with one's own body and with sensoriality as ontological conditions of one's belonging to oneself and to one's ethological matrix. The mental experience of the body is characterized by continuous evolution and change – as is the case with the condition of "becoming" that Bion describes for O – since the world of sensations is in constant and unpredictable motion.

In this sense it seems to me that Bion's scrutiny of O leads his gaze to a condition that in certain ways corresponds to the body–mind relationship: and surely Bion is admitting that there is a relationship between O and feeling when he says that "its presence can be recognized and *felt*" (Bion, 1970: 30; my italics). Obviously this does not mean that Bion's vertex is directed towards the body–mind relationship, since it is declaredly focused on mental functioning *tout court*: but nevertheless this observation of his about O and what is felt is still significant because it takes him back to a more human and subjective dimension of feeling.

In fact, Bion's insistent emphasis on the ineffable meaning of the psychoanalytic experience and on O as "ultimate reality, absolute truth, the godhead" leaves his approach open to an interpretative tendency of a spiritualistic, religious, even mystical nature, even though it is evident from his whole output that his work is distinctly empirical in method. Hence it seems to me that a dialectical juxtaposition of Bion's propositions and the "ineffable" dimension of physical sensations as an expression of the deepest and most concrete levels of the unconscious might broaden the pragmatic implications of his hypotheses.

My attempt to effect a meeting between O and the body–mind relationship might seem less paradoxical if we were to think of the importance that Freud attributed to the relationship between the body and the unconscious (cf. Freud, 1915c, 1915b; Freud and Groddeck, 1973), even in the conclusion to the *Outline of Psychoanalysis*, in which he states:

> there would thus be no alternative left to assuming that there are physical or somatic processes which are concomitant with the psychical ones and which we should necessarily have to recognize as more complete than the psychical sequences, since some of them would have conscious processes parallel to them but others would not. If so, it of course becomes plausible to lay the stress in psychology on these *somatic processes*, to see in them *the true essence of what is psychical*.
>
> (1938: 157; my italics)

It is in this sense that we can see the experience that Bion calls O as connected – with full respect for the difference in the implied vertices – with the concrete levels of the unconscious (Freud, 1915b), as well as with the body, understood as the primary object of the mind (Ferrari, 2004).

Bion stresses the importance of reaching the unsaturated condition characteristic of O, by tolerating the depression and feelings of persecution that are associated with it. If we alter the vertex and take a look at the area involving body–mind that Bion explored, we might conclude that the "unknown, incoherent, formless void" state of O (Bion, 1970: 52) is actually *empty only cognitively*, if it corresponds to approaching the subject's sensory world. Approaching one's sensations coincides with the void to the extent that we are speaking of an area that is difficult to describe or define and structurally alien to thought (Lombardi, 2009a, 2009b). The feeling of persecution that Bion describes as deriving from elements of an O in evolution can then be viewed, alternatively, as the expression of the experience of approaching the overwhelming and incandescent nucleus of primitive sensations, which is unknowable and unthinkable precisely because it is structurally alien to thought.

On the other hand, Bion was anything but unaware of the motive power that the body represents for the mind: it was not by chance that he stated that "the inescapable bestiality of the human animal is the quality from which our cherished and admired characteristics spring" (Bion, 1970: 65–66). The analytic experience becomes a decisive challenge for the development and awareness of the animal and bodily matrices of the personality: "love, hate, dread, are sharpened to a point where the participating pair may feel them to be almost unbearable" (1970: 66). Thus there seems to be no doubt that Bion was aware of the propulsive role played by the investigation of the connection of the mind with its bodily matrices (cf. also Lombardi, 2008b). But then however did Bion come to place this repeated emphasis on the value of the mental level to the point of setting it against the sensory dimension?

Differentiation between sensory and mental

If we are to increase our understanding of this question we should not forget that Bion was interested first of all in revaluing an orientation towards thinking; his reference point is Freud's hypothesis (1911a) of the two principles of mental functioning, according to which the pleasure principle involves a sensual pressure towards fulfilment, which is in contrast with setting in motion an orientation towards thinking, based on the capacity for tolerating frustration and the containment of motor discharge. With this presupposition in mind, we can observe that Bion was interested in contrasting the mental and the sensory dimensions, relegating the role of the body to the sphere of the pressure of desire and its satisfaction. As Bion consistently pursued this line, he inevitably *left unexpressed* the active role that the experience of the body plays in constructing the ego and in the differentiation of the personality: an absolutely central role, as Freud had indicated that

> The ego is first and foremost a bodily ego" (1923: 26), further specifying, in a note added in 1927 to the same work, that "the ego is ultimately derived from bodily sensations, chiefly from those springing from the surface of the body. It may thus be regarded as

a mental projection of the surface of the body, besides, as we have seen above, representing the superficies of the mental apparatus.

(1923, 26)

In keeping with an approach comprising the opposition of the two principles of mental activity, Bion considered that "the 'act of faith' has no association with ... sensation" (1970: 35) and that "the central phenomena of psychoanalysis have no breakdown in sense data" (35). Bion meant thereby to emphasize that symbol formation requires a distancing from the sensory level: from this perspective the revaluation of the sensory level would in fact expose thought to a risk of confusion with sensation and desire, whereas thought must quite properly accentuate its difference from the sensory level and from the domination of the pleasure principle: otherwise it would be unable to have any containment function for sensory and affective events.

Thus, for the sake of conceptual clarity, we must keep the two components of the body–mind relationship well differentiated: whereas, at the *first level* – as Bion underscores – we must free ourselves from the restrictive conditioning of sensory data dominated by the pleasure principle if we are to approach mental activation, at the *second level* – which needs a specific working-through in primitive mental states – there must be activated a functioning body–mind relationship, as a prerequisite for the setting in motion and continuation of mental functioning. This involvement of sensory data is necessary, both as a safeguard against the danger of self-referential and abstract thinking that loses all connection with the concrete levels of the personality, and as a protection of an orientation towards thinking in the presence of emotions, which Bion (1962) considered fundamental.

An exclusive emphasis on the phenomena of thought and the analytic relationship, such as can occasionally be seen in certain followers of Bion, runs the risk of obscuring the role of the sensory dimension which perforce accompanies the phenomena of thought – those basic ineffable experiences that can at times be so urgent that "the participating pair may feel them almost unbearable." Spotlighting this "almost unbearable" sensory dimension that arises from the relationship with sensations and feelings can lead to a more effective value of the contributions of the individual subjectivities of analyst and analysand: each is, in fact, endowed with a different constitutional sensitivity to the impact of sensations and emotions, so that they tend to develop different characteristics of thought on the abstract plane. As regards the importance of mental activity that develops on the evolutive axis of body, affect, and thought (Lombardi, 2009b), the very concept of "thought without a thinker" risks fostering the erroneous notion of *disembodied thought*, in which the role of feeling is secondary and unimportant. With this assertion I do not, of course, intend to deny the argumentative value that this hypothesis can, in other ways, have in the context of Bion's theory of thinking.

The hidden tsunamis of the analytic encounter

When we are facing clinical experience, we discover that one of the extreme aspects of the challenge that work with so-called serious cases offers us derives from the *almost unbearable ineffable sensations* we discover within ourselves, at the border between the unconscious and the conscious, as a result of the broadening of experience consequent upon our relationship with the analysand. Failing to recognize the development of our own emotional life as it takes place in the analytic relationship can lead to an impasse in the evolution and growth of the analysis.

Facing our feelings can involve the risk of fragmentation, with ruptures on the mental and physical sides, when the analyst is not up to working through, internally, the great sensory and emotional burden to which she is exposed. The famous sequence in *Alien* (dir. Ridley Scott, 1979) comes to mind, in which Kane, played by the actor John Hurt, is contaminated by the creature and, prey to choking and convulsions, suddenly gives birth to the monster alien, which (fatally) lacerates him as he emerges. Similarly, the analyst who is not prepared to recognize as her own the new feeling that is being activated by the analytic relationship is in danger of being the object of an alienating laceration on the part of her sensations.

On the sensory level, we find that we are discovering within ourselves a new world, which has those terrifying and evolutive characteristics that Bion assigned to O. We discover that *we* – inside ourselves – are the patient in front of us. This opening up of the analyst to an *otherness in herself* becomes the condition of the patient's being able, in his turn, to *recognize himself within himself*: a condition that is necessary but not sufficient, given the possibility that the analysand may balk at the attendant internal evolution.

These sensations have a specifically invasive quality as well as a specific weight that must be borne, and they have a decisive effect on the analyst's personal order and, indeed, life. When the difficult analysands under his care number more than one, the situation creates a burden on the analyst that has multidimensional implications, because of both the multidimensionality connected to profound emotions (Matte Blanco, 1988) and the multiplicity of analytic relationships that are in play. The evolution that takes place on the sensory level in the analyst involves the tolerance of unknown phenomena with explosive characteristics that last until some representative and symbolic definition is found.

By way of example, I shall briefly mention the case of Giovanni, a frigid analysand who was particularly impermeable to emotions. This impenetrability was most evident on the occasion of his return from the Far East, when he told me, without the least ruffle of his glacial comportment, that he had been somewhere that was involved in the violent tsunami of December 2004: an event that is still impressed on the collective memory as one of the most catastrophic disasters of the modern age, with hundreds of thousands of victims in Asia and Africa. Giovanni and his family had managed to get themselves to safety on their hotel terrace, whence they could witness the devastation wrought by the tsunami. Unsettled by the information, I nevertheless continued to listen to Giovanni's account, which he delivered with the inflection and control of someone who is describing the delivery of today's edition of the newspaper, instead of an overwhelming natural happening that placed his own life in serious danger.

Some time later I awoke in the night in the grip of a terrifying nightmare, in which a gigantic lion leapt at my head, his jaws gaping. The next day Giovanni told me about a strange dream in which he was sitting in a room when he became aware of an unfamiliar presence just behind him: indeed, out of the corner of his eye, he could just make out the form of a lion's body, whose head was hidden.

This bizarre and unforeseen parallelism of our two dreams revealed a complementary progression of the analytic couple towards an approach to very intense feelings of hatred. For my part, the direct confrontation with the lion's head showed that I was exposed to a more direct and conscious contact with the hatred of which the patient was just beginning to have an indirect inkling, opening himself then gradually to a conscious working-through. The situation finally became explicit when, after some weeks of psychoanalytic work, my unflappable analysand told me about having had an extremely violent impulse to fling his little son, only a few months old, out of the window when he had him in his arms. The urge had been sudden and very intense and he had "miraculously" managed to contain it: this discovery had left him profoundly worried about the disastrous consequences of such an act. From that moment, Giovanni's condition of emotional insensibility began to recede little by little, until it left him space for a more normal working-through of his emotions.

This clinical illustration may perhaps give some idea of the burden the analyst must bear during all those long phases in which the relation to sensations and feelings is built up in the analytic relationship, following a *progressive incubation* in which only a few indirect elements rise to the conscious level: nonetheless, these "almost unbearable" sensory pressures take root within the analyst, a condition for a gradual approach to them and for their working-through in the analytic setting.

I should like at this point to move on to another clinical case, and to explore in greater detail some moments of its analytic development, starting from a dangerous condition of acute psychosis. In this case, it will become manifest that there had to be an at-one-ment – not by any means easy for the analyst – with swamping violent emotions. We shall also see how the analysand initially lacked not only the ability to contain motor discharge, but also the resources that derive from an internal container, of which the body is the first concrete representative. I hope it may serve as an example of how, in a clinical context, Bion's vertices of O and of the container–contained relationship can prove to be intertwined with the vicissitudes of the body–mind relationship, thus extending the implications of psychoanalytic intervention and increasing the comprehension of clinical cases.

Karl

Karl was apparently icy and impassive, but from what he related it emerged that he was capable of turning into a volcano in full eruption that threatened to destroy everything around it. When he began his four-session-a-week analysis he showed the characteristics of a delusional state alternating with moments of lucidity, with intensely paranoid experiences at work and attacks of uncontrolled fury that put various people at risk, even his own family: on one occasion he came close to killing his baby son with the ferocity of his blows. In these violent situations Karl entered into action automatically and was completely incapable of containing the impulse to act.

The initial work in analysis was very difficult because Karl felt that whatever I said was hostile. For my part, I felt a great internal weight and I followed with considerable anxiety and concern the situation of this patient who was at risk of doing concrete harm through his attacks. In my dreams of that period I found myself in enormous refrigerators in the midst of hanging animal carcasses dripping with blood. These slaughter-related dream experiences seemed to represent my own O, in which hatred had infinite and lethal features: something that corresponded to what the patient was experiencing on his side in a very concrete way as a conjunction of frost and rage.

One day during a session I happened to move in my chair, producing a noticeable noise. Karl reacted with impatience and irritation, saying that he could not bear noises of that sort, and that he could not understand where they came from. I forced myself to overcome my immediate reaction, which would have led me to deny my physical presence, just to avoid confronting Karl's hatred. I said to myself that I couldn't not exist physically, so that making no noise was not a thing I could ask of myself.

And so I answered Karl, saying that it was I – in fact that it was my body – that had produced that noise: clearly he had no idea that there could be an actual body that was capable of producing noises. Used as I was to his reactions of scornful intolerance, I was astonished to hear him placidly say that he was feeling more at ease on the couch.

It is interesting to note the analysand's positive reaction to a working-through based on a non-symbolic, concrete level that referred to an actual body. We had started from the perception of a noise produced by my body, followed by his irascible exclamation. My comment, then, instead of offering a symbolic interpretation of his reaction as an expression of aggressive transference towards my person, had brought us back to the concrete bodily level that had generated it. Evidently the concrete level based on a recognition of the body met the analysand's need, giving rise to that positive reaction, so unlike the annoyance he would generally express when I sought to introduce a more symbolic level of elaboration, which ran the risk of widening the fracture of dissociation from his own body instead of mending it.

This episode proved to be decisive, because thenceforth Karl embarked on a working-through focused on localizing his bodily presence. During the next session it happened that a beep was emitted by the pager in Karl's pocket: he took it out to look at it. Then he said it had never occurred to him that his body also produced beeps, or signals that he could receive and in some way place. It seemed to me an interesting development of the preceding session, with the difference that *this time it was* his *body that was producing sensory signals*, not mine. He also demonstrated that he was capable of connecting the beep sound to other undefined signals coming from his body: bodily signals waiting to be received by his mind.

This model reappeared in subsequent sessions, to the point that when he felt submerged by mental confusion, he activated the beep of his pager, which helped him to track down his bodily presence and begin to be aware of something moving inside him. This working-through led to greater attention to his bodily needs, like the need for rest and for sleep, which he was in the habit of ignoring completely. His first awareness of his body and of what was moving inside it, together with increasing respect for his need for rest, led to clinical improvement and to a first containment of emotional violence.

This working-through, which placed Karl in relationship to himself and to his actual body, opened the door, not by chance, to the first forms of self-representation, so that, in a later dream, Karl saw himself before a mirror: but in the dream *his face appeared without a mouth*. The dream gave rise to no associations, but it did anticipate a phase centered on the working-through of his sense perceptions regarding taste, from which there arose a greater containment of his feral impulses towards disembowelment.

A few comments

This material shows how the psychoanalytic office can constitute an undifferentiated space in which the sensations of the participants in the analytic relationship are superimposed on one another: a "massive body" that the working-through enables to give birth to the subjective experience of the analysand's body. So we see how, in a mobilization of experience characterized by sensory predominance and non-symbolic, pre-verbal levels, the analyst's intervention can be oriented towards concrete and non-symbolic levels, emphasizing the analysand's discovery of sensations and of his body, and helping to set up his internal body–mind relationship: while working in this manner the analyst can make use of the events that occur in the horizontal analyst–analysand relationship (his intolerance of the movements and noises originating in my body) so as to highlight the analysand's vertical body–mind relationship (his hatred and denial of sensations and of his body).

Thus a first internal relationship is set up in the analysand – a prerequisite for the discovery of an internal space – and there can then be containment of the patient's fragmenting tendency to expand aggressively and "omnipotently" outside himself. These developmental steps lead us back to some interesting reflections of Bion on the elaboration of O, and the passage from a formless infinite in the "omnipotent" patient to his more realistic and finite perception of himself.

Bion writes that "The individual's realization of a gulf between his view of himself as omnipotent and his view of himself as an ordinary human being must be achieved ... as in ordinary analysis" (1970: 76–77). Karl's "omnipotence" involved the absence of any limits regarding his violent impulses: this conspired with his unbearable helplessness about recognizing his limits as a person and within his actual body. Bion continues: "In the first stage there is no real confrontation between the god and the man because there is really no such distinction. In the second stage the infinite and transcendent god is confronted by the finite man" (1970: 76–77).

In the sequence above "the infinite and transcendent god" of Karl's violence finds, "concretely," a container, when he recognizes in my body the source of the irritating "noises." The discovery of the body can in fact make possible a first passage from an omnipotent, transcendent, and infinite dimension of the emotions to a more realistic conception, according to which, impulses – even if they are experienced as infinite – belong to a finite body, to a finite man, and hence are themselves finite.

The prerequisite of this working-through is the analyst's willingness to develop his or her own O, which corresponds to the patient's, so that I found myself first of all bearing an indistinct "felt" weight of unthinkable violence, after which I passed on to a phase in which the infinite world of my violent impulses found representation in my dreams of carcasses that dripped with blood. Thus it became possible to refrain from interpreting Karl's hatred, when he was faced with the noises originating in my body, in terms of the transference. Such an interpretation would have driven those emotions he was already having trouble dealing with back inside him, now aggravated by a dangerous, guilt-infused coloration. If the analyst is willing to recognize as her own the savage hatred belonging to the infinite level, she can accept joint possession of the very hatred that the patient is experiencing, and be open to the recognition of her actual body. Thanks to this relational exchange mediated by the analyst's *rêverie*, the analysand discovers that infinite hatred is connected to an actual body and hence to an actual and finite person.

In this context, both of clinging to the infinite of a sensation, and of uncertain access to a "finite" conception of affects and of oneself, Karl's missing mouth in the dream in which he saw his reflection in a mirror seemed to make visible the missing integration between the fact of the body and mental experience, so that the body and its sensory emanations were sealed, like a body without a mouth, without any form of connection with the external world or with mental phenomena. Most significantly, Frances Tustin (1981) pointed out the importance of bodily orifices in autistic children and the profound terror of recognizing the natural cavities that make the child aware of its own sensory self, its own separateness, and the existence of the world.

The hat on top of the volcano

Karl's further development in analysis, which brought him closer to an awareness of his body, is significantly represented by a dream he had after he had lived through a frustrating situation that earlier would have led him to explode in violent acting out. Instead of behaving aggressively, this time Karl showed that he was capable of dreaming.

> There's quite a short fellow with a big top hat in his hand. He approaches a kind of pyramid with smoke coming out of its apex, as if it were a volcano, and he puts the hat over the smoke. The hat begins to act like a fire-balloon, and starts to rise. The fellow is still anchored to his hat and finds that he's being raised into the air, and then he returns to earth, describing a semicircle.

This dream was accompanied by marked physical participation, so that, in the course of that same night, Karl was seized by a sudden fever that left him prostrate.

I said to Karl that when he felt stirred up by hatred, he managed to discover that there is a way of recognizing the explosive volcano within himself, by orienting his mind to recognize his internal sensations. Karl reacted by saying that the weakness he had felt was unbearable, so I pointed out that the counterweight of this physical weakness was the mental strength he was beginning to discover within himself as he dealt with his hot and explosive emotions. At this point he began for the first time to associate experiences of a depressive nature, particularly those having to do with memories of his childhood and the family he came from.

The dream shows how an intense sensory current headed towards muscular discharge managed to find a check thanks to a new frame of mind, so that Karl actively prepared to accept his internal sense experiences. His new frame of mind is seen to be at work when he begins to approach the volcano and then places his mind/hat over the fumes emanating from the pyramid. The smoke from the volcano does however show that we are dealing with live, incandescent material, something that is burning and could explode, as he had observed in his experience of episodes of violence.

Although it took place quite a bit later, we shall now consider a development that was very significant, in part because of the way it was transmitted by a dream, in which:

> Karl sees himself sitting on a potty, such as is used by small children. Through the doorway he can see a very beautiful woman, whom he finds attractive and with whom he would like to have sexual relations, but he prefers to allow himself the time to finish his bowel movement, instead of interrupting it to run after the woman.

This dream displays Karl's further integration in his relationship with himself, such that he is capable of favoring the needs suggested by his bodily functions rather than the satisfaction of his sexual desires. Karl had been dominated by a propensity for control of what was outside him: his relationship with himself was completely overshadowed by his tendency to move in a world of concrete objects to be controlled and possessed, in which human beings were also ranked as inanimate objects. In this dream, on the other hand, he makes progress with his ability to relate to a physical, actual self, as he tolerates his connection with the temporal requirements of his body – in this case his intestinal functions.

A few comments

Karl was distinctly wanting, not only in muscular containment, but also in his capacity to think abstractly. To give you an idea of his concreteness: I recall that Karl once arrived for his session in a rage because he had seen a television program in which a public figure spoke well of his own analysis, saying that it had profoundly changed him. Karl was furious with a psychoanalysis that manipulates people and transforms them into someone else. The metaphoric meaning of change as evolution completely escaped him: he grasped only the concrete aspect of change, which for him was the same as manipulation and depersonalization.

The dream about the hat on top of the volcano thus seems to represent his approach to his *own personal O*, with decisive developmental, and also terrifying, characteristics, together with his assuming a *transcendent position* (Bion), such that the patient discovers that he is capable of mental transformations. The dream-hat's upward movement seems to evoke a first separation from concreteness and a start of abstraction, associated with a containment of paranoia and an orientation towards the depressive position.

At the same time the hat/mind's drawing nearer to the burning and fuming manifestations of the body catches an elaborative movement of the *eclipse of the body* (Ferrari), through which the patient sets in motion a mental orientation towards recognition of the body itself and of emotions, so that the chaotic pressure of the emotions can begin to find containment.

The later dream about defecation on the potty and sexual attraction gives us a further stage of body-and-mind integration, whereby the patient succeeded in conceiving of himself with a differentiated inside – with a stomach and a digestive system that became the model of independent mental functioning. There had been a great developmental step forward since the earliest phases of the analysis, in which a spatial definition of Karl's body just did not exist; and also since the first attempts at self-representation, in which his anxiety banished his mouth from the dream representation because it was an element of intolerable vulnerability; and further, since when his body assumed the geometric and impersonal features of a pyramid that was on fire inside.

By this time Karl was able to recognize his bodily needs and to show *respect for interior space and for time*, which was connected with the experience of his body: thus he achieved *a first in the vertical body–mind relationship linked to excitatory satisfaction and to discharge*. The dream sequence with the choice between sexual gratification and respect for the body's time requirements makes it possible to differentiate between a more evolved level connected to sexual desire and a more basic organizing level connected to the space-time of the body and to its needs, on which level the patient is ready to recognize his own actual body as the basis of an incipient humanization.

We first looked at Bion's criticism of sensoriality and desire, which leave one open to the risk of saturating the mental apparatus. From this tossing of excitatory desire and the bodily senses into the same category there seemed to arise the danger that Bion might have been "throwing the baby out with the bath water," to the point of considering everything connected to the body as antagonistic to mental functioning. But here we can see how Karl succeeds in differentiating between, on the one hand, sexual desire (the pleasure principle) and, on the other, a basic respect for sensoriality, linked to his own body–mind relationship, to temporality and to loss (the reality principle) – i.e., to parameters capable of fostering integrated mental functioning that opens the door to the depressive position.

Conclusion

In this chapter I have attempted to bring together two concepts – Bion's O and the body–mind relationship – with some of their ramifications, leaving the very different vertices just as they are. Considering them together makes possible a clearer placement of Bion's contribution to the exploration of the mysterious experience of our sensations and of corporeity, as well as their decisive influence on our understanding of the development of the mind. Without denying that Bion's vertex is oriented towards mental functioning, I feel that recognizing those components of his thinking connected to the body and sense experience can perhaps help to free our reading of his approach from an intellectualistic tendency, which could easily get in the way of "patience" and the "negative capability," as well as the activation of our resources of common sense and evidence.

An example of working-through according to Bion's ideas about O in conjunction with the activation of a body–mind relationship seems to me to have been offered unwittingly by a piece on late Bion by Rudi Vermote, in which the patient's "transformations in O (T(O))" are described in relation to a dream in which he sees "protrusions in his belly, like tumours which were growing fast. Later these became bulbs pushing through his skin, and his abdomen becomes a field of tulips" (Vermote, 2011: 1095). In this material there emerges, it seems to me, a clearly bodily component as a result of Bion's approach. Vermote also reports the dream of another patient, in which an object that is rooted inside the patient's body is extracted from behind the patient's sternum (1096).

I find evidence, in both fragments of material, of a strong pressure from the body heralding the patients' integrated evolution, in which the body can play a part in the analytic relationship and in a representative dimension, becoming a foretoken of mental development. Nonetheless we must acknowledge that Vermote completely overlooks the reference to the body–mind relationship, both in dialogue with these patients and in his scientific reconstruction. Taylor (2011), in his commentary, underlines the risks inherent in Vermote's approach, in which a patient's responses have too much of an aura of mystery, thus inhibiting analytic thought and limiting the development of the analyst's understanding of the patient. For my part, I believe that an explicit reference to the setting in motion of a body–mind relationship could, in both cases, have introduced a hypothesis – to be verified empirically with the analysands – thus offering a parameter of comprehension of the evolution that was under way: a comprehension whose absence is rightly regretted by Taylor.

What I have learned from my experience with Karl – which I have also found with many other patients – is that placing the hat/mind on top of the incandescent volcano of the body involves the cost of contact with the sensory world, which often leads us to the limits of our human resources for managing and containing: it is, all the same, the resonance with the profound vibrations of our corporeity that organizes our capacity for empathy and makes possible a more than superficial understanding of the patient's world. I hope that the perspective I have presented here can contribute to a greater openness of clinical vision, as well as to an increased flexibility in interpreting Bion's contribution on thinking.

Chapter 10

Bodily claustrophobia and the music
A psychoanalytic note on Beethoven's *Fidelio*

Freud held that creative writers – and this might be extended to artists generally – could arrive intuitively at the same knowledge that psychoanalysis acquires through a laborious empirical process (Freud, 1907). Of all the arts, music, by its nature, is the one that lends itself most particularly to evoking the most profound aspects of a human being: indeed, Schopenhauer claimed, with good reason, that it allowed one to apprehend the nature of the world without the mediation of representations.

I have, in the past (Lombardi, 2008b), explored the clinical implications of the analyst's musical associations as a part of the more general function of psycho-sensory *rêverie*, whose roots reach into the unconscious and the pre-verbal dimension: the presence of music in the analyst's mind collects the scattered sense impressions of the session, arranging them in an organized spatio-temporal flow, thus facilitating the emerging temporal organization of the analysand's mind. The development of an awareness of time fosters the development of one's own spatio-temporality, which is rooted in the body: in this way the subject organizes the sensory matrices of her own identity and is less subject to the pressures of imitative dynamics.

In connection with my interest in the role of music in the analytic relationship, I have also repeatedly observed how the appearance of musical references in the analysand's communications can coincide with the activation of significant dynamics of change, in which the subject begins to be aware of and identify with his own bodily dimension and to develop inexpressible sense experiences. I maintain, in fact,

This chapter was translated by Karen Christenfeld.

that we can now no longer take for granted the coherence between body and mind in those difficult patients we are used to treating in analysis: indeed, we often find this condition reaching even to the point where the body and the mind have become mutually inaccessible (cf. Lombardi, 2002, 2007). Consequently the analytic working-through should be oriented towards these deep levels of functioning.

I would define bodily claustrophobia as that area of primal phenomena in which the subject begins to recognize that she exists within the confines of her own body, and also that she has a direct and indissoluble relation to her own intimate sense experiences. I attribute no pathological connotation to this definition: I use the term "claustrophobia" to underscore the anxious and conflictual component that generally accompanies these experiences. The sense of claustrophobic constriction thus indicates constructive development in the direction of a functioning body–mind dialogue, i.e., towards access to the world of one's own bodily sensations and the realistic perception of living within physiological boundaries, here specifically those defined by one's own body.

I have on various occasions been flabbergasted at how even patients with some previous experience of analysis could present evident signs of dissociation from their bodies, as a result of which they were incapable of identifying their bodies as their own or of having access to a sensory dimension of their own. These are often subjects who give the impression of having solid relationships, being able to adapt easily to external situations, and being successful in their social lives. Despite their good interpersonal integration, there remains in these subjects a sense of dissatisfaction, of being unfulfilled, which contrasts markedly with the social regard they are able to inspire in others.

Music and the body in analytic development: Two clinical vignettes

To give you an idea of the phenomena I refer to, I should like to introduce two brief clinical vignettes.

Giorgio's family and work situations were apparently satisfactory, but he felt he was not really equal to them. The most evident sign of his profound internal detachment was the cessation of sexual relations with his partner, and, more generally, a total disappearance of sexual desire. The analytic relationship very gradually paved the way to a heightened and more direct perception of the sensations, impressions, and personal opinions that he had long repressed or constantly opposed. His markedly self-critical attitude had become a fine-tuned instrument for staving off awareness of any form of internal sensory manifestation. At a certain point Giorgio found himself unexpectedly faced with the symptoms of bodily claustrophobia. He was traveling on a high-speed train when, as the result of engine trouble, the train had to make an unscheduled stop in the middle of the countryside, and no precise information was available about when it would be able to start up again. Suddenly, Giorgio had a violent sense of oppression in his chest and an impulse to rush right out of his carriage. He had to make a tremendous effort not to jump up from his seat and try to force open the doors of the train. His sense of panic was accentuated by his not understanding what was happening to him, or rather by the lack of any apparent reason for his extreme anxiety. He then began to associate it with other experiences of oppression he had experienced in my presence during his sessions, when he had been able to calm himself by concentrating on the rhythms of his breathing: as if focusing on the rhythmic element of the movement of his lungs as he inhaled and exhaled were in itself comforting and gave him a more definite sense of actually being located in real space-time. So he began to take deep breaths, and he noticed that if he counted the cycles of breath, almost metronome-like in their regularity, his anxiety would tend to diminish. Connecting the rhythmic nature of his breathing with metronomes and, consequently, music, Giorgio then recalled that he had an iPod with him with music on it, so he put on his earphones. He found the presence of music flowing into his ears quite comforting, and his sense of oppression continued its gradual abatement. Thus he discovered he was able to tolerate his claustrophobic anxiety for the remaining time until the train finally started up again. With this experience, Giorgio began to develop a growing awareness of the reality of his body and of his inner sensations: a starting-point for a working-through that had Giorgio himself – a self that was not generic and abstract, but real and bodily – as its focus.

The second case is that of Guglielmo, a pianist who asked to be analyzed because of a series of complex situations that I shall not describe in detail for obvious reasons of confidentiality. I simply mention that he was just coming out of a particularly unsatisfactory and punitive relationship. It was during the phase of recovery from his considerable relational and affective disappointments that Guglielmo dreamed he was playing the piano with great concentration and satisfaction when, to his immense surprise, he saw a cockroach emerging from under the skin of his arm. His sense of horror and disgust at the sight of the insect was accompanied by a feeling of relief that he was getting rid of it. When he told me about it, Guglielmo connected the dream scene with his recently intensified dedication to his instrument and his increasing sense of satisfaction at feeling comfortable in his own skin. In this period he found the study of J. S. Bach particularly congenial: it was what gave him the greatest sense of well-being. In the course of our conversation I asked him, from the perspective of someone who, unlike him, did not have a professional knowledge of music, whether he did not find a form of internal dialogue in Bach, which he then recognized as similar to his own internal dialogue. Guglielmo replied that that was not it, that lots of other composers also seemed to offer the interpreter this possibility. What he found in Bach was the thoroughness with which the hand and the arm were called into play and exercised, so that it transmitted a sense of the complete mastery of one's own bodily instrument with which one related to the piano. He added that there were emotions, such as, for example, fear, whose existence he had discovered not from a generic abstract perception of them, but from precise bodily sensations. When he had to face the start of a concert, fear was, for him, the very concrete physical fact of the distance that he keenly perceived between his fingertips and the keys.

In the first case, we can see how Giorgio's perception of intracorporeal location emerged just when he was faced with claustrophobic anxiety. It became possible for him to bear staying in a place where he felt physically constricted when he discovered that he could organize a sort of musical exercise with his respiratory movements and then associate his bodily experience with a sensory-emotional datum that had musical connotations. The presence of music organized the concrete experience of suffocating through being walled inside the confines of his own body while it also fostered the conditions for cohabitation between a body that allows the mind to inhabit it and the mind that discovers that it inhabits a real and specific body.

In the second case, Guglielmo's experience of music was closely associated with regaining the ability to have an intimate sensory dialogue with his body: the arm exercise involved in playing Bach's scores allowed the subject to feel increasing mastery over his body, a body that became the evidence of a definite corporeal identity, and that helped him define his personality as differentiating him, as distinct from that of others. The cockroach emerging from his arm thus served to indicate – alongside the acquisition of a body of his own by means of the "pragmatic" and muscular mediation of music – his emancipation from a parasitic relationship (Bion, 1970) that had threatened and undermined his own resources and abilities.

Encountering the boundaries of one's own body

Now that I have marked off the psychoanalytic area of the phenomena I shall be exploring, I can focus on the experience of approaching the sensory and corporeal nucleus of the personality as it is revealed by a psychoanalytic interpretation of Beethoven's opera *Fidelio*. It seems to me that in *Fidelio* there emerge various themes connected with claustrophobia, such as imprisonment, and the conflicts and vicissitudes of a sort of voyage of initiation towards the darkest part of the prison, or what can be seen as a journey towards a sensory and corporeal nucleus of the personality. The vicissitudes of conjugal love that Beethoven set out to describe in *Fidelio* will thus be reinterpreted here in the light of a dialectic that focuses on the voyage of the mind in search of a more intimate relationship with the body, as well as some experiences connected with the body–mind dialogue that can be established within the personality (cf. Lombardi, 2002, 2003a; Ferrari, 2004).

Beethoven's *Fidelio*

In the rich assortment of works by this prolific composer, *Fidelio* (1805–1814) is the only complete opera, and was itself subject to numerous rewritings. In it, Beethoven wished to express the ethical and humane values that inspired him, and first of all the love of liberty and of psychic growth through the affective force of the heart. And the highest form of affect is represented, for Beethoven, by conjugal love. Beyond the explicit intentions of the composer, which are focused on the force of certain moral values, the opera lends itself to a psychoanalytic interpretation that is so oriented as to catch some aspects of the deepest levels of the mind and of primary anxiety typical of primitive mental states. The action takes place in a prison. Even in his choice of subject Beethoven focuses on the question of freedom and the privation of freedom that afflicts prisoners. In psychoanalytic terms, incarceration calls into play claustro-agoraphobic levels, which are involved in many forms of severe mental illness. Structurally, the subject of prison also refers to the defining of boundaries: the boundaries of the body contribute to defining one's identity, but they can also be experienced as oppressive. If the body can be said to be the house inhabited by the mind, then it is also true that the body – with its attendant limits and mortality – can be experienced as a malign and oppressive prison from which the mind feels the need to escape. If it is true – as I have sought to show in various studies – that the body–mind relationship is prominent in many serious conditions that psychoanalysis can treat, then *Fidelio* may be of great interest to psychoanalysts. Focused as it is on the subject of incarceration and the quest for freedom, *Fidelio* lends itself to the exploration of profound conflicts that lay the body open to being perceived as a prison; but the opera can also help to explore a passage of personal growth that can lead to experiencing the body and its attendant confines as the expression of a personal subjectivity that is a rich source of creativity.

We can now proceed to consider the plot of the opera, and then to identify some crucial points, in both the aesthetic or musical, and the psychoanalytic, sense.

How the story unfolds

The action takes place in a Spanish prison near Seville. Before the action begins, Don Pizarro, the governor of the prison, has confined numerous political prisoners in it, amongst them his enemy Florestan, who had sought to reveal some of Don Pizarro's malefactions. Florestan's wife, Leonore, who fears for her husband's life, succeeds, by disguising herself as a man, in getting a job as a prison guard. So Leonore, now known as Fidelio, soon manages to gain the trust of Rocco, the head jailer. His daughter Marzelline falls in love with Fidelio/Leonore, causing the embarrassment of the latter and the jealousy of Jacquino, prison gatekeeper and adorer of Marzelline. The opera opens with a duet in which Jacquino confesses his love to Marzelline, who rejects him. In the following aria she sings of her hopes for a happy married life with Fidelio. So initially we encounter characters who are not finding requited love in a stable relationship. This contagious lack of reciprocity seems to find an expressive outlet in the mysterious music of the quartet in canon form. After Rocco has revealed his character – that of a simple man with a taste for concrete things – in an aria that extols the value of gold, Fidelio can offer "his" contrasting vision, in which "the union of two hearts that beat as one is the source of true married happiness" ("dass die Vereinigung zweier gleichgestimmter Herzen die Quelle des wahren ehelichen Glückes ist"). From conversations with Rocco, Fidelio learns of a prisoner who has been kept for two years in the deepest dungeon and, for the last month, reduced to a diet of bread and water. Fidelio asks if he may accompany Rocco on his visits to the prisoner, although, as Marzelline sings in the following trio, "Your tender heart will be oppressed in that tomb" ("Dein gutes Herz wird manchen Schmerz in diesen Grüften leiden"). Thus the descent to see the prisoner in the subterranean vault is compared to a sort of direct confrontation with death. Rocco, too, refers to death, when he announces that he will justify his need for Fidelio's help, when he asks Don Pizarro's permission, by explaining that he is old and has one foot in the grave. In this situation of anxiety and uncertainty, Fidelio turns to Hope for comfort ("Du, Hoffnung, reichst mir Labung dar"). Preceded by the march of a detachment of guards, the governor, Don Pizarro, enters, and receives a confidential letter warning him that the Minister will be coming for an inspection, since he has had reports of arbitrary violence in the prison. Pizarro is terrified by the possibility that the Minister will discover that Florestan is not dead, but confined to a dungeon. In an aria, Pizarro proclaims his cruelty and craving for revenge on Florestan. He attempts to bribe Rocco with a purse of gold to murder his enemy, but the jailer refuses. So Pizarro decides to kill Florestan himself, and Rocco agrees to get everything ready, telling himself that killing him is a way of saving him from the martyrdom he is enduring in the depths of his dungeon.

Fidelio, who has witnessed the scene, is terrified by Pizarro's complete lack of mercy and feelings of common humanity. Once again "he" invokes Hope, the last star shining for the afflicted ("Komm Hoffnung, lass den letzten Stern der Müden nicht erbleichen!"). Now

Fidelio and Marzelline convince Rocco, in the absence of Pizarro, to let the prisoners out into the prison courtyard to enjoy a few minutes of the fine day. Thus, with the moving Prisoners' Chorus, one of the great high points of the opera, we approach the end of the first act. Rocco, in need of help in executing Florestan, engages Fidelio, to "his" extreme horror: "Am I to dig the grave of my own husband? Oh, what could be more frightful!" ("Vielleicht das Grab des Gatten graben, O was kann fürchterlicher sein?"). Finally Fidelio overcomes "his" horror at the descent into the dungeon of bondage and violent death ("Ich muss ihn seh'n, den Armen seh'n, und müsst' ich selbst zugrunde geh'n!") ("I must see him, the poor man, even if it means the end of me!"). When Pizarro discovers that prisoners have been allowed out into the courtyard he explodes with anger, somewhat calmed only by Rocco's invention that it was just in honor of the King's name day that the prisoners were granted this unusual privilege. The act finishes with Pizarro ordering Rocco to descend into the dungeon to prepare for the murder of Florestan.

Act II takes us to the subterranean dungeon where Florestan is wasting away in the gloom. He sings of the torment of his misfortunes and his solitude. On the verge of madness, he hallucinates a refreshing breeze accompanied by a vision of his wife Leonore arriving to console him; then, in the exaltation of delirium, he faints. Fidelio and Rocco appear with the tools for burying Florestan's corpse. Fidelio, while digging, shakes with fright. Florestan regains consciousness and sees two men, and now the trio sung by Rocco, Fidelio, and Florestan glows with humane sentiments. Pizarro arrives completely enveloped in a black cloak, which he then unwraps so that Florestan can recognize the man who is about to kill him: Florestan must pay with his life for daring to denounce him. But just as Pizarro is on the point of stabbing Florestan, Fidelio rushes between them and reveals "his" true identity as Leonore, the prisoner's wife. Pizarro's fury is countered by Leonore's open defiance, together with Florestan's joy and Rocco's trepidation. Pizarro is about to strike Leonore when she draws out a pistol and threatens him. But now a trumpet fanfare can be heard, announcing the arrival of the King's Minister, Don Fernando. Pizarro is obliged to withdraw, while Florestan and Leonore sing of their ineffable joy ("O namenlose Freude!"). The finale of the second act opens with Don Fernando's rejection of tyranny in a statement that anticipates the choral finale of the Ninth Symphony ("Es sucht der Bruder seine Brüder, / Und kann er helfen, hilft er gern") ("A brother will seek his brothers, and if he can help, he does so gladly"). Fernando sees that Florestan is the friend he thought he had lost forever. Leonore sings of the love that allowed her to free Florestan from his shackles. The finale concertato celebrates conjugal love ("Nie wird es zu hoch besungen, Retterin des Gatten sein") ("Never can a woman who rescues her husband be too highly praised").

Fundamental conflict

The characters of *Fidelio* are modeled as if in a marble bas-relief: in this they show their affinity with Beethoven's dramatic sonata style, which encompasses the logic of conflict and contrast. One is particularly struck by the contrast between Leonore's affective trust, Florestan's oppressive sense of powerlessness, and the inexorable thirst for revenge and inhuman cruelty of Don Pizarro. The entire first act seems like a progressive approach to the deepest dungeon of the fortress, the darkest point towards which Beethoven proceeds: a sort of Dantesque journey towards the lowest and deepest place in one's own personal inferno. The introduction to Act II and Florestan's aria mark the arrival at the destination of this voyage towards the darkness of night, of solitude, despair, and probable imminent death.

Levels of meaning

It is well known that Beethoven suffered from a serious existential crisis with all the features of suicidal depression: in fact, when he had to come to terms with his deafness he experienced a brief period of dramatic isolation and unshakable dejection that threatened to end in suicide. Documentary evidence of this dramatic period is to be found in the "Heiligenstadt Testament" (a reference to the village near Vienna where he was staying at the time [1802; see Solomon, 1977]). Thus one is struck by the parallel between the anguish Leonore undergoes to save her husband and the effort that Beethoven had to make to save himself, to emerge from his period of crisis and rediscover his faith in life and in his own creative abilities. Deafness was, of course, particularly onerous for Beethoven, as it involved mourning for the sense organ that was of greatest importance to him. And mourning can be complicated by hatred and paranoid feelings (Klein, 1940). The murderous hatred and intolerance of the primitive super-ego towards the limits imposed by reality and mourning are represented in *Fidelio* by the character of Don Pizarro. Leonore, however, seems to embody the values of the ego in contrast to the punitive intolerance of the super-ego.

Body–mind conflict

The body–mind relation is an essential organizing element of mental functioning. As the neuroscientist Antonio Damasio has noted, "consciousness is rooted in the representation of the body" (1999: 37). At the same time, conflicts between respect for and rejection of the connection between the body and the mind develop. At these primitive body–mind levels, Don Pizarro represents the mind's omnipotent ambition to be independent of the limits imposed by the body, and to rise above the weight and the pain inherent in the senso-affective world connected with it. Florestan's experience, however, represents the point of contact with the dark and puzzling world of primitive sensations: a world that is in danger of being dissociated from the most abstract levels of the personality, as happens, for example, in the organization of the so-called autistic nuclei described by Tustin (1981). Leonore can be seen as representing the mind's tendency to approach sensory experience, and to value and love it, even when that experience is painful and hard to bear. The descent to the deepest dungeon would then stand for confronting the most remote levels of the body–mind conflict, in which a would-be omnipotent and controlling mind (Don Pizarro) tends to prevail – even to the point of annihilation through murder – over the body and sensory experience. Leonore/Fidelio's anguish then represents the vicissitudes that the mind is willing to confront in order to remain connected to the profound sensations of the body; it also makes possible the formation of an internal body–mind couple symbolized by the re-establishment of the married couple Leonore–Florestan.

Bodily claustrophobia

In the light of the body–mind conflict – as I mentioned earlier – the impact on the mind of the reality of the body is characterized by strong claustrophobic anxieties. Where there is a strong tendency for the mind to function without connection to the body, the psychoanalytic process tends to foster the growth of a capacity to listen to one's internal sensations, thus favoring a body–mind dialogue. As I attempted to show in the foregoing clinical vignettes, the mind's drawing nearer to the world of the senses tends to be associated with claustrophobic elements, causing the body to be experienced as a prison. In the course of the analytic process this claustrophobic condition can become progressively tolerable, to the point where inhabiting one's own body can become the source of enrichment and creativity – as was the case for the analysand who discovered in the musical exercise of his arms at the piano a source of definition and consolidation of his basic identity.

About a few key moments of the opera

I should now like to speak more specifically about certain moments of the opera in which Beethoven seems to convey the claustrophobic oppression and profound conflicts of the body–mind relationship, while also expressing the poetic and creative sense that derives from the ability to integrate bodily experience and mental horizons.

Quartet: "Mir ist so wunderbar" ("How strange it seems to me")

This quartet, which appears shortly after the beginning of the opera, already reveals the incomparable range of Beethoven's genius. The four characters, Marzelline, Leonore, Rocco, and Jacquino, come in vocally one by one, following a strict canon sequence with a theme that is at once lofty, mysterious, and beguiling. The quartet suits our case in that it expresses a general relational situation in which everyone is eagerly talking to him-/herself: Marzelline is pursuing a fantasy of happiness, Leonore is anguished and confused, Rocco is benevolently satisfied, and Jacquino feels jealous and discontented. Although these concerted asides respect certain theatrical conventions, it is as if Beethoven were portraying a common human condition in which everyone is circumscribed by the boundaries of him-/herself. Thus there already emerges what I described as the overall subject of the opera, i.e., being confined within the boundaries of one's own enclosed bodily identity. This restricted condition does not give rise to relational incompatibility: thanks to its contrapuntal nature, the music marks the respective autonomy of the characters. At the same time, the gentle musical climate creates a general concord that is not without a note of melancholy and remoteness.

The ability to respect the autonomy of the different parts while putting together divergent lines of thought, as well as differing emotions, is also to be found in Beethoven's treatment of the orchestra, with the strings creating an initially dark and mysterious atmosphere; the bassoon supporting Rocco's part; the clarinet softening the outpourings of the two female voices; and, finally, the violins backing up the vocal ensemble with a sublime melody that anticipates the contemplative ecstasy of the Adagio from the Ninth Symphony.

Prisoners' chorus: "O welche Lust" ("O what joy")

I shall skip over Leonore's great aria "Komm Hoffnung" – which nonetheless deserves attention because of its perspective of temporal openness, which the feeling of hope introduces – and go straight on to the Prisoners' chorus. Rocco's initiative, inspired by Leonore, to let the prisoners out into the sunlight of the prison courtyard leads to the finale of Act I, which opens with this moving chorus in which Beethoven treats, together with imprisonment and freedom, the subjects of solitude and silence. He gives full expression here to a universal feeling of suffering humanity. Let's look at the text:

> O welche Lust in freier Luft
> Den Atem einzuheben;
> Nur hier, nur hier ist Leben,
> Der Kerker eine Gruft.
>
> [O what delight to draw one's breath in the open air! Here alone, here alone is life: prison is a tomb.]

The first voices to enter are the basses, thus determining a crescendo of sound intensity that reflects the Beethovenian tension of the anguish that leads from the darkness to the light. We can hear the same expressive method – the movement from lower to higher notes – as we find in the cello theme that opens the Third Symphony after the awe-inspiring double striking of the kettledrum, and also the same emancipatory ascending tension of the cello melody at the beginning of the "Rasumovsky" Quartet, Op. 59 no. 1.

In the Prisoners' chorus, their precarious breathing is emphasized by their almost whispered tone, as well as by the labored progression of the musical discourse, so that the theme seems to double back on itself, creating an immediate suffocating and claustrophobic effect. In addition, the opening up to freer breathing, liberty, communication, creativity, and life is explicitly accompanied by a great sense of instability and a strong paranoid menace: the solo intervention of the Second Prisoner makes unequivocally plain the looming threat of prison.

> Spricht leise; – haltet Euch zurück –
> Wir sind belauscht mit Ohr und Blick.
>
> [Speak softly; restrain yourselves; We're spied upon by ear and eye.]

The words can convey only partially the warring senses of anxiety and relief expressed by this unforgettable chorus, which transforms into a peerless poetic vision not only emotions of the proto-sensory and bodily level that correspond to the oppression and liberation of the pulmonary function, but also the oppression and liberation of personal identity.

Introduction to Act II and Florestan's aria

> Gott! Welch ein Dunkel hier!
>
> [God! How dark it is!]

The second act leads us directly to the dungeon where Florestan is confined. The intensely dramatic music moves forward on anguished, harrowing chords; the suffocating pain depicted by the strings is answered by a theme of some sweetness from the woodwinds, which becomes increasingly *cantabile*, although opposed by a dramatic contrasting melody played by the cellos. The tenor aria is, at the outset, evocative of darkness – with an immediate dramatic answer from the strings – as well as of the terrifying silence of Florestan's infernal prison. The warm voice of the clarinet prefigures his painful evocation, Lied-like in style, of his loss of happiness and decline into imprisonment and misfortune. A sudden breeze awakens a hallucinatory vision – reassuring and liberating – of his wife. His agitation blends with delirium to create an ambiguous atmosphere of dramatic tension and trusting openness to new and unforeseen developments.

In terms of a body–mind reading, this scene shows the characteristics of a dramatic isolation of sensory-emotional experience when it is disconnected from mental reception. The hallucination of the refreshing breeze in the darkness of the dungeon seems a visionary anticipation of the reuniting of the Florestan–Leonore couple, which, as we indicated earlier, corresponds to the re-establishment of a body–mind connection: a connection in which the most unbearable sensations can find a possible reception.

Quartet: "Er sterbe!" ("He must die!")

With this quartet we reach the moment of supreme conflictual confrontation. Don Pizarro has arrived to exact his revenge by killing Florestan. From the perspective of the body–mind conflict, Don Pizarro represents the violence of a mind that rejects the restraints of the body and reacts punitively and homicidally towards that same body. Fidelio/Leonore now springs between Pizarro and his victim, Florestan: Leonore thus acts like a mind that is disposed to acknowledge its place in a connection with the body and to afford protection and reception even towards emotions replete with impotence and mortal danger.

This is one of the most stirring moments of the opera. The music Beethoven has written for Pizarro is charged with savage power. Leonore's opposition unleashes a dramatic crescendo that leads to the revelation of her real identity as a woman. The soprano Jeannine Altmeyer offered, on the stage, a particularly thrilling interpretation of this revelatory moment, suddenly letting her abundant blonde female tresses cascade down from out of her man's hat. Thus it seems that the revelation of the body–mind conflict also serves to restore her real sexual identity to the character.

When Pizarro attempts to kill Florestan, Leonore draws out a pistol, stopping him short, as she declaims the words "One more sound and you're dead!" ("Noch einen Laut – und du bist tot!").

Richard Wagner, in his autobiography, dwells on this sudden passage from lyrical singing to recitative, starting with what he felt when he witnessed a performance of *Fidelio* featuring the great nineteenth-century soprano Wilhelmine Schröder-Devrient. Wagner speaks of the height of the sublime that he experienced when the word "tot" was pronounced on the stage:

> an astounding terror that took hold of me as I felt that I was suddenly plunging, as if struck by an executioner, from the ideal sphere, in which music relieves even the most horrifying situations, down to the bare earth of terrible reality ... the sublime flash of lightning that illuminates the two completely different worlds, at the point where they touch and yet they altogether diverge.
> (quoted by Petrella, 2004: 104; translated by Karen Christenfeld)

It would seem that Wagner had intuited Beethoven's fusional power when the latter succeeds in conveying – at the same moment – the ideal tension of the mind together with the concreteness and mortality of our bodily condition. And the moment is sublime, to the extent that the body–mind conflict, displayed at its height, is nonetheless suddenly resolved thanks to the catalyzing force of Beethoven's genius: mind and body, two completely different worlds – as Wagner says – do here touch, revealing their separateness and diversity.

This all takes place on stage just before one hears the fateful trumpet announce the arrival of Don Fernando, which provides a redemptive resolution to the drama. The intervention of the trumpet underscores the emergence from darkness: a key moment that, hardly by chance, Beethoven preserves intact in his various versions of the overture to the opera, the most well-known being the "Leonore" Overture no. 3 (1806), which has become a popular concert piece. The most striking things about "Leonore" 3 are the emphasis he gives to the prisoner's theme during the entire development and the majesty and epic proportions of the coda, which shows how a tragic situation and mourning are employed by Beethoven as the basis for the musical expression of distinctly heroic and affirmative themes that announce the affirmation of life over death.

My familiarity with "Leonore" was in a sense forged by my being able, some thirty years ago, to witness the rehearsals of Leonard

Bernstein and the Orchestra Nazionale di Santa Cecilia, in which the great American conductor, with patient, painstaking perfectionism, succeeded in marking the first bars of the coda with an irresistible forward and upward drive, which then developed progressively into a heroic and overwhelming finale. It was difficult not to believe that one was listening to some of the greatest music in the world.

In conclusion, this chapter has elaborated the theme of the emergence of musical elements in the analytic material of patients in the process of evolving an internal dialogue between the mind and the body. The model of Beethoven's opera *Fidelio* seemed particularly suitable for illustrating various characteristics of the claustrophobic emotions and the conflicts that can surface in analysis in the course of the integration of these deep levels.

Conclusion
Art, bodily experiences, and internal harmony

Aldo was an analysand who discovered in music and dance a resource for activating a sensation of being alive and for resisting his persecutory annihilation anxiety, which threatened to overcome him. He associated his experience with what is portrayed in *Awakenings* (dir. Penny Marshall, 1990), the film based on a book by the neurologist Oliver Sacks, which deals with patients who temporarily emerge from their encephalitis lethargica thanks to a new medicine. Aldo himself experienced an actual "awakening," in the course of his analysis, that allowed him to take possession of his body, which had formerly seemed foreign to him. His anxiety in a subsequent phase of analysis was manifested as the fear that he would lose the sensations that made him feel alive, and that his experience of awakening would not be repeated.

This is how he described his experience:

> Music moves me inside: then I feel I'm alive. I started to experience this when I listened to cassettes in the car. I moved while I was driving, as if I were dancing. Then I decided to take dancing lessons. I have to keep discovering it like a whole new thing for it to have meaning: first the blues, then jazz, then Brazilian music. First they'd be fleeting manifestations, then I'd fall back into a depression that was a sort of nothingness. I was terrified that the awakening would just vanish and never come back. Now, though, I sense more continuity in my feeling I'm alive.

We'll go from Aldo to a brief consideration of another case in which psychoanalysis makes contact with a musical experience. Anita was

This chapter is translated by Karen Christenfeld.

a young adult who asked to be analyzed because of her anxious fear that she was invisible. If the paranoid feels the constant threat of others watching him, Anita instead felt that when people looked her way she was virtually transparent. When we started working together it became clear that her problem was in feeling alive and recognizing her inner needs and desires. Sessions with Anita were quite demanding because of her very soft and distant tone of voice, as if she were being engulfed by fog.

We'll have a look at a phase in which she was starting to give signs of a more definite personal presence. In a dream, Anita saw me during a session: she was lying on the couch, while I was standing next to her, singing an operatic verse from Puccini's *Turandot*, "Il mio mistero è chiuso in me" ("My secret is enclosed within me"). This line comes from the famous aria "Nessun dorma" ("Let no one sleep"), which works up to the triumphant final line "All'alba vincerò" ("At dawn I will win"), with the tenor's voice going up to an exultant high B. Together we observed that in her dream she was assigning to me her new capacity to recognize herself in the "mistero" – the secret or mystery – of being alive within herself. In other words, she was, in the dream, declaring her burgeoning ability to recognize herself in a body that could display itself, as is the case with an opera singer, in contrast with a body that disappears, as had been the case with her. With this evolution she was bringing to the foreground her own internal music, however ineffable and mysterious it was.

In an immediately subsequent dream, Anita saw herself shut in behind a gate. This "imprisonment" was accompanied by a paradoxical feeling of tranquility and well-being. Thus we could discover how her acceptance of being in an enclosed space, defined by distinct borders, corresponded for her with feeling in charge of her own private area, responsible for a space that belonged to her: a space where she could co-habit with 'the mystery enclosed within her' of being herself. After this phase of working-through, Anita was increasingly able to accept being seen and recognized by others, as happens to a real person.

Musical experiences became, for Aldo and Anita – as occurs with many of our analysands' aesthetic experiences – a creative spur to body–mind integration. Familiarity with art, and music in particular, supports the construction of a contact network through which body and mind can converse with each other, not unlike what can take place within the dream-work (Lombardi, 2000b).

The orchestra conductor Carlo Maria Giulini (1914–2005), whose incomparably intense interpretations engraved themselves on my inveterate music-lover's sensibility for decades, caught and condensed the profound sense of musical experience as a harmonious convergence of body and mind in a simple remark: "I don't know if I conduct Brahms correctly. But I feel Brahms's music in my blood. *It's a part of my body.*"[1] Discovering Giulini's Brahms made a great impression on me, because of his supreme capacity to combine the fire of passion and the contemplative lucidity of form. Music organizes and translates internal conflicts and discord, especially the most primitive ones of the body–mind relationship, giving rise in the composer–interpreter–listener nexus to a communicational and creative continuity that involves, at different levels, both bodily experience and mental representations.

I could hardly imagine myself without the daily contribution that music offers me in keeping my emotional sensibility alive and attentive: as a passionate lover of music I have learned a lot about emotions and about empathy from attending concerts. "On a tant besoin de beauté aux côtés de la mort" ("One has a great need of beauty, with death near at hand"; libretto based on Maeterlinck for Debussy's *Pelléas et Mélisande*, Act IV, Scene 1). The analyst who is faced with the *primitive agonies* (Winnicott, 1974) of body–mind dissociation experiences the aesthetic response to beauty as being momentarily in harmony: an instant in which the mind is able, through the experience of art, to contemplate the ineffable sensations of the body.

But now we can consider another analysand who seized on art – literature this time – as a helpful stimulus to the attempt at self-perception. Romolo, in his early thirties, suffered from serious agoraphobia that had a paralyzing effect on his life. When he read George Orwell's *1984*, he was greatly struck by its description of a totalitarian state that requires all of its citizens to conform to the dictates of the regime. The only alternative to the aridity of the regime is the two minutes of hatred displayed when a terrorist manages to intrude on official television. Romolo then equated this narrative to his own condition of total conformity to external requirements, except during his brief but acute attacks of hatred, during which he destroyed whatever he came into contact with: indeed, he arrived at one session limping because of a bad contusion he had given himself when he kicked his record player to pieces.

Another literary inspiration for Romolo then came from the short story "I sette messaggeri" ("The Seven Messengers") by Dino Buzzati, which tells of the son of a king who sets off with messengers to find the borders of his father's realm. The messengers, dispatched one by one, serve to maintain written contact with the capital, but the epistolary news that eventually reaches him during his endless voyage always tells of a long-gone past and reports plans for a now-passed future, and he also never succeeds in finding the boundaries of the kingdom. Romolo connected this story to his own lack of personal boundaries, as well as to his detachment from himself, as a result of which he always felt as if he were elsewhere, while also feeling chronically untouched by every present experience.

This growing awareness of his virtual non-existence made it possible for him to add increasingly to his understanding of the nature of his problems. In a later session Romolo described an evening with his father in which he "had the most substantial meal I've ever eaten" – in clear contrast with his decided anorexic tendency: he had consumed tortellini and drunk wine and, to finish, grappa. He told me he'd never had such a distinct sensation of his body's taking center stage. "It was as if my body, revolving, had turned a somersault and entered straight into my mind."

Romolo made use of his literary sensibility to approach important perceptions of his state of virtual non-existence and his lack of personal boundaries or of any relation to the present. At this point his orientation became concrete, in a manner that was decisive in bringing about change. His experiential body stepped forward: his body was "revolving" – a revolution suggestive of rebellion against the "non-existence" attendant upon body–mind dissociation – and it urgently summoned the attention of his mind.

With Romolo, analytic experience once again demonstrates how the body with its concreteness can offer resistance to the lethal guise of non-existence, becoming the foundation-stone of being. Although Romolo's new experience with food and wine is extreme in its exclusive focus on the body – in distinct contrast to his former denial of it – it brings to mind my own experience, in which bodily activities such as food, cooking, and wine-tasting play an important role.

Writing about the pervasive tendency of certain well-educated people to disparage bodily activities, Don Greif discusses their attitude towards sports, stating that:

> Sports are thought of as less "serious" pursuits than, say, opera, theater, dance, or film. Unlike the arts, sports do not set out to address serious issues. Sports are seen – at least among "serious" people – as a form of light entertainment, a diversion or escape from the important issues of life."
>
> (Greif, 2010: 551)

Paraphrasing what Greif writes about sports, I'd say that, in a world where virtual experience has largely supplanted embodied experience, involvement in cooking, wine-tasting, and certain other experiences such as gardening or playing with pets may be quite a good way to stay connected to an ancient, profound, and partially lost aspect of ourselves.[2]

Unlike engagement in the fields of abstract knowledge, involvement in cookery and wine-tasting encourages mental integration in a direct confrontation with the body, placing the body–mind dialogue at the center of one's mental activity. To wine in particular I have dedicated extensive research, and for years have contributed articles on the wines of Burgundy to a prominent enological journal in Italy.[3]

Wine-tasting is not to be considered a simply hedonistic gratification, given that the perception/consciousness system is faced with bodily sensations that are difficult to note, differentiate among, and express, as well as with the containment of instinctual pressure (Freud, 1911a). The tasting experience is a solitary one, even when it takes place within a relational context, in which the individual's taste and style are compared with the objective and shared parameters of sensory notation. It fosters the capacity for independence of opinion in the presence of sensations and emotions that emanate directly from the body, as well as promoting thought based upon sensory experience, rather than upon interpersonal conditioning or external parameters such as prestigiousness or price.

The devaluation of somatic activities is the expression of *an anthropological discord* that leads to the overestimation of the mental as opposed to the bodily, even though we know that "the mind" in its most extreme form can be more of an obstacle than an advantage – as Bion (1970) notes in relation to mental saturation caused by an overloading of knowledge, or Winnicott (1958b) observes, when he speaks of "mind activity" as "a threat to the psyche-soma."

As in the cases of some of Italo Calvino's literary characters – such as the "cloven Viscount," later put back together – who are characterized by incompleteness, the psychoanalyst who is consistently heedful of her relationship with her body, or, one might say, open to cookery and wine, or – according to one's personal prospensities – to sports, gardening, or caring for and playing with pets, has a chance to reconstruct the link between her mind and the "other half" of her nature, and "to heal an unhealable breach at the core of our identity" (Malcolm Slavin, quoted by Greif, 2010).

It is my hope that this volume has usefully explored body–mind dissociation as a new horizon in psychoanalysis that might offer protection against the danger that body and mind inhabit two disparate realms, leaving analysts, hardly less than their analysands, "cloven" when they confront the great responsibility of the clinical encounter.

Notes

1 From the sleeve notes to Johannes Brahms, Piano Concertos, Claudio Arrau (piano), conducted by Carlo Maria Giulini, LP (German Edition, 1962).
2 I've learned a lot from my analysands about the considerable contribution to body–mind integration that one's relationship with pets can offer.
3 Burgundy offers a unique culture of *climat*: namely, the identity of a small area in which "the quality of the grapes, the soil, the subsoil, the aspect, the climate and the history form the characteristics of a unique personality" (Bazin, 1996: 15); Bazin also declares that "King Minos' labyrinth on Crete was nothing compared to vine-growing, wine-making Burgundy" (1994: 3). For Jean Laplanche, psychoanalyst and owner/wine-maker of Château de Pommard – whom I had the opportunity to interview – wine and psychoanalysis both "comprise the involvement of knowledge," as well as being "part of a vaster whole which is the art of living … and they are part of the culture of mankind" (*Il gambero rosso*, 153 [October 2004]: 140).

References

Ammaniti, M. and Trentini, C. (2009). "How new knowledge about parenting reveals the neurobiological implications of intersubjectivity: A conceptual synthesis of recent research." *Psychoanal. Dial.*, 19: 537–555.

Aron, L. and Anderson, F. S. (2003). *Relational Perspectives on the Body*. New York, Other Press.

Bach, S. (1998). "Two ways of being." *Psychoanal. Dial.*, 8: 657–673.

Baker, R. (1994). "Psychoanalysis as a life line: A clinical study of a transference perversion." *Int. J. Psychoanal.* 75: 743–753.

Balsam, R. H. (2003). "The vanished pregnant body in psychoanalytic female developmental theory." *J. Amer. Psychoanal. Assn.*, 51: 1153–1179.

Bazin, J. F. (1996). *Le Vin de Bourgogne*. Paris: Hachette.

Bick, E. (1968). "The experience of the skin in early object-relations." *Int. J. Psychoanal.*, 49: 484–486.

Bion, W. R. (1955). "Il linguaggio e lo schizofrenico." In *Nuove vie della psicoanalisi*, ed. M. Klein: Heimann, and R. Money-Kyrle. Milan: Il saggiatore, pp. 294–317.

───── (1962). *Learning from Experience*. London: Karnac.

───── (1963). *Elements of Psychoanalysis*. London: Karnac.

───── (1965). *Transformations*. London: Karnac.

───── (1967a [1950]). "The imaginary twin." In *Second Thoughts*. London: Karnac, pp. 3–22.

───── (1967b [1957]). "Differentiation of psychotic from the non-psychotic personalities." In *Second Thoughts*. London: Karnac, pp. 43–64.

───── (1967c [1959]). "Attacks on linking." In *Second Thoughts*. London: Karnac, pp. 93–110.

───── (1967d [1962]). "A theory of thinking." In *Second Thoughts*. London: Karnac, pp. 110–119.

───── (1970). *Attention and Interpretation*. London: Karnac.

───── (1988 [1979]). "Making the best of a bad job." In *Clinical Seminars and Other Works*. London: Karnac, pp. 321–332.

—— (1990 [1973/1974]). *Brazilian Lectures*. London: Karnac.
—— (1992). *Cogitations*. London: Karnac.
Blechner, M. J. (2011). "Listening to the body and feeling the mind." *Contemp. Psychoanal.*, 47: 25–34.
Blos, P. (1967). "The second individuation process of adolescence." *Psychoanal. St. Child.*, 22: 162–186.
Blum, H. P. (1973). "The concept of erotized transference." *J. Amer. Psychoanal. Assn.*, 21: 61–76.
Bolognini, S. (1994). "Transference: Erotised, erotic, loving, affectionate." *Int. J. Psychoanal.*, 75: 73–86.
Bonaminio, V. (2004). "Commentary on Dr. Riccardo Lombardi's 'Three psychoanalytic sessions.'" *Psychoanal. Q.*, 78: 793–799.
Bon de Matte, L. (1988). "An account of Melanie Klein's conception of projective identification." In I. Matte Blanco, *Thinking, Feeling and Being*. London and New York: Routledge, pp. 319–330.
—— (1994). "Introduction." In A. Ferrari, *Adolescenza: La seconda sfida*. Rome: Borla, pp. 9–15.
—— (1998). "L'età dell'inquietudine." *MicroMega*, 3: 209–217.
—— (1999). "Anorexic syndrome in adolescence and anorexia." In *Psychotherapeutic Issues on Eating Disorders: Models, Methods and Results*, ed. A. Ciocca, P. Bria, and S. De Risio. Rome: Società Editrice Universo, pp. 41–48.
Bria, P. (1996). "El infinito en la mente: Ignatio Matte Blanco entre Galileo y Freud." *Rev. Chilena de Psicoanalisis*, 13: 48.
—— (2000). Review of A. Ferrari and A. Stella, *L'alba del pensiero*. *Int. J. Psychoanal.*, 81: 609–612.
Bromberg, P. M. (2001). "Treating patients with symptoms – and symptoms with patience: Reflections on shame, dissociation, and eating disorders." *Psychoanal. Dial.*, 11(6): 891–912.
Bucci, W. (2000). Panel report from 41st IPA Congress: "Biological and integrative studies on affect." *Int. J. Psychoanal.*, 81: 141–144.
—— (2007). "New perspectives on the multiple code theory: The role of bodily experience in emotional organization." In *Bodies in Treatment: The Unspoken Dimension*, ed. F. S. Anderson. Hillsdale, NJ: The Analytic Press, pp. 51–77.
Calvino, I. (1988a). *Lezioni americane: Sei proposte per il prossimo millennio*. Milan: Garzanti.
—— (1988b). *Six Memos for the Next Millennium*. Cambridge, MA: Harvard University Press, 1988.
Caparotta, L. and Ghaffari, K. (2006). "A historical overview of the psychodynamic contributions to the understanding of eating disorders." *Psychoanal. Psychother.*, 20: 175–196.
Carignani, P. (1999). "La finta calma della latenza." *Parolechiave*, 16: 77–91.

Ciocca, A. (1998). "La dissociazione psicosomatica." In *Festschrift sul pensiero e l'opera di A. B.Ferrari, ed.* A. Ciocca, C. LaRosa, R. Lombardi, and M. Turno. *Psicoterapia e istituzioni*, 4: 183–120.

Damasio, A. (1994). *Descartes' Error: Emotion, Reason and the Human Brain.* New York: Putnam.

——— (1999). *The Feeling of What Happens: Body and Emotion in the Making of Consciousness.* New York: Harcourt Brace.

Damasio, A. and Carvalho, G. B. (2013). "The nature of feelings: Evolutionary and neurobiological origins." *Nat. Rev. Neurosci.*, 14(2): 143–152.

Davies, J. M. and Frawley, M. G. (1994). *Treating the Adult Survivor of Childhood Sexual Abuse: A Psychoanalytic Perspective.* New York: Basic Books.

De Masi, F. (2012). "Erotic transference: Dream or delusion?" *J. Amer. Psychoanal. Assn.*, 60: 1199–1220.

Del Greco, E. (1996). "Problemi di tecnica psicoanalitica nel passaggio dall'infanzia all'adolescenza." *Richard e Piggle*, 4: 201–213.

Delion: (2010). *Le Corps retrouvé.* Paris, Hermann.

Delli Ponti, M. and Luban Plozza, B. (1986). *Il terzo orecchio: Musica e psiche.* Turin: Centro Scientifico Torinese.

Ellenberger, H. F. (1976). *La scoperta dell'inconscio.* Turin: Boringhieri.

Emde, R. N. (2009). "From ego to 'we-go': Neurobiology and questions for psychoanalysis. Commentary on papers by Trevarthen, Gallese, and Ammaniti and Trentini." *Psychoanal. Dial.*, 19: 556–564.

Fast, I. (1992). "The embodied mind: Toward a relational perspective." *Psychoanal. Dial.*, 2: 389–409.

——— (2006). "A body-centered mind." *Contemp. Psychoanal.*, 42: 273–295.

Ferrari, A. B. (1982). "Relação analitica: Sistema ou processo?" *Rev. Brasil. Psican.*, 16: 335–349.

——— (1992). *L'eclissi del corpo.* Rome: Borla.

——— (1994). *Adolescenza: La seconda sfida.* Rome: Borla.

——— (2004). *From the Eclipse of the Body to the Dawn of Thought.* London: Free Association Books.

——— (2005). *Il pulviscolo di Giotto.* Milan: Angeli.

Ferrari, A. B. and Garroni, E. (1979). "Schema di progetto per uno studio della 'relazione analitica.'" *Riv. di psicoanal.*, 25: 282–322.

Ferrari, A. B. and Lombardi, R. (1998). "Il corpo dell'inconscio." *MicroMega*, 3: 197–208.

Ferrari, A. B. and Stella, A. (1998): *L'alba del pensiero.* Rome: Borla.

Finelli, R. (1995). "Mente e corpo tra due e tre." *Almanacchi nuovi*, 2/3: 132–139.

Fink, K. (1993). "The bi-logical perception of time." *Int. J. Psychoanal.*, 74: 303–312.

Flanders, S. (2007). Discussion of Riccardo Lombardi's paper, "The body in the analytic session." Fourth British–Italian Conference, British Society, London, 2–3 February.

Fonagy, P. and Target, M. (2000). "Playing with reality. III: The persistence of dual psychic reality in borderline patients." *Int. J. Psychoanal.*, 81: 853–873.

Fornari, F. (1979). *I fondamenti di una teoria psicoanalitica del linguaggio*. Turin: Boringhieri.

Fosshage, J. L. (1994). "Toward reconceptualising transference: Theoretical and clinical considerations." *Int. J. Psychoanal.*, 75: 265–280.

Freud, S. (1893–1895). *Studies on Hysteria*. In *The Standard Edition of the Complete Psychological Works of Sigmund Freud*, ed. J. Strachey, A. Freud, C. L. Rothgeb, A. Richards, et al. Vol. II. London: Hogarth Press.

—— (1900). *The Interpretation of Dreams*. In *The Standard Edition of the Complete Psychological Works of Sigmund Freud*, ed. J. Strachey, A. Freud, C. L. Rothgeb, A. Richards, et al. Vols IV–V. London: Hogarth Press.

—— (1901). *The Psychopathology of Everyday Life*. In *The Standard Edition of the Complete Psychological Works of Sigmund Freud*, ed. J. Strachey, A. Freud, C. L. Rothgeb, A. Richards, et al. Vol. VI. London: Hogarth Press, pp. 1–279.

—— (1905). *Three Essays on the Theory of Sexuality*. In *The Standard Edition of the Complete Psychological Works of Sigmund Freud*, ed. J. Strachey, A. Freud, C. L. Rothgeb, A. Richards, et al. Vol. VII. London: Hogarth Press, pp. 123–246.

—— (1907). "Delusion and dream in Jensen's *Gradiva*." In *The Standard Edition of the Complete Psychological Works of Sigmund Freud*, ed. J. Strachey, A. Freud, C. L. Rothgeb, A. Richards, et al. Vol. IX. London: Hogarth Press, pp. 7–96.

—— (1910). "Leonardo Da Vinci and a memory of his childhood." In *The Standard Edition of the Complete Psychological Works of Sigmund Freud*, ed. J. Strachey, A. Freud, C. L. Rothgeb, A. Richards, et al. Vol. XI. London: Hogarth Press, pp. 57–138.

—— (1911a). "Formulations on the two principles of mental functioning." In *The Standard Edition of the Complete Psychological Works of Sigmund Freud*, ed. J. Strachey, A. Freud, C. L. Rothgeb, A. Richards, et al. Vol. XI. London: Hogarth Press, pp. 218–226.

—— (1911b). *Psycho-Analytic Notes on an Autobiographical Account of a Case of Paranoia ("Dementia paranoides")*. In *The Standard Edition of the Complete Psychological Works of Sigmund Freud*, ed. J. Strachey, A. Freud, C. L. Rothgeb, A. Richards, et al. Vol. XII. London: Hogarth Press.

—— (1912). "The dynamics of transference." In *The Standard Edition of the Complete Psychological Works of Sigmund Freud*, ed. J. Strachey, A. Freud, C. L. Rothgeb, A. Richards, et al. Vol. XII. London: Hogarth Press, pp. 97–108.

—— (1914a) "The Moses of Michelangelo." In *The Standard Edition of the Complete Psychological Works of Sigmund Freud*, ed. J. Strachey, A. Freud, C. L. Rothgeb, A. Richards, et al. Vol. XIII. London: Hogarth Press, pp. 211–236.

——— (1914b). "Narcissism: an Introduction." In *The Standard Edition of the Complete Psychological Works of Sigmund Freud,* ed. J. Strachey, A. Freud, C. L. Rothgeb, A. Richards, et al. Vol. XIV. London: Hogarth Press, pp. 67–102.

——— (1915a). "Instincts and their vicissitudes." In *The Standard Edition of the Complete Psychological Works of Sigmund Freud,* ed. J. Strachey, A. Freud, C. L. Rothgeb, A. Richards, et al. Vol. XIV. London: Hogarth Press, pp. 117–140.

——— (1915b). "Observation on transference-love." In *The Standard Edition of the Complete Psychological Works of Sigmund Freud,* ed. J. Strachey, A. Freud, C. L. Rothgeb, A. Richards, et al. Vol. XII. London: Hogarth Press, pp. 159–171.

——— (1915c). "The unconscious." In *The Standard Edition of the Complete Psychological Works of Sigmund Freud,* ed. J. Strachey, A. Freud, C. L. Rothgeb, A. Richards, et al. Vol. XIV. London: Hogarth Press, pp. 166–215.

——— (1920), "Beyond the pleasure principle." In *The Standard Edition of the Complete Psychological Works of Sigmund Freud,* ed. J. Strachey, A. Freud, C. L. Rothgeb, A. Richards, et al. Vol. XVIII. London: Hogarth Press, pp. 7–64.

——— (1923). "The ego and the id." In *The Standard Edition of the Complete Psychological Works of Sigmund Freud,* ed. J. Strachey, A. Freud, C. L. Rothgeb, A. Richards, et al. Vol. XIX. London: Hogarth Press, pp. 3–66.

——— (1926). *Inhibitions, Symptoms and Anxiety*. In *The Standard Edition of the Complete Psychological Works of Sigmund Freud,* ed. J. Strachey, A. Freud, C. L. Rothgeb, A. Richards, et al. Vol. XX. London: Hogarth Press.

——— (1929). *Civilization and Its Discontents*. In *The Standard Edition of the Complete Psychological Works of Sigmund Freud,* ed. J. Strachey, A. Freud, C. L. Rothgeb, A. Richards, et al. Vol. XXI. London: Hogarth Press.

——— (1932). "New introductory lectures on psychoanalysis." In *The Standard Edition of the Complete Psychological Works of Sigmund Freud,* ed. J. Strachey, A. Freud, C. L. Rothgeb, A. Richards, et al. Vol. XXII. London: Hogarth Press, pp. 1–182.

——— (1938). *Outline of Psychoanalysis*. In *The Standard Edition of the Complete Psychological Works of Sigmund Freud,* ed. J. Strachey, A. Freud, C. L. Rothgeb, A. Richards, et al. Vol. XXIII. London: Hogarth Press.

Freud, S. and Groddeck, G. (1973). *Carteggio*. Milano: Adelphi.

Gabbard, G. (1995). "Countertransference: The emerging common ground." *Int. J. Psychoanal.,* 76: 475–485.

Gaddini, E. (1992). *A Psychoanalytic Theory of Infantile Experience: Conceptual and Clinical Reflections*. London: Karnac.

Gallese, V. and Ebisch, S. (2014). "Embodied simulation and tact: The sense of touch in social cognition." Read at the Roman Training Program of the Italian Psychoanalytic Society, 1 February.

Gallese, V., Eagle, M. N., and Migone, P. (2007). "Intentional attunement: Mirror neurons and the neural underpinnings of interpersonal relations." *J. Amer. Psychoanal. Assn.*, 55: 131–176.

Garroni, E. (1975). *Pinocchio uno e bino.* Bari: Laterza.

——— (1992). "Che cosa si prova ad essere un *Homo sapiens*?" Introduction to A. B. Ferrari, *L'eclissi del corpo.* Rome: Borla, pp. 7–16.

Ginzburg, A. (1993). "Psicoanalisi ed educazione: La ricostruzione di un percorso di ricerca." *Psiche*, 1: 39–45.

——— (1999). Review of *Festschrift sul pensiero e l'opera di A. B. Ferrari,* ed. A. Ciocca, C. LaRosa, R. Lombardi, and M. Turno. *Riv. di psicoanal.*, 2: 403–406.

Good, M. I. (2006). "Perverse dreams and dreams of perversion." *Psychoanal. Q.*, 87: 939–952.

Green, A. (1984a). "Realtà psichica, realtà materiale." In *Livelli di realtà,* ed. M. P. Palmarini. Milan: Feltrinelli, pp. 376–408.

——— (1984b). "Le langage dans la psychanalyse." In *Langages.* Paris: Editions Les Belles Lettres, pp. 19–250.

——— (1990 [1976]). "Le concept de limite." In *La Folie privée: Psychanalyse de cas-limites.* Paris: Gallimard, pp. 103–140.

——— (2002). *La Pensée clinique.* Paris: Editions Odile Jacob.

Greenberg, J. (2004). "Commentary on Dr. Riccardo Lombardi's 'Three psychoanalytic sessions.'" *Psychoanal. Q.*, 78: 801–805.

Greenberg, J. and Mitchell, S. (1983). *Object Relations in Psychoanalytic Theory.* Cambridge, MA: Harvard University Press.

Greenson, R. (1971). "The 'real' relationship between the patient and the psychoanalyst." In *The Unconscious Today*, ed. M. Kanzer. New York: International Universities Press, pp. 213–232.

Greenspan, S. I. (1981). *Psychopathology and Adaptation in Infancy and Early Childhood: Principles of Clinical Diagnosis and Preventive Intervention.* New York: International Universities Press.

——— (1989). *The Development of the Ego: Implications for Personality Theory, Psychopathology and the Psychotherapeutic Process.* New York: International Universities Press.

Greif, D. (2010). "Revaluing sports." *Contemp. Psychoanal.*, 46: 550–561.

Grotstein, J. S. (1997). "Integrating one-person and two-person psychologies: Autochthony and alterity in counterpoint." *Psychoanal. Q.*, 64: 403–430.

——— (2004). "Commentary on Dr. Riccardo Lombardi's 'Three psychoanalytic sessions.'" *Psychoanal. Q.*, 78: 787–792.

——— (2007). *A Beam of Intense Darkness.* London: Karnac.

IJzerman, H. and Semin, G. R. (2009), "The thermometer of social relations: Mapping social proximity on temperature." *Psychological Science*, 20: 1214–1220.

Isaacs, S. (1991 [1948]). "The nature and function of phantasy." In *The Freud/Klein Controversies, 1941–1945*, ed. P. King and R. Steiner. London: Routledge, pp. 264–321.

Jacobs, T. J. (2001). "Reflections on the goals of psychoanalysis, the psychoanalytic process, and the process of change." *Psychoanal. Q.*, 70: 149–181.

Jaques, E. (1965). "Death and the Mid-Life Crisis." *Int. J. Psychoanal.*, 46: 502–514.

James, M. (1960). "Premature ego development: Some observations on disturbances in the first three months of life." *Int. J. Psychoanal.*, 41: 288–294.

Joseph, B. (1975). "The patient difficult to reach." In *Melanie Klein Today*. Vol II, ed. E. Bott Spillius. Routledge: London.

Kernberg, O. (1993). "Convergences and divergences in contemporary psychoanalytic technique." *Int. J. Psychoanal.*, 74: 659–673.

Khan, M. R. (1960). "Regression and integration in the analytic setting: A clinical essay on the transference and counter-transference aspects of these phenomena." *Int. J. Psychoanal.*, 41: 130–146.

——— (1974 [1964]). "Ego-distortion, cumulative trauma and the role of reconstruction in the analytic situation." In *The Privacy of Self*. London: Hogarth Press, pp. 67–78.

Killingmo, B. (1989). "Conflict and deficit: Implication for technique." *Int. J. Psychoanal.*, 70: 65–79.

Kohut, H. (1979). "The two analyses of Mr. Z." *Int. J. Psychoanal.*, 60: 3–27.

Korbivcher, C. F. (2014). Plenary Address of the Seventh International Tustin Conference: "Spilling, Falling, Dissolving." Boston, MA, July 24–27.

Klein, M. (1940). "Mourning and its relation to manic-depressive states." *Int. J. Psychoanal.*, 21: 125–153.

——— (1975a [1923]). "Early analysis." In *"Love, Guilt and Reparation" and Other Works 1925–1945*. London: Hogarth Press.

——— (1975b [1925]). "A contribution to the psychogenesis of tics." In *"Love, Guilt and Reparation" and Other Works 1925–1945*. London: Hogarth Press.

——— (1975c [1928]). "Early stages of the Oedipus complex." In *"Love, Guilt and Reparation" and Other Works 1925–1945*. London: Hogarth Press.

——— (1975d [1935]). "Contribution to the psychogenesis of manic-depressive states." In *"Love, Guilt and Reparation" and Other Works 1925–1945*. London: Hogarth Press.

——— (1975e [1936]) "Weaning." In *"Love, Guilt and Reparation" and Other Works 1925–1945*. London: Hogarth Press.

——— (1975f [1946]). "Notes on some schizoid mechanisms." In *"Envy and Gratitude" and Other Works 1946–1963*. London: Hogarth Press.

——— (1975g [1952]). "Some theoretical conclusions regarding the emotional life of the infant." In *"Envy and Gratitude" and Other Works 1946–1963*. London: Hogarth Press.

Laforgue, J. (1986). *Oeuvres complètes*. Vol. I: *1860–1883*. Lausanne: Editions L'Age d'Homme.
Langer, S. (1953). *Feeling and Form: A Theory of Art*. New York: Scribner.
Laufer, M. and Laufer, M. E. (1989). *Developmental Breakdown and Psychoanalytic Treatment in Adolescence: Clinical Studies*. New Haven and London: Yale University Press.
Lecours, S. and Bouchard, M.-A. (1997). "Dimensions of mentalisation: Outlining levels of psychic transformation." *Int. J. Psychoanal.*, 78: 855–876.
Lieberman, J. (2000). *Body Talk: Looking and Being Looked at in Psychotherapy*. Northvale, NJ: Aronson.
Loewald, H. (1960). "On the therapeutic action of psycho-analysis." *Int. J. Psychoanal.*, 41: 16–33.
Loewenstein, R. and Ross, D. (1992). "Multiple personality and psychoanalysis: An introduction." *Psychoanal. Inq.*, 12: 3–48.
Lombardi, R. (1987). "Funzione di guida dell'analizzando nel trattamento psicoanalitico delle psicosi." *Neurologia psichiatria scienze umane*, 7(1): 1–14.
——— (1992). "La psicosi e il corpo." In A. Ferrari, *L'eclissi del corpo*. Rome: Borla, pp. 177–206.
——— (2000a [1998]). "Le narrazioni oniriche e la rete di contatto corpo-mente." In *Il sogno cento anni dopo*, ed. S. Bolognini. Turin: Boringhieri, pp. 162–177.
——— (2000b). "Corpo, affetti, pensieri: Riflessioni su alcune ipotesi di I. Matte Blanco e A. B. Ferrari." *Riv. di psicoanal.*, 46(4): 683–706.
——— (2002). "Primitive mental states and the body." *Int. J. Psychoanal.*, 83: 353–381.
——— (2003a). "Catalyzing the dialogue between body and mind in a psychotic analysand." *Psychoanal. Q.*, 72: 1017–1041.
——— (2003b). "Knowledge and experience of time in primitive mental states." *Int. J. Psychoanal.*, 84: 1531–1549.
——— (2003c). "Mental models and language registers in the psychoanalysis of psychosis: An overview of a thirteen-year analysis." *Int. J. Psychoanal.*, 84: 843–863.
——— (2004a). "Stanley Kubrick's swan song: *Eyes Wide Shut*." *Int. J. Psychoanal.*, 85: 209–218.
——— (2004b). "Three psychoanalytic sessions." *Psychoanal. Q.*, 73: 773–814.
——— (2005a). "On the psychoanalytic treatment of a psychotic breakdown." *Psychoanal. Q.*, 74: 1069–1099.
——— (2005b). Review of A. B. Ferrari, *From the Eclipse of the Body to the Dawn of Thought*, trans. I. Chigi. London: Free Association Books, 2004. *Int. J. Psychoanal.*, 86: 579–584.
——— (2006a). "Catalizzando il dialogo tra il corpo e la mente in un analizzando psicotico: Una prospettiva biologica." *Riv. di psicoanal.*, 52: 743–765.

——— (2006b). "Passioni e conflittualità nelle istituzioni psicoanalitiche." *Riv. di psicoanal.*, 52: 191–212.

——— (2007). "Shame in relation to the body, sex and death: A clinical exploration of the psychotic levels of shame." *Psychoanal. Dial.*, 17: 385–399.

——— (2008a). "The body in the analytic session: Focusing on the body–mind link." *J. Int. Psychoanal.*, 89: 89–109.

——— (2008b). "Time, music, and *rêverie*." *J. Amer. Psychoanal. Assn.*, 56: 1191–1211.

——— (2009a). "Body, affect, thought: Reflections of the work of Matte Blanco and Ferrari. *Psychoanal. Q.*, 78: 126–160.

——— (2009b). "Symmetric frenzy and catastrophic change: A consideration of primitive mental states in the wake of Bion and Matte Blanco." *Int. J. Psychoanal.*, 90: 529–549.

——— (2009c). "Through the eye of the needle: The unfolding of the unconscious body." *J. Amer. Psychoanal. Assn.*, 57: 61–94.

——— (2010). "The body emerging from the 'neverland' of nothingness." *Psychoanal. Q.*, 79: 879–909.

——— (2011). "The body, feelings, and the unheard music of the senses." *Contemp. Psychoanal.*, 47: 3–24.

——— (2013a). "Death, time, and psychosis." *J. Amer. Psychoanal. Assn.*, 61: 691–726.

——— (2013b). "Object relations and the ineffable bodily dimension." *Contemp. Psychoanal.*, 49: 82–102.

Lombardi, R. and Carignani, P. (1998). "La scoperta del corpo: Sviluppo senso-motorio ed integrazione corpo-mente nell'analisi di una bambina." *Psicoterapia e istituzioni*, 4: 183–202.

Lombardi, R. and Pola, M. (2010). "The body, adolescence, and psychosis." *Int. J. Psychoanal.*, 91: 1419–1444.

Mahler, M. and McDevitt, J. (1982). "Thoughts on the emergence of self, with particular emphasis on the body self." *J. Am. Psychoan. Assn.*, 33: 827–848.

Mancia, M. (1994). Review of A. B. Ferrari, *L'eclissi del corpo*. Rome: Borla. *Int. J. Psychoanal.*, 75: 1283–1286.

Marty, P. (1976). *Les Mouvements individuelles de vie et de mort*. Paris: Payot.

——— (1980). *L'Ordre psychosomatique*. Paris: Payot.

——— (1985). "Les psychothérapies des malades somatiques." In *Terapia in psicosomatica: Atti del IX Congresso della Società Italiana di Medicina Psicosomatica, Torino, 26–29 maggio 1983*. Turin: Università, pp. 53–64.

Mathis, I. (2000). "Sketch for a metapsychology of affect." *Int. J. Psychoanal.*, 81: 215–227.

Matte Blanco, I. (1975). *The Unconscious as Infinite Sets*. London: Duckworth.

——— (1988). *Thinking, Feeling and Being*. London and New York: Routledge.

McDougall, J. (1989). *Theaters of the Body*. London: Free Association Books.

——— (1995). *The Many Faces of Eros*. London: Free Association Books.

Meissner, W. W. (1997). "The self and the body. I: The body self and the body image." *Psychoanalysis and Contemporary Thoughts*, 20: 419–448.
—— (1998a). "The self and the body. II: The embodied self. Self vs. nonself." *Psychoanalysis and Contemporary Thoughts*, 21: 85–111.
—— (1998b). "The self and the body. III: The body image in clinical perspective." *Psychoanalysis and Contemporary Thoughts*, 21: 113–146.
—— (1998c). "The self and the body. IV: The body on the couch." *Psychoanalysis and Contemporary Thoughts*, 21: 277–300.
—— (2005). Review of A. B. Ferrari, *From the Eclipse of the Body to the Dawn of Thought*, trans. I. Chigi. London: Free Association Books, 2004. *Psychoanal. Q.*, 74, 603–609.
Meltzer, D. (1964). "The differentiation of somatic delusions from hypochondria." *Int. J. Psychoanal.*, 45: 246–250.
—— (1982). "Implicazioni psicosomatiche nel pensiero di Bion." *Quaderni di psicoterapia infantile*, 7: 199–222.
Milana, G. (1992). "Rapporto verticale e rapporto orizzontale." In A. B. Ferrari, *L'eclissi del corpo*. Rome: Borla, pp. 113–140.
Miles, L. K., Nind, L. K., and Macrae, C. N. (2010), "Moving through time." *Psychological Science*, 21: 222–223.
Milner, M. (1969). *The Hands of the Living God*. New York: International Universities Press.
—— (1987 [1977]). "Winnicott and overlapping circles." In *The Suppressed Madness of Sane Men*. London: Tavistock, pp. 279–286.
Money-Kyrle, R. (1968). "On cognitive development." *Int. J. Psychoanal.*, 49: 691–698.
Nagel, T. (1981). "What is it like to be a bat?" In *The Mind's I: Fantasies and Reflections on Self and Soul*, ed. D. R. Hofstadter and D. C. Dennett. New York: Basic Books.
Nancy, J.-L. (2000). *L'Intrus*. Paris: Galilée.
Nemiah, J. and Sifneos, P. (1970). "Affect and fantasy in patients with psychosomatic disorders." In *Modern Trends in Psychosomatic Medicine*, ed. O. W. Hill. Vol. II. London: Butterworth, pp. 26–34.
Ogden, T. H. (1989). "On the concept of an autistic-contiguous position." *Int. J. Psychoanal.*, 70: 127–140.
—— (1994). "The analytic third: Working with intersubjective clinical facts." *Int. J. Psychoanal.*, 75: 3–19.
Petrella, F. (2004). "Spazio artistico e umorismo in musica." In *Cantando e scherzando: Il comico in psicoanalisi e musica*, ed. R. Carollo. Cremona: Cremonabooks.
Piperno, R. (1992). "Il riemergere dell'Oggetto Originario Concreto nelle condizioni psicotiche." In A. B. Ferrari, *L'eclissi del corpo*. Rome: Borla.
Pohlen, M. (2009). *In analisi con Freud: I verbali delle sedute di Ernst Blum del 1922*. Turin: Boringhieri.

Pollak, T. (2009). "The 'body-container': A new perspective on the 'body-ego.'" *Int. J. Psychoanal.*, 90: 487–506.

Prigogine, I. (1988). *Entre le temps et l'éternité*. Paris: Fayard.

Rabih, M. (1991). "The body as a stage for criminal acting out." *Int. J. Psychoanal.*, 72: 499–510.

Reale, G. (1999). *Corpo, anima e salute: Il concetto di uomo da Omero a Platone*. Milan: Cortina.

Reeder, J. (2004). *Hate and Love in Psychoanalytic Institutions: The Dilemma of a Profession*. New York: Other Press.

Renik, O. (1993). "Analytic interaction: Conceptualizing technique in light of the analyst's irreducible subjectivity." *Psychoanal. Q.*, 62: 553–571.

——— (2003). "Standards and standardization." *J. Amer. Psychoanal. Assn.*, 51S: 43–55.

Resnik, S. (1973). *Personne et psychose*. Paris: Payot.

——— (1976). *Persona e psicosi*. Turin: Einaudi, 1976.

——— (1982). *Il teatro del sogno*. Turin: Boringhieri.

——— (1987). *The Theatre of the Dream*. Trans. A. Sheridan. London: Tavistock.

——— (2001). *The Delusional Person: Bodily Feelings in Psychosis*. London: Routledge.

Rizzuto, A.-M. (1988). "Transference, language and affect in the treatment of bulimarexia." *Int. J. Psychoanal.*, 69: 369–387.

Robbins, M. (2008). "Primary mental expression: Freud, Klein, and Beyond." *J. Amer. Psychoanal. Assn.*, 56: 177–202.

——— (2011). *The Primordial Mind in Health and Illness*. New York: Routledge.

Rosenfeld, H. (1964). "The psychopathology of hypochondriasis." In *Psychotic States: A Psycho-Analytical Approach*. London, Hogarth Press, 1965, pp. 180–199.

——— (1971). "A clinical approach to the psychoanalytic therapy of the life and death instincts: An investigation into the aggressive aspects of narcissism." *Int. J. Psychoanal.*, 52: 169–178.

Sandler, J. and Sandler, A. M. (1984). "The past unconscious, the present unconscious and interpretation of the transference." *Psychoan. Inq.*, 4: 367–399.

Scott, W. C. (1948). "Some embryological, neurological, psychiatric and psycho-analytic implications of the body scheme." *Int. J. Psychoanal.*, 29: 141–155.

Segal, H. (1958). "Fear of death: Notes on the analysis of an old man." *Int. J. Psychoanal.*, 39: 178–181.

——— (1964) *Introduction to the Work of Melanie Klein*. London: Heinemann Medical.

——— (1984). "Joseph Conrad and the mid-life crisis." *Int. R. Psychoanal.*, 11: 3–9.

Seligman, S. (1999). "Integrating Kleinian theory and intersubjective infant research: Observing projective identification." *Psychoanal. Dial.*, 9: 129–159.

Sletvold, J. (2013). "The ego and the id revisited: Freud and Damasio on the body ego/self." *Int. J. Psychoanal.*, 94: 1019–1032.

Smith, H. (2006). "Analyzing disavowed action: The fundamental resistance of analysis." *J. Amer. Psychoanal. Assn.*, 54: 713–737.

Solano, L. (2000). "Glycaemic dysregulation and relational/affective dysregulation in a patient with diabetes mellitus." *Int. J. Psychoanal.*, 81: 291–305.

Solms, M. and Nersessian, E. (1999). "Freud's theory of affects: Questions for neuroscience." *Neuro-psychoanalysis*, 1: 5–14.

Solomon, M. (1977). *Beethoven*. New York: Schirmer Books.

Steiner, J. (1993). *Psychic Retreats: Pathological Organization in Psychotic, Neurotic and Borderline Patients*. London: Routledge.

——— (2006). "Seeing and being seen: Narcissistic pride and narcissistic humiliation." *Int. J. Psychoanal.*, 87: 939–52.

Steiner, R. (1975). *Processo di simbolizzazione nell'opera di Melanie Klein*. Turin: Boringhieri.

Steinman, I. (2009). *Treating the "Untreatable."* London: Karnac.

Symington, N. (2007). *Becoming a Person through Psychoanalysis*. London: Karnac.

Tausk, V. (1933). "On the origin of the 'influencing machine' in schizophrenia." *Psychoanal. Q.*, 2: 519–556.

Taylor, D. (2011). "Commentary on Vermote's 'On the value of "late Bion" to analytic theory and practice.'" *Int. J. Psychoanal.*, 92: 1099–1112.

Turno, M. (1998). "Disarmonia mente-corpo nelle crisi di panico." In *Festschrift sul pensiero e l'opera di A. B. Ferrari,* ed. A. Ciocca, C. LaRosa, R. Lombardi, and M. Turno. *Psicoterapia e istituzioni*, 4: 121–132.

Tustin, F. (1981). *Autistic States in Children*. London: Routledge.

——— (1986). *Autistic Barriers in Neurotic Patients*. London: Karnac.

Tylim, I. (2012). "The techno-body and the future of psychoanalysis." *Psychoanalytic Inquiry*, 32: 468–479.

Untersteiner, M. (1955). *Le origini della tragedia e del tragico*. Turin: Einaudi.

Valéry, P. (1973). *Cahiers*. Paris: Gallimard.

Vermote, R. (2011). "On the value of 'late Bion' to analytic theory and practice." *Int. J. Psychoanal.*, 92: 1089–1098.

Williams, A. H. (1983). *Nevrosi e delinquenza*. Trans. G. Pasquali. Rome: Borla.

Williams, P. (2004). "Incorporation of an invasive object." *Int. J. Psychoanal.*, 85: 1333–1348.

——— (2007). "The body and mind (including of the analyst) in the treatment of a psychotic state: Some reflections. Commentary on paper by Riccardo Lombardi." *Psychoanal. Dial.*, 17: 401–409.

——— (2010). *Invasive Objects: Minds under Siege*. New York: Taylor and Francis.

Winnicott, C. (1978). "D. W. W.: A reflection." In *Between Reality and Fantasy: Transitional Objects and Phenomena*, ed. S. A. Grolnick, L. Barkin, and W. Muensterberger. New York: Jason Aronson, pp. 17–33.

Winnicott, D. W. (1958a [1935]). "The manic defence." In *Through Paediatrics to Psycho-Analysis: Collected Papers*. London: Tavistock, pp. 129–144.

―――― (1958b [1949]). "Mind and its relation to the psyche-soma." In *Through Paediatrics to Psycho-Analysis: Collected Papers*. London: Tavistock, pp. 243–254.

―――― (1958c [1954]). "Withdrawal and regression." In *Through Paediatrics to Psycho-Analysis: Collected Papers*. London: Tavistock, pp. 255–261.

―――― (1965 [1960]). "Ego distorsion in terms of the true and false self." In *The Maturational Processes and Facilitating Environment*. London: Hogarth Press.

―――― (1971a [1969]). "L'uso di un oggetto e l'entrare in rapporto attraverso identificazioni." In *Playing and Reality*. London: Tavistock.

―――― (1971b). "Creativity and its origins." In *Playing and Reality*, London: Tavistock.

―――― (1974). "Fear of breakdown." *Int. Rev. Psychoanal.*, 1: 103–107.

Zhong, C. B. and Leonardelli, G. J. (2008). "Cold and lonely: Does social exclusion literally feel cold?" *Psychological Science*, 19: 838–842.

Index

abstraction 10, 22, 38, 58, 79, 86–7
acting out: in adolescence 80–1, 113; in analytic relationship 63, 65, 67, 86, 107, 108; as favorable to working-through 147
adolescence 90, 110–24, 127; and bodily sensations 72; and the COO 80–1, 107; eclipse of the body and 86; second challenge of 112–15; violence in 64, 65–6
aggression 177–8; *see also* violence
agoraphobia 117, 126, 205
Aldo 203, 204
Alien (Ridley Scott) 175
Almodóvar, Pedro 126
alpha elements 68, 92, 99, 167
animals 122–3, 124, 139, 158, 173
Anita 203–4
Anna 146
anorexia *see* eating disorders
anthropological conflict, contemporary 25–6
Antonia 94–100
Antonio 28–32
anxiety 84, 101, 103, 115, 118, 134–5, 140, 146; adolescent 113; persecutory 51; phobic 120, 121; and seeing 56; sexual 121, 156–7; *see also* panic; *specific phobias*
appearance, personal 130, 136, 137
Aquinas, Thomas 10
Aristotle 8
Artaud, Antonin 124–5
artificial intelligence 59–60, 145
arts, the 1–2, 105, 144–5, 187, 205–6
Arturo 86–91
authenticity 136, 145, 150
autism 12, 15–16, 181
"autistic-contiguous position" 72

auto-eroticism 76, 107
Awakenings (Marshall) 203

baby 9, 24; *see also* children
Bach, J.S. 190, 191
Bacon, Francis (artist) 144
Baker, Ronald 70–1
basic mental organization (BMO) 70
Beethoven, Ludwig van, *Fidelio* 191–202
being 20, 26; vs. not being 147
beta elements 68, 92, 167
Bion, W.R. 14, 16, 22, 81; the container 24–5, 53; on counter-transference, unconscious 4; on emotion 12; on failure to be 39; grid, beta and alpha sensory levels 68, 92; "The imaginary twin" 40–5, 57; on lies 145; negative capability 10–11; and neurophysiological model 68–9; O 166–86; *theoretical simplification* 8–9; "A theory of thinking" 58; on vertical axis 83
birth 112
birth, psychological 73
Blechner, Mark 19, 60
blindness, theme 129, 141
blushing 47, 49–50, 53
bodily functions 146, 151–3, 164, 179, 182–3
bodily representation, absence of 15–16
body: as COO 75, 76, 79–81; eclipse of 12–14, 75–81, 85–91, 166–7, 183; as enemy (in adolescence) 110–12, 115–16; hallucinations about 116–17; as "non-mental" object 10; patient's non-perception of 95; physical illnesses and mental working through 63; psychoanalytic status, lack of 163

body image 94
body-language 73
Bouchard, Marc-André 73
breast: baby's attacks on 9; symbolic significance of 106; and thinking phenomena 81
breathing 189
British Psychoanalytical Society 40

Carlo 104–9
change, fear of 133, 183
child analysis 86
childhood 64, 106, 151, 182
children: autistic 15–16, 181; development 9, 17–18, 24, 70, 81, 82–3; psychotic 77, 111, 127; *see also* mother–child relationship
cinema *see* films
Claudio 120–2
claustro-agoraphobia 71, 114
claustrophobia 28–32, 72, 90; and music 188–202
Clockwork Orange, A (Kubrick) 110–11, 115, 116
clothes, patients' 130, 133, 136, 139
color perception 55
compliance 34, 106, 149
compulsive tendencies 122, 123
computer science 59–60, 145
concrete original object (COO) 75, 76, 79–81, 104, 107, 163
concreteness 12, 38, 40, 41, 52, 183, 206
confusion, transitory, in analysis 142
consciousness: birth of 141–2; organizational role of 22
constant conjunction 167–9
contact network 79, 84, 97, 101, 204
container, internal 177, 180
container–contained relationship 24–5, 53, 91, 162, 168, 177
control 150; anticipatory 51–2, 135
control, parental 151
cookery 207
counter-transference 4, 34, 35–8, 97, 140, 150
creativity 26, 126, 148; lack of, in analysis 171; *see also* arts, the; music
Crying Game, The (Neil Jordan) 105
curiosity 103

Damasio, A. 19, 25, 69, 163, 196
Dario 115–17, 120

death 109, 112, 146, 154, 159; *see also* mourning
death instinct 9
Delion 15
delusions 72
depression 73, 100, 172, 182, 195
desire *see* sensuality; sex/sexuality
detachment 206
developmental structuralist approach 17
diabetes 78–9
disappearance: of analyst 63–6; of the body 96, 98, 99, 100; of patient 61–3
disruptive impulsion 73, 74–5
dissociative identity disorder 6
dreams 69, 72, 178
dreams, interpretation 6, 33, 41–2, 83, 185–6; Anita 204; Antonia 94–5, 99; Arturo 89–90; Carlo 104–8; Dario 116; Giovanni 176–7; Guglielmo 191; Karl 181–4; Laura 118, 119; Magda 122–3; Maria 93; Marta 129–35, 142; Mauro 49; Roberta 101–3; Rosa 56–7; Sandra 154–6, 159; Vittoria 149, 151–3
drives 60, 120; *see also* sex/sexuality
drug use 159

earthquakes 52–3, 57, 133, 134, 135
eating disorders 77, 78, 80, 86, 90, 114, 117–20, 128, 146
ego 120, 173–4, 196
ego–body relationship 14, 18, 72, 79
Eliot, T.S. 165
emotions 13, 161; absence of 86–7; crying 161; paralyzing force of 66; *see also* senses/sensations
empathy 34, 114, 186
endings, patient's difficulty with 98
entropic area 77, 85, 114
erotic transference 105, 107, 108, 154–5, 156–8, 163–4
erythrophobia 47, 49–50, 53
existential conflict 28
eyes and looking *see* visual power
Eyes Wide Shut (Kubrick) 48

fainting, fear of 120
fathers 3, 106, 116, 122, 134, 151
"feeling" vs "not feeling" 51
Fernando 64–6
Ferrari, A. B. 12, 34, 84–5; on adolescence, second challenge 112–15; on eclipse of the body 12–13, 75, 76,

79–81; one-person model 69–70; on vertical and horizontal axes 81–2, 84
Ferrari, A.B. 163, 166–7
Fidelio (Beethoven) 191–202
Filippo 126–7
films: adolescent hatred in 110–11; on body–mind conflict 48, 144–5; by Pedro Almodóvar 126; on sexuality/possession 158; *see also individual film titles*
Fonagy, Peter 74
Fosshage, James 82
fragmentation 103, 175
France 73
freedom, quest for 192
Freud, Sigmund 25, 38, 59, 163, 172; on artists 187; on conflict 21, 147; on consciousness 22; on dissociation and the unconscious 6; on ego 72; on instinctual body 26–7; *The Interpretation of Dreams* 33, 83; on reality 9, 22, 38, 142, 184; on the self 19; on sexuality 12; on thinking in abstractions 22, 38; on transference in dreams 83; on the unconscious 23, 33, 112
functional dualism 25

Gaddini, E. 70
Giorgio 116, 120, 146, 188–9, 190
Giovanni 176–7
Goethe, W. 168–9
gravitation, based on the body 54, 57
Grazia 148
Green, André 33
Greenberg, Jay 67; *Object Relations in Psychoanalytic Theory* 59
Greenspan, Stanley 17
Greif, Don 207
growth, sexual, in adolescence 115
Guglielmo 189–90, 191

hallucinations 87–8, 89, 116–17
hatred 9, 30–1, 45, 47, 181; of analyst/analytic relationship 9, 41, 65, 98, 99, 178; of the body 89–90; of body(ies) in adolescence 110–12, 114, 115–16; and love 158; of responsibility 130, 139; of surprises 109; of time 137; *see also* self-hatred
hearing 30, 49, 62, 160
heart transplants 124–5
holding 16

homicidal fantasies 116
homicidal impulses 177, 178
homicidal transference, risk of 60
homosexuality 100, 107
horizontal and vertical axes 81, 82–3, 94–100, 103, 166, 180

identity 79, 109, 126, 127
"imaginary twin" 40–5, 57
imitation 34, 70, 106
immune response 125
Independent Tradition 60
instincts 162
intellectualization 124–5, 208; in analysis 8, 86–7, 145
International Psychoanalytical Association 59
intersubjectivity 59–67, 148
invisibility, fear of 204
Italian psychoanalytic culture 59

Janet, Pierre 6, 25
Joseph, B. 71

Kafka, Franz 90
Karl 177–84
Keats, John 10, 164, 171
Klein, Melanie 7, 9
Kraepelin, Emil 111

language, body 73
language proper, psychoanalysis and 80
Laura 117–20
Lecours, Serge 73
Lee, Paul 1, 2
lesbianism *see* homosexuality
linking, attacks on 9, 61
literature 205–6
loss *see* mourning
love 164; and hatred 158

madness, fear of 153
Magda 123–4
Maria 92–4
Maria (anorexic patient) 146
Mario 148
Marta 128–43; change and experience 140–1; first session 128–31; second session 132–5; third session 135–8
Marty, P. 73
Mary 61–3
Matte Blanco, I. 84–5
Mauro 46–53

McDougal, J. 73, 80
memory 169
mental growth, and perception 44
mental pain 54, 56–7, 71
mentalization: compulsive 74–5; hyperactive 74
Milner, Marion 81, 111
mirror neurons 16
Mitchell, Stephen 67; *Object Relations in Psychoanalytic Theory* 59
mother–child relationship 9, 17–18, 23–5, 106, 115; *see also* children; *rêverie*
mourning 54, 56–7, 195–6, 201
music 1, 95, 111, 160, 203–5; in analysis 187–91; *see also* Beethoven, Ludwig van
mystery 10, 168
mystics and poets 9–10

Nancy, Jean-Luc 124–5
narcissism, destructive 71
negation, tendency towards 55–6
"negative capability" 10, 171, 185
negentropic area 77, 85
neosexuality 7, 73
neuropsychoanalysis 19
neurosciences, and psychoanalysis 68–9, 70

O 166–86
object relations 22, 23, 59–67, 103, 147–8, 163
observation: psychoanalytic 10, 24; of self 50
obsessive syndrome 105–6; obsessive thoughts 108, 122
Ogden, T.H. 72
omnipotence 120, 150, 180
opera 191–202
Orwell, George 205
otherness 175
"packing" 15–16

panic 78, 92, 94, 189
paralysis, sense of 52, 64, 66, 99, 122, 146, 149, 162
paranoia 178, 183
parenting 151; *see also* fathers; mother–child relationship; *rêverie*
patience 171, 185
Peeping Tom (Powell) 48
persecution, feeling of 31, 51, 172–3
persecutory state 106

personality: adolescent 112; and authenticity 145; psychotic and non-psychotic areas 9
philosophers 21, 124–5
phobic-obsessional symptoms 104
Plato 21
pleasure principle 170
Poe, Edgar Allan 13
poets and mystics 9–10
pregnancy, as theme 148–50
primitive mental states 12, 68–91; autistic-contiguous position 72; psychoanalytical research on 70–5
prison 31, 32, 111, 114, 159; in *Fidelio* 191–4, 197, 198–9
projective identification 9, 84, 89, 103, 129
psychic reality 69, 107
psychoanalysis: inception of 22; Independent Tradition 60; status of the body in 107, 163
psychoanalytic research, on primitive mental states 70–5
psychoanalytic training 59
psycho-sensory pentagram 36–8
psychosis 4, 22, 53–7, 146, 170, 177; in adolescence/children 77, 111, 127; body-eclipse hypothesis and 85–91; disintegration in boundaries 15; narcissism and ego structure in 71–2
psychosomatic illness 28, 45, 78

reality principle 9, 22, 38, 142, 184
relational model 60
repression 21, 44–5, 147, 164, 189
Resnik, Salomon 71–2, 80
responsibility 27, 39, 41, 44, 130, 139
rêverie 9; analytic 13, 34, 58, 80, 139, 142, 151, 187; maternal 163, 166; maternal/parental 6, 18, 23–5, 79, 141
Rey, Henry 71
Roberta 100–4
Romolo 205–6
Rosa 53–8, 146

Sandra 154–62
Sappho 164
schizophrenia 46, 72, 111
seeing *see* visual power
seeming 20, 26
self-awareness 17, 19; *see also* mental growth

self-hatred 142
self-mutilation 15, 74–5
senses/sensations 62–3, 72, 162–5;
  hearing 30, 49, 62, 160; sight *see* visual power; smell, sense of 72, 122, 123, 142, 160; taste 160, 179, 206, 207; touch 142; *see also* bodily functions
sensory integration, and parenting 17–18
sensory perception: and conflict 13; and emotion 31; organizing role of 13
sensory registration 91; onset of 75
sensuality 93, 94, 156, 169–70, 173
separateness 57, 198
separation 99–100, 132
separation of mind and body 95
sex/sexuality 12, 95, 104–5, 148, 162, 182–4, 188; adolescent difficulties with 119, 121, 122, 124; vs. sensuality 93, 94; *see also* erotic transference
sexual identity 109, 126
shame 107, 123, 133
sleep 99, 136, 179
smell, sense of 72, 122, 123, 142, 160
Solano, L. 78
solitude 57, 198
splitting 44–5, 130, 138, 161
sport 207
Steiner, R. 71
suicide: attempts 53, 74–5, 116, 117, 146; risk of 64, 111, 120, 195
super-ego 106, 126, 163, 196
surgeons, surgery 3–4, 43, 94, 154
surprises, hatred of 109
"surrogates" 144, 145
Susan 111
symbol saturation 170

Target, Mary 74
taste 160, 179, 206, 207
Taylor, D. 185–6
temperature, influence on emotions 19
tempo 48
"thing presentation" 22, 26, 38
thinking/thought 51–2, 53, 80, 93, 94, 146, 164; *see also* abstraction
time: in adolescence 114, 119; hatred of 137; and human limits 112, 184; and the infinite 85; and music 187; "pause" 50; and space-time perception 48
touch 142
transference 163; distinction between content and process 82
transference, interpretation, analyst's tendency towards 145
transference onto external objects 97
transference onto internal objects 70–1
transference onto the analyst 33, 84; erotic *see* erotic transference
transference onto the body 16, 21–39, 42–3, 49
transference onto the word 33
transparency, analyst's 140
transplants, heart 124–5
transvestism 126
trauma 74
tsunami 176
Tustin, Frances 13, 72, 77, 181, 196

uncertainty *see* "negative capability"
unconscious 21, 33–4, 147, 172
unconscious falsehood 25

Valéry, Paul 11
Vermote, Rudi 185
vertical and horizontal axes 81, 82–3, 94–100, 103, 166, 180
violence 64, 65–6; adolescent 110–11, 116–17; adolescent anxieties relating to 115–16; emotional 102; impulses to 177–9; possessive/sexual 158–9; *see also* suicide
visual power 40–58, 131, 139; "imaginary twin" 40–5; Mauro 46–53; Rosa 53–8
Vittoria 148–53, 162

Wagner, Richard 201
weather *see tempo*
Wilde, Oscar 144
wine 206, 207
Winnicott, Donald 6, 16, 59, 72, 81, 109, 208
"word presentation" 22, 26